Many VOICES, Many TONGUES

From Indonesia—the impassioned love poems of Chairil Abwar, whose life was tragically cut off at the age of twenty-six.

From Turkey—a story of a female in Islamic society by the remarkable woman novelist, Halide Edib.

From Egypt—the momentous blueprints for the future by the then young Gamal Abdel Nasser.

From India—the shining genius of the peerless master of modern Urdu poetry, Mirza Ghalib.

From Jordan—vivid memories of Lawrence and Churchill by King Abdullah, founder of the modern Jordanian state.

From the vast and varied world of Islam, a superlative selection of prose and poetry that bridges an historic gulf between alien cultures . . .

"A major contribution to the cultural resources of the West . . . a book to be read slowly and savored."

—*Florida Times-Union*

ABOUT THE AUTHOR: JAMES KRITZECK is Professor of Oriental Languages and History at Notre Dame University and Director of the Institute for Advanced Religious Studies. In addition to the companion to this volume, ANTHOLOGY OF ISLAMIC LITERATURE (also available in a Mentor edition), he has published ISLAM IN AFRICA, SONS OF ABRAHAM, PETER THE VENERABLE AND ISLAM, and THE WORLD OF ISLAM.

MENTOR Books of Special Interest

Modern Islamic Literature from 1800 to the Present

With an Introduction and Commentaries by

James Kritzeck

A MENTOR BOOK from
NEW AMERICAN LIBRARY
TIMES MIRROR
New York and Scarborough, Ontario
The New English Library Limited, London

For
Arthur Ross
and
George Anderson

Fellow Mozarabs

Library of Congress Catalog Card Number: 66-10269

This is an authorized reprint of a hardcover edition published
by Holt, Rinehart and Winston. The hardcover edition
was published simultaneously in Canada by Holt, Rinehart and
Winston of Canada, Limited.

MENTOR TRADEMARK REG. U.S. PAT. OFF. AND FOREIGN COUNTRIES
REGISTERED TRADEMARK—MARCA REGISTRADA
HECHO EN CHICAGO, U.S.A.

SIGNET, SIGNET CLASSICS, SIGNETTE, MENTOR AND PLUME BOOKS
are published *in the United States* by
The New American Library, Inc.,
1301 Avenue of the Americas, New York, New York 10019,
in Canada by The New American Library of Canada Limited,
81 Mack Avenue, Scarborough, 704, Ontario,
in the United Kingdom by The New English Library Limited,
Barnard's Inn, Holborn, London, E.C. 1, England.

FIRST PRINTING, DECEMBER, 1972

PRINTED IN THE UNITED STATES OF AMERICA

Acknowledgments

For their wonderful hospitality I gratefully acknowledge the American Universities of Beirut and Cairo. To the innumerable other institutions of learning throughout the Islamic world which have given me so much assistance I offer my heartfelt thanks. I wish to thank my colleagues and students at Princeton and Notre Dame for their help; and in particular I wish to mention, omitting their many titles: Georges Anawati, Arthur J. Arberry, Richard Armentrout, Peter Avery, R. J. C. Broadhurst, Edmund Burke, Lawson Cashdollar, Bahram Jamalpur, Bruce Lawrence, Omar Pound, Mahmud Ridwan, Gregor Roy, Wilfred Cantwell Smith, Muhsin Tayyibji, Wheeler Thackston, Michael Van Dusen, and Gustave von Grunebaum. To Arthur A. Cohen I owe the idea of the book; to Joseph E. Cunneen I owe its plan; and to Catherine Oleson, the finest editor in the world, I owe its accomplishment.

I wish to thank the following for their kind permission to include in this anthology excerpts from the books listed:

George Allen & Unwin Ltd., London, and Columbia University Press, New York, for excerpts from *The Autobiography of a Turkish Girl*, by Resat Nuri Güntekin, translated by Sir Wyndham Deedes, copyright 1949; *Turkish Nationalism and Western Civilization: Selected Essays of Ziya Gökalp*, translated and edited with an Introduction by Niyazi Berkes, © Niyazi Berkes, 1959; and *The Theology of Unity*, by Muhammad ʿAbduh, translated by Isḥāq Musaʿad and Kenneth Cragg, © George Allen & Unwin Ltd., 1966.

The Asia Society, Burton Raffel, and the University of California Press for poems from *An Anthology of Modern Indonesian Poetry*, edited by Burton Raffel, © 1962, 1963, 1964 by The Asia Society.

Basil Blackwell, Oxford, for a poem from *Poems from the Persian*, translated by John Charles Edward Bowen, Oxford, 1948.

Curtis Brown Ltd., London, for extracts from *Tales from the Arab Tribes* (1949), *From Town and Tribe* (1952), and *Told in the Market Place* (1954), translated by C. G. Campbell.

Calder and Boyars Ltd., London, and Grove Press, New York, for a passage from *The Blind Owl*, by Sadegh Hedayat, translated by D. C. Costello, © by John Calder (Publishers) Ltd., December 1957.

Cambridge University Press, New York, for selections from *Modern Arabic Poetry*, by A. J. Arberry (1949).

The Clarendon Press, Oxford, for a chapter from *The Reconstruction of Religious Thought in Islam*, by Sir Mohammed Iqbal (1934); and excerpts from *Somali Poetry*, by B. W. Andrzejewski and I. M. Lewis, © Oxford University Press, 1964.

Collins, Publishers, London, for a chapter from *As Others See Us*, by Marmaduke Pickthall, copyright W. Collins & Co. Ltd., 1922.

Congress for Cultural Freedom and Vanguard Press, New York, for a portion of *Twilight in Djakarta*, by Mochtar Lubis, translated by Claire Holt, Copyright © mcmlxiii, by Congress for Cultural Freedom.

J. M. Dent & Sons Ltd., London, and E. P. Dutton & Co., New York, for several poems from *Persian Poems*, translated by A. J. Arberry (1954).

Djambatan N.V., Amsterdam, for an excerpt from M. Kamel Hussein, *City of Wrong*, translated by Kenneth Cragg, © Djambatan N.V. 1959.

Ferozsons Ltd., Lahore, for poems from *Whispers from Ghaalib*, by Sufee A. Q. Niaz, Copyright with Author, n.d.

Grove Press, Inc., New York, and George Weidenfeld and Nicolson, Ltd., London, for a selection from *A Life Full of Holes*, by Driss Ben Hamed Charhadi, © 1964 by the Grove Press, Inc.

The Harvill Press Ltd., London, for passages from *Maze of Justice*, by Tewfik el Hakim, translated by A. S. Eban (1947); and *Land of Enchanters*, edited by Bernard Lewis (1948).

Taha Hussein, Alexandria, and the Longman Group Ltd., Harlow, for a chapter from *The Stream of Days*, by Taha Hussein, translated by Hilary Wayment (1948).

Ibadan University Press, for lines from *Tazyīn al-Waraqāt*, by ᶜAbdullāh ibn Muhammad, edited by M. Hiskett, © 1963 Ibadan University Press.

Intercultural Publications Inc., New York, for selections from *Perspectives of the Arab World*, © 1956 by Intercultural Publications Inc., reprinted by permission of Intercultural Publications, Inc.

Intertrade Publications (India) Pvt. Ltd., Calcutta, for poems from *Mirza Ghalib*, by R. K. Kuldip (1967).

Macmillan & Co. Ltd., London, for poems from *The Secrets of the Self*, by Sir Muhammad Iqbal, translated by R. A. Nicholson (1920).

John Murray, London, and the Wisdom of the East Series, for selections from *Poems from Iqbal*, translated by V. G. Kiernan (1955).

His Imperial Majesty, Mohammed Reza Shah Pahlavi, Shahanshah of Iran, for an extract from *Mission for My Country*, © H.I.M. Mohammed Reza Shah Pahlavi, Shahanshah of Iran, 1960.

Oxford University Press, London, for two stories from *Modern Arabic Short Stories*, translated by Denys Johnson-Davies, © Oxford University Press, 1967; Oxford University Press, Bombay, for an extract from *Twilight in Delhi*, by Ahmed Ali, first edition, Hogarth Press, 1940, published by the Oxford University Press, Bombay, 1967.

Philosophical Library, New York, for portions of the *Memoirs of King Abdullah of Transjordan*, translated by G. Khuri, published, 1950, by the Philosophical Library, Inc.

Public Affairs Press, Washington, D.C., for selections from *Egypt's Liberation: The Philosophy of the Revolution*, by Gamal Abdel Nasser, copyright 1955 by Public Affairs Press.

Simon & Schuster, Inc., New York, for a selection from *World Enough and Time*, by H.H. the Aga Khan, Copyright, 1954, by Simon and Schuster, Inc.

University of California Press, Berkeley and Los Angeles, for a chapter from *Arab Nationalism: An Anthology*, edited by Sylvia G. Haim, copyright 1962.

University of Toronto Press and *The University of Toronto Quarterly* for poems from *The Islamic Near East* (1960).

I should also like to acknowledge that I have drawn upon the following for some source material:

Cambridge University Press, Cambridge, *The Press and Poetry of Modern Persia*, by Edward G. Browne (1914).

The Colonial Press, New York, *Turkish Literature*, introduced by Epiphanius Wilson (1901).

M. Walter Dunne, Washington and London, *Ottoman Literature*, edited by Theodore P. Ion (1901).

Ibn-i Sina, Teheran, for *Hazar Sokhan*, by Mohammed Hejazi (1967).

Kitapçılık ve Kağıtçılık Ltd. Şti., Istanbul, *Works of Ömer Seyfettin* (1958).

Luzac and Co., London, *A History of Ottoman Poetry*, by E. J. W. Gibb, Vol. V, edited by E. G. Browne (1907).

John Murray, London, *The Diary of H.M. The Shah of Persia*, translated by J. W. Redhouse (1874).

The Pilot Press, London, *Images from the Arab World*, translated by Herbert Howarth and Ibrahim Shukrallah (1944).

Contents

Introduction

Modern Islamic literature may seem an odd title for what follows. We do not consider the nineteenth century, or much of the twentieth, as "modern" any more. And Islamic literature since 1800 has become increasingly difficult even to define.

Granted that classical Islamic literature, except for such curiosities as *The Thousand and One Nights* and the *Rubaiyat* of Omar Khayyam, remains generally unknown outside the Islamic world, what can be said about the recognition and appreciation of modern Islamic writers? Certainly every great modern Russian author has been translated into English, usually more than once, and his works have been studied in depth and inserted into the curricula of most of our universities. Nearly every great modern Japanese author enjoys similar recognition. We always hear of, whether or not we actually read, books by prominent Latin American, Asian, and African writers. We could hardly avoid learning the names of the great and semigreat European and North American writers. Yet there is scarcely one modern Moslem author whose name is familiar to most of us, and not a single one, all of whose works are available in translation.

This incredible state of affairs is but a recent manifestation of a very old cultural pattern. Islam and Europe, in particular, have managed to make for themselves a long and cruel history of cultural misunderstanding.[1] It is only a few miles from Gibraltar to Tangiers, let alone Ceuta; the trip takes a matter of minutes and is now grinningly plowed by even the most bored and casual of tourists. But in terms of understanding, those few miles might as well be millions of light years. Even from Gibraltar, the British Crown Colony whose very name ("Mountain of Al-Tariq")

[1] The best overall study of the misunderstanding, with great sensitivity to its religious background, is Norman Daniel, *Islam and the West: The Making of an Image* (Edinburgh, 1960); and *Islam, Europe and Empire* (Edinburgh, 1966).

9

immortalizes the Islamic conquest of Spain, and from the great Spanish culture beyond, which certainly owes an immense debt to Islam, there breaks no sympathetic surf.

The distance is the distance of thirteen and a half centuries. It extends, with but few exceptions, all around the boundaries of the *Dār al-Islām* (The "Abode of Islam," customarily distinguished by Moslems from the *Dār al-Harb*, the "Abode of Warfare"), and is well known among the component cultural segments of the Islamic world itself. One is inevitably close to an enemy in war or any opponent at loggerheads; Moslems and Europeans have always experienced that sort of proximity. Simultaneously they have begged, borrowed, and stolen each other's scientific and philosophical wisdom. But in radical cultural matters, they must be accused of paying each other the supreme insult of mutual indifference. What has been basically at play and at fault, of course, is the preventive exclusivity of their religions, in these cases commonly supposed to be brotherly or at least cousinly in their relationship to the faith of Abraham.[2] Their religions, to tell the simple truth, have held their cultures together and apart. The consequences of that fact are today, perhaps desperately, at stake in the game of human survival.

It was a weak and unprepared Islamic world that was forced to bear the brunt of European power at the turn of the nineteenth century. Earlier tastes of defeat by the Ottoman empire and its Islamic associates and rivals had been replaced, to some extent, by the bittersweet tastes of international diplomacy. Only the Mughal empire, largely consumed by Great Britain (an important factor in the events to follow), had already experienced the fate that was more or less immediately in store for nearly all of the Islamic lands.

In 1798 an army under the command of Napoleon Bonaparte landed in Egypt. Ostensibly, its mission was to overthrow the Mamluks and restore full Ottoman authority; in fact, the ambitious Corsican intended to counter British interests in the Mediterranean, the Red Sea, and beyond by annexing the country. His attempt was thwarted, it is true, but he opened the central Islamic world to the realities of the times and a completely new vision of itself, and forever changed the course and pattern of Islamic history.

[2] See the editor's *Sons of Abraham: Jews, Christians, and Moslems* (Baltimore, 1965).

Borrowing heavily from European technology, the Albanian Mehmet (Muhammad) Ali Pasha initiated from Egypt the first large-scale internal attempt at carving up the Ottoman empire. He and his son succeeded to a very remarkable degree in achieving that goal. After the Suez Canal was opened in 1869, however, Egypt necessarily fell prey to outside forces greater than it could cope with. In 1882 it was invaded by Great Britain.

In the meantime, much else in the Islamic world had fallen prey to similar forces. A large portion of North Africa had been occupied by France. The coast of East Africa had been divided among Great Britain, Italy, France, Germany, and Portugal. Coastal Arabia was under British "protection." Russia had annexed enormous portions of Central Asia and Transcaucasia, as well as Bessarabia, while the Balkans, Greece, Crete, Cyprus, and Lebanon had successfully revolted, with various forms and sources of help, against the Ottoman empire. That empire, still for all its losses the greatest single Moslem power, reacted with more conviction than foresight and became an unwitting partner in a series of losing causes.

New intellectual forces were also at work within the Islamic world. Nationalism of the European type was first planted in the Arab world by some Lebanese and Syrian Christians who belonged to literary societies sponsored by American Presbyterians and French Jesuits in the middle of the century.[3] Except insofar as it was willing to be accounted an apology for the East against the West (which was not far), Arab nationalism was ruled subversive by the Turkish government in Istanbul, and many of its leaders were obliged to seek refuge in Egypt or in Europe. At almost the same time a Pan-Islamic movement was being advocated by Jamal al-Din al-Afghani. The Ottoman sultan at first reacted favorably to this latter movement, sensing in it a means of strengthening his own fugitive powers; but when the Arab nationalists and some Islamic reformers, such as Muhammad Abduh and Rashid Rida in Egypt, began seriously considering and rigorously applying its principles, he had no recourse but to oppose it.[4]

[3]The now classic study of this development is that of George Antonius, *The Arab Awakening* (London, 1938).

[4]See Sylvia G. Haim, *Arab Nationalism: An Anthology* (Berkeley, 1964). Malcolm Kerr's *Islamic Reform* (Berkeley, 1966) admirably fills out the crucial period during which those Egyptian thinkers prepared the theories for what was to come. On the Turkish experience, Niyazi Berkes' *The Development of Secularism in Turkey* (Montreal, 1964) is an excellent guide.

The Ottoman empire entered World War I on the side of the Central Powers, and the "Arab Revolt" under British direction hastened its defeat. But the hopes of the Arab nationalists were dampened or dashed completely by the terms of the peace settlements. The so-called "Great Powers" divided the Islamic world along lines and according to arrangements which best suited their own strategic interests. If anything, Turkey, Persia, and India fared rather better than the awkward new kingdoms and protectorates in the Arab world. The years between the wars deepened resentments, but at least partially disengaged some national aspirations from international politics.

The dislocations attending World War II placed several of the Islamic states in stronger positions than they had recently known. The subsequent creation of the United Nations and its expressions of world opinion generally seemed to encourage all efforts in the direction of national independence and to deplore efforts in the direction of obstructing such an aim. Whether by negotiation or revolution, nearly every Moslem state has now achieved some form of self-government.

The Islamic world came into the nineteenth century without a Renaissance, a Reformation, an Enlightenment, or anything closely resembling those movements of minds and time to assist it in understanding the tangled European thought of the age.[5] In consequence it is all the more to its credit that it succeeded in doing so as well and as rapidly as it did.

The early literature of this period was no greater than one could expect it to be, considering that imitation of the older forms had gone so far as to appear dull and sterile, confessedly, even to its authors. As new foreign influences made themselves felt, however, Islamic literature entered an exciting and tremendously vital new period. Even in its earliest stages, those influences had the twin effects of liberating Islamic writers from their reliance upon traditional forms and exposing them to forms entirely new to them. Nationalism encouraged the deeper study of their languages and heritage; new dictionaries and encyclopedias were produced. A great many works of European literature were made available in translation and a great many Moslems learned European languages and studied in Europe. The effect of newspapers and magazines was

[5]H. A. R. Gibb, *Modern Trends in Islam* (Chicago, 1947).

suddenly phenomenal. The time-honored dichotomy between the oral and the more formal written literature was
now effaced, as many presses published a deluge of new
works which were eagerly sought after.

These rapid innovations had far-reaching effects on the
Islamic languages themselves. Nationalist purists made new
use of old words; young liberals borrowed both vocabulary
and syntax from European languages: many writers aimed
at bringing literature closer to the spoken idiom of the
times. A few authors resisted the new influences. Some
went all the way and preferred to write in French or
English. By far the majority, however, welcomed the new
spirit in literature and found the new forms both suited to
their tastes and challenging to their art.

Arabic and Persian poets were among the first to wrench
themselves out of the old ways. Writers of prose discovered
a carnival of new genres: the novel, the short story, the
essay, and drama. There were, of course, clumsy imitations
of European models, but not a few of the imitations deserve at least such applause as one willingly accords their
counterparts within European literature. Chauvinism and
politics often cluttered the new works, but a lively competition among the new writers supplied a self-correcting
and self-improving mechanism for them.

Modern Islamic literature, as a result, presents a very
marked contrast to classical Islamic literature. Its forms,
impulses, and messages are usually quite different; and 1800
is as good a round-numbered date as any to mark the start
of that difference.[6]

Literature, to be great, must be vital; and to be vital, it
must both be responsive to the cultural situation in which
it is created and expressive of some universality in the
human condition. At the start of the nineteenth century,
Islamic literature seemingly could only improve itself. With
so many languages and cultural traditions at work, it had
always been random as the stars; yet it had tended lately to
adhere, with predictable regularity, mediocrity, and lack of
enthusiasm, to certain accepted forms. It was then true that

[6] G. E. von Grunebaum, "The Spirit of Islam as Shown in its
Literature," in *Islam* (London, 1955), pages 95–110, is the finest way
to start. The best recent surveys of the major modern Islamic
literatures, in the editor's opinion, are the articles by Niyazi
Berkes, G. M. Wickens and P. J. E. Cachia in *The Islamic Near
East* (Toronto, 1960).

one could quite easily identify most Islamic literature from its static forms.

The unfettering which took place during the nineteenth and within the twentieth centuries went much farther than the abandonment of traditional literary forms, of course; it was the liberation of the whole creative impulse within the Islamic peoples, of which this was only one artistic result. It also gave rise to a paradox: If the Islamic peoples considered themselves newly enslaved by the West, why did they take so sharp a turn toward Westernization?

The explanation is to be sought not merely in the ambivalence and force of the acceptance of relatively more advanced foreign influences, as some have asserted, but also in the fact that the Islamic peoples had experienced lengthy seasoning along these lines, and had even performed particularly well under such circumstances. When the history of Islam became the history of Europe, and vice versa, both were at an epic moment in their destinies.[7]

We could not possibly, in the space of a few paragraphs, retrace the progressively more complicated factors necessary for an understanding of even the major faceting of Islamic history since 1800. The "Selected References" at the end of this book have been chosen particularly to provide the reader with guides to such background material, if he wishes to have it. Here let us simply consider a few of the characteristics of modern Islamic literature in relation to classical Islamic literature and other modern literatures.

To begin with, modern Islamic literature is far more broadly representative of the Islamic peoples, both geographically and socially, than was classical literature. The writers from what had formerly been the outskirts of the Islamic world have gradually taken positions of great importance in the field of letters; and what was once an almost casual hobby for an elite few has been brought, with the rise in literacy and the communications media, to the masses.

Next, one has to recognize that many modern Islamic writers seem far less Islamic, somehow, than their predecessors. Not that within the realm of belles-lettres, at any rate, the classical Moslem authors were always very pious. Far from it. But the modern authors have concerned themselves with the age-old situations less complacently, and have discovered new ones. They have drawn away from

[7] A point well made by Wilfred Cantwell Smith in his *Islam and Modern History* (Princeton, 1957), pages 3–92; the reader is also referred generally to the argument of this brilliant book.

the magnificently dreamy resolutions of dilemmas immortalized in *The Thousand and One Nights,* and have come to see them as social ills to be cured. They do not satirize the way the classical authors did; they satirize just as humorously and devastatingly, but they are less whimsical and more compassionate. Islam often rests aside.

Further, and this is an especially delicate matter, many non-Moslems no longer take quite the same pride in being part of Islamic culture as their ancestors used to take. The chemistry of this situation is very complicated indeed. The nationalisms behind European imperialisms in the nineteenth century seeded their counterparts throughout the Islamic world. It was really the Christian missionaries and their already Christian pupils, for example, who invented Arab nationalism; and the Christians who helped begin the *nahdah* (the movement of revival and renaissance, making twin the term for ecumenical reasons) cannot be classified as Islamic writers.[8]

By eliminating distinctly non-Moslem writers, one gets a lopsided view of the development of the various national literatures. Thus, for notable examples, one has to eliminate Albert Camus, the best North African writer of this century, and Kahlil Gibran, the immensely popular Lebanese writer, as obviously non-Moslem; while on the other hand one can include Marmaduke Pickthall, the gifted English convert to Islam, perfectly well.

If there is one apt simile for these writings generally, it is perhaps the oyster's pearl. They are mainly bright substances, produced by quite hard-shelled beings within soft insides, around irritants. They are valued on a complicated and strangely fickle scale, largely dependent upon ignorance that there are as many of them as there are. They have also been produced by means which, though somewhat artificial, are still perfectly natural. They are best appreciated individually when they come in sets. And above all, they are for people who prefer sheen to sparkle.

This book continues and complements the *Anthology of Islamic Literature* which was published in 1964.[9] In some

[8]See Albert Hourani, *Arabic Thought in the Liberal Age, 1798–1939* (London, 1962); compare Aziz Ahmad, *Islamic Modernism in India and Pakistan* (London, 1967).

[9]In addition to the edition by Holt, Rinehart and Winston (New York, 1964), there were the editions of Penguin Books in England (Pelican A648) and Mentor Books (MT 666) in the United States and Canada.

ways it is very similar to that book, and in others very different from it. The books are approximately the same length. The length of the selections and the general manner of introducing them conform with those of the *Anthology*. *Modern Islamic Literature* tries its best to reflect the salient qualities of that immense new literature, qualities enumerated and discussed above. Although the total volume is somewhat shorter than the *Anthology*, the obvious may be emphasized, namely that the representation of Islamic writers from 1800 to the present is vastly greater than that of its predecessor, which covered some twelve centuries. Donald Keene, whose fine anthologies of Japanese literature I am proud once again to acknowledge as the principal examples I have striven to follow, said simply: "The disproportion is largely to be explained in terms of the amount of literature that has poured from the printing presses in recent times. All the literature which survives from, say, the thirteenth century can hardly compare in bulk with what any single year now produces. But it is not only by mere numbers that literature earns the right to be heard; its quality is remarkably high, and compares with that written anywhere in the world."[10]

The scope of this volume is considerably wider than that of the first; its base has been broadened to include selections on subjects such as political philosophy and speculative theology, which the *Anthology* pointedly omitted. The inherent nature and dynamism of modern Islamic literature strongly suggested that; and once having accepted the suggestion, one practically had to include some more selections which ran along the same lines. I am the first to admire the other fine anthologies that have been produced along other lines.[11]

In the *Anthology* I was generally able to follow a consistent system of transliteration of proper nouns which, deriving from their connections with Islam and often unsuitably, employ the Arabic alphabet.[12] In this book I have tried to follow the same system, particularly in giving the titles of the original works. However, I must concede defeat, after great frustration, in the matter of personal names and tech-

[10]*Modern Japanese Literature* (New York, 1956), page 9; its companion volume was *Anthology of Japanese Literature* (New York, 1955).

[11]For example the *Anthologie de la littérature arabe contemporaine*, 2 vols. (Paris, 1964–1965).

[12]*Anthology of Islamic Literature*, pages 17–18.

nical terms within copyrighted material and even my own. Surely men and women must have the right to spell their own names any way they please. Though I was once a purist myself, you are not likely to discover me ever again making *al-Makkah* out of Mecca, or *abū-Ruqaybah* out of Bourguiba.

Finally, I am afraid this anthology, attempting so much, accomplishes very little. More, many more, recipes will have to be tried before we get what we want. Nothing could be more conducive to a better understanding and appreciation of that huge body of literature, of the persons who have produced and enjoyed it, or more clearly my intention in braving this attempt, than to see that come to pass.

J. K.

Hong Kong, 1969

AL-JABARTI: THE FRENCH IN CAIRO

[from *ʿAjɑʾib al-Āthar fī Tarājim w-al-Akhbār*, The Marvels of Evidence Concerning Interpretations and News]

> *Abd al-Rahman al-Jabarti was born in Cairo in 1754. His was a family of scholars that had originally emigrated from Abyssinia. He became an important religious official, and was appointed by Napoleon to the Grand Divan, by means of which the French hoped to rule the country. But he is best known for his sharp-eyed chronicling of events in Egypt during the period of the end of the Mamluk beys, the brief French occupation, and the beginnings of modernization and nationalism under Muhammad Ali.*
>
> *Al-Jabarti approached the new era with an open mind and a calm curiosity that cannot be regarded as typical. His literary style is not genuinely distinctive or distinguished, yet his prose does exhibit a little of the abandonment of ornament in favor of a simpler, more direct narration that was to gain popularity among the Islamic writers as the decades went on.*

THE MONTH OF JUMĀDA AL-THĀNIYAH [AL-ĀKHIRAH], 1213 (NOVEMBER 1798)

The mosque of [Sultan] Al-Zahir Baybars was converted into a fortress and cannons were installed on the roof. The minaret became a lookout tower. The inside of the mosque was fitted out to serve as a barracks for the soldiers to live in. This mosque had fallen into ruins a long time before and had been abandoned by the ministry of religious endowments, which had sold many of its pillars as well as the grounds whose revenues had been marked for its upkeep. A fortress was built on the hill at Nasiriyyah, known

18

as The Hill of the Scorpions, and several towers were also
built there in which soldiers were quartered and munitions
stored. Many of the houses that had belonged to the
mamluks were demolished to provide building materials for
new constructions.

The houses situated on Nasiriyyah Street were put at the
disposal of mathematicians, astronomers, architects, artists,
and writers, houses such as those of Qasim Bey, of Abu
Yusuf (the leader of the pilgrimage to Mecca), and of
Hasan Kashif the Circassian. The French also occupied the
new house which Hasan Kashif had had built with the
treasures from his tax exactions. This house had been furnished very luxuriously. When it was finished the French
arrived and Hasan Kashif was forced to flee with the other
mamluks.

The French installed in this latter house a large library
with several librarians who looked after the books and
brought them to the readers who needed them. This library
was open every day from ten o'clock. The readers gathered
there in a large room adjoining the room in which the
books were kept; they sat on chairs placed around large
tables and set about their work. Even ordinary soldiers
went to work in this library. If a Moslem wished to come
in to visit the place he was not in the least prevented from
doing so; on the contrary, he was warmly received. The
French especially enjoyed it when the Moslem visitor appeared to be interested in the sciences. They welcomed
him immediately and showed him all sorts of printed books
with maps representing various parts of the world and pictures of animals and plants. There were also many books
on ancient history. In some of them there were pictures
portraying the miracles of the Apostles and the Apostles
themselves. One was positively astounded at the sight of all
these beautiful things.

I had occasion to visit this library quite a few times. I
saw there, among other things, a large volume on the history of our Prophet (may God bless him). His holy visage
was represented there as exactly as the knowledge of the
author permitted. He was standing, looking up worship-
fully toward the heavens, and holding in his right hand a
sword and in his left hand a book; around him were his
Companions (may God be pleased with them), also holding swords. On another page, the four first caliphs were
portrayed; on a third, the ascension of the Prophet to
heaven—he was mounted on his steed Buraq. On other
pages one saw the Temple of Jerusalem and those of Mecca

and Medina and portraits of the great Imams, the founders of the sects, and other caliphs and sultans. One saw, too, a panoramic view of Istanbul with its great mosques, such as Hagia Sophia and the mosque of Sultan Muhammad. In this last picture one saw the ceremony of the Prophet's birthday celebrated in the presence of a considerable crowd. The mosque of Sultan Suleyman was represented during the Friday prayer and that of Abu-Ayyub during a funeral ceremony. One also saw pictures of other countries, shores, and seas, and of the Pyramids and the ruins of Upper Egypt with all the statues they contain. I saw many other books which treated of natural history, medicine, and applied mechanics.

They also had many Islamic books translated into French. I saw Qadi Ayad's book *Al-Shifa*, and Al-Busayri's poem on the Prophet entitled *Al-Burdah*. The French had learned some verses of the poem by heart and they had also translated it into their language. Some among them had also learned verses of the Koran. In short, they were great scholars and loved the sciences, especially mathematics and philology. They applied themselves day and night to learning the Arabic language and conversation. They possessed grammars of all languages which helped them to translate rapidly into their own language everything they wished to express.

An astronomer and his students had very precise astronomical instruments. One saw among them instruments constructed in absolutely remarkable ways and which were obviously very expensive. All of these instruments were composed of many parts. They went up and down by means of a knob; when they were down they were very small, but when they were up they were quite bulky. They also had telescopes which contracted and closed themselves in little boxes. They helped to observe the stars and determine their distances, volumes, conjunctions, and oppositions. They also had all sorts of time devices, including very valuable clocks which indicated the seconds very precisely, and many other instruments.

The artists were installed in the house of Ibrahim Bey. Among them was one who did portraits. He was so expert at it that when you saw them you would say that they were three-dimensional and ready to speak. He did a portrait of one of the *shaykhs* and of other notables. These paintings were placed in the salons of the general-in-chief and others. Another artist was occupied with drawing animals and insects. A third drew fish. When an animal or a fish was discovered that was unknown in France, they put it into a sort of liquid that preserved it indefinitely without any alteration.

The engineers also had a special house at their disposal. The chief doctor installed himself with all his instruments and chemicals. He had furnaces constructed to distill water and produce oils and salts. He had two laboratories, one on the ground floor and the other on the first floor. There one saw containers and bottles of all shapes and sizes. Many other doctors and surgeons were there.

Another group of learned men occupied Hasan Kashif's house. There, too, were all sorts of vats and instruments which had been installed for distillations, evaporations, and the analysis and synthesis of the elements. All the chemical products were kept in glass bottles of every shape, lined up on shelves.

Here is the most curious thing that I saw in this last establishment. One of the assistants in the laboratory took a bottle containing a certain liquid and poured a part of it into an empty glass. Then he took another bottle and poured another liquid into the same glass. It gave off a colored smoke, and when the smoke cleared, the liquid had solidified and had a yellowish color. I touched this solid mass and found it to be hard as a rock. The same demonstration was repeated with other liquids and one got a blue stone, and a third time when one got a stone as red as a ruby. Then the assistant took some white powder and placed it on an anvil. He struck it with a hammer and there was a great explosion like that of a gunshot. We were terrified, and that made the assistants laugh. Then one of them took an empty tube and immersed it in clear water kept in a wooden tank reinforced on the inside with lead. Then he immersed another tube of a different shape and joined the tubes in such a way that air was retained in only one of them. Then another assistant brought a flame to this tube and that, too, produced a great explosion. Later we witnessed other scientific demonstrations of this sort, based on the combination of simple elements and their reactions one on another.

We also saw a machine in which a glass went around which gave off sparks and crackled whenever a foreign object was brought near it. If a person put one of his hands on the machine and touched the glass with the other one, his body received an immediate shock that made the bones of his arms and shoulders crack. The same shock would pass into the body of any other person who touched the first one—or even the edge of his clothing—and with anybody in contact with that person. This way a thousand persons or more could instantly receive the same shock.

We had other experiences even more extraordinary than the first ones, and untutored intellects like ours could not conceive how they happened or give any explanations for them.

TRANSLATED BY IBRAHIM ABDEL AKHER

ABDULLAH DAN FODIO: HOLY WAR IN AFRICA

[from *Tazyīn al-Waraqāt*, The Adorning of Leaves]

While Islam was generally at low ebb, and suffering humiliations in many parts of its world, an outburst of fervor among the Fulani clerics of West Africa produced a rapid "old-time" expansion into the territories of what is now northwestern Nigeria. The most successful of these "holy wars" was led by Shehu Usumanu dan Fodio between 1804 and 1810.

Usumanu's brother Abdullah was a leading intellectual behind this movement, tied with a surprising erudition to the "classical" Islamic patterns of the north. His panegyrical poem to his (and his brother's) catechist conveys something of the excitement of their cause, and suggests the coarse vigor of pre-Islamic poetry in its local, bridled imagery.

The face of religion has become white after its nadir,
And the face of unbelief has become black after dawning
   brightly.
And religion is mighty, and on a straight way.
Unbelief is in disgrace, and in worn clothes,
And the splendid *sunna*[1] is a morning revealed,
And black heresy is a night which darkens,
Its signposts become obliterated, and its garments wear
   out,
And religion walks proudly in embroidered raiment,
And a spring of life for religion flows abundantly from
   his blessings;
Displacing the water of the muddy hollow.

And brooks flow to the drinking places filled with water
Whose purity says "Is there one who comes?"

[1]The path of "orthodox" Islamic behavior, based on the traditions.
[Ed.]

23

Until religion appears like a full moon, rising
On clear nights; or like a bright morning;
Or a meadow whose flowers laugh with it,
The tops of whose tender branches blossom;
Or like tender shoots or a garden
Or grasses in a glade, or on a hill, or in a sandy place.
Copious rain gives it the gift of generosity;
Upon it blows the east wind after the south wind has
    drawn down rain from the clouds.

Its branches multiply and its birds coo
Like a poet humming verses in the thrilling metre of
    hazaj.[2]
Its branches become tangled with foliage,
It gives abundant fruit, pleasant to eat.
It becomes luxuriant, and its scents diffuse
With beauty, verdure and fragrance.
It is as if his light among the chief men
Is meadow flowers, or minarets of silver,
And it is as if the thunder of their companies
Is the noise of pasturing camels, or flocks of goats.

TRANSLATED BY MERVYN HISKETT

---

[2]The delicate and sole antispastic meter of Arabic poetry, which
consists of a single repetition of $\smile - - \smile$, varied by $\smile - - -$.
[Ed.]

THE HISTORY OF THE FORTY VEZIERS

[from *Qïrq Vezīrin*]

Reworked old tales called masal *remained, in the first part of the nineteenth century, the most popular form of light reading and entertainment in the Ottoman empire and generally throughout the Islamic world. When pressed into cohesive literary form of some sort, as many of them had been long before 1800, they rather resembled the* Thousand and One Nights. *But the forms were, to say the very least, fluid and unstable. The stories, so many of which had begun in antiquity or had changed materially even between two tellings, refused to be confined to the written word.*

Still, form was imposed often enough, and not always badly. The History of the Forty Veziers, *for example, is one popular Turkish attempt, dating from the 15th century, it is thought, but here excerpted from a 19th-century redaction. Even the unifying plot is less exciting than that of the* Thousand and One Nights, *but the stories are still marvelously entertaining. "They are like all Oriental tales," their first English editor says, "barely tinged with any ethical significance; they aim principally at amusing and distracting the mind by a series of quickly changing incidents; there is no attempt at character-drawing, and an amazing element of the improbable spices the whole series. They form, however, the most notable work in prose produced in that period which saw the dawn of a Turkish literature."*

The Merchant's Bequest

There was of old time a great merchant, and he had two sons. One day the merchant laid his head on the pillow of death, and he called his sons before him, and brought together some wise persons, and said, "Moslems, if it

25

please God most high, these boys will live for many years; reckon at the rate of a hundred years from today, and allow to each of them a daily grant of a thousand aspres, and whatever the sum may amount to, that sum will I give them, that after me they may stand in need of no one till they die, but pass their lives in ease in this transient world." Then they reckoned up, and he gave them much money; and a few days afterward he passed to the abiding home.

The sons buried their father, and then began to waste that money. Their father's friends gave them much advice, but they would not accept it. One of them would enter the shop of a confectioner and buy up all the sweetmeats that were therein, and load porters with them, and take them to the square of the city, and cry out, "This is spoil!" and the folk would scramble for them, and he would laugh. And his business was ever thus. The other youth would buy wine and meat, and enter a ship with some flattering buffoons, and eat and drink and make merry; and when he was drunk he would mix up gold and silver coins before him and throw them by handfuls into the sea, and their flashing into the water pleased him, and he would laugh. And his business likewise was ever thus. By reason of these follies, the wealth of both of them came to an end in little time, in such wise that they were penniless, so that they sat by the way and begged.

At length the merchants, their father's friends, came together, and went to the king and said, "The sons of such and such a merchant are fallen a prey to a plight like this; if they be not disgraced now, tomorrow will our sons also act like them. Do thou now put them to death, for the love of God, that they may be an example, and that others may not act as they." Then the king commanded that they bring them both into his presence, and the king said to them, "O unhappy ones, what plight is this plight in which ye are? Where is the headsman?" And he ordered them to be killed. They said, "O king, be not wroth at our having fallen into this plight, and kill us not; our father is the cause of our being thus, for he commended us not to God most high, but commended us to money; and the end of the child who is commended to money is thus." Their words seemed good to the king, and he said, "By God, had ye not answered thus, I had cleft ye in twain." And then he bestowed on each of them a village.

Now, O king, I have related this story for that among youths there is nor shame nor honor, neither is there zeal for friend or foe. Beware and beware, be not negligent,

ere the youth kill thee do thou kill him, else thou shalt
perish. When the king heard this story from the lady he
said, "On the morrow will I kill him."

When it was morning, and the darkness of night, like
the wealth of that merchant, was scattered, the king sat
upon his throne and commanded the executioner, saying,
"Smite off the youth's head." Then the eleventh vezir came
forward and said, "O king of the world, hurry not in this
affair, and whatsoever thou doest, do according to the
command of God and the word of the Apostle; and the
holy Apostle hath said that when the resurrection is near,
knowledge will vanish and ignorance will increase and the
spilling of blood will be oft. O king, leave not the Law,
and spill not blood unjustly on thine own account, and
pity the innocent; for they have said that whoso taketh a
fallen one by the hand to raise him shall be happy; but
whoso, having the power, raiseth him not shall himself
burn in the fire of regret. Mayhap the king has not heard
the story of a certain king and a vezir's son." The king
said, "Tell on, let us hear." Quoth the vezir:

The King and the Vezir's Son

"Of old time there was a king, and that king had a sage
vezir. God most high had given that vezir a son; and the
people of the world were bewildered at the beauty of that
boy. And the king loved him so that he could not endure
to be a moment without seeing him, and he never parted
from him. So his parents yearned for the boy, but what
avail? they had needs have patience through fear of the
king. One day, the king while drunk entered the palace
and saw this boy playing with another page, and thereupon
was he wroth and he commanded the executioner, 'Smite
off the head of this degenerate boy.' And they dragged
the boy out. Thereupon word was sent to the vezir, and he
came straightway, and crying, 'My life! my son!' went up
to the headsman and said, 'O headsman, now is the king
drunk and senseless and he knows not the words he says;
if thou kill the boy to-night, to-morrow the king will not
spare thee; but will kill thee likewise.' The headsman said,
'How shall we do? he said to me, 'Quick, smite off his
head and bring it.'

"The vezir answered, 'Go to the prison and smite off the
head of some man meriting death, and bring it; at this
time the king has not his senses and will believe it.' And

he gave the headsman much gold. The headsman took the
sequins and was glad, and went forthwith to the prison and
smote off the head of a robber and brought it to the king.
The king was pleased and gave the headsman a robe of
honor. And the vezir took the boy and brought him to his
own house and hid him there. When it was morning and
the king's senses returned, he asked for the boy, and they
said, 'This night thou didst command the executioner that
he smote off the boy's head.' As soon as the king heard this
he fell senseless and his understanding forsook him. After
a while his understanding returned and he sat beating his
knees and he fell a-weeping. Then the vezir, feigning not
to know, came before the king and said, 'O king, what
plight is this?' Quoth the king, 'O vezir, where is that
source of my life? where is that spring of my soul?' The
vezir said, 'O king, whom meanest thou?' The king replied,
'Thy son, who was the joy of my heart.' And he cried and
wept beyond control, and the vezir rent his collar and
wailed and lamented.

"For two months the one business of the king was sigh-
ing and crying; during the nights he would not sleep till
dawn for weeping, and he would say, 'My God, shall I
never behold his face? mayhap I shall behold it at the resurrection. To me henceforth life is not beseeming.' Mad
words like these would he utter. And he ceased from eating
and drinking, and retired from the throne and sought a
private house and wept ever, and it wanted little but he
died. When the vezir saw this, he one day decked out the
boy like a flower and took him and went to the private
place where the king dwelt. He left the boy at the door
and went in himself and saw that the king had bowed his
head in adoration and was praying to God and weeping and
thus saying, 'My God, henceforth is life unlawful for me,
do thou in thy mercy take my soul'; and he was lamenting,
recalling the darling fashions of the boy.

"The vezir heard this wail of the king and said, 'O king,
how thou weepest! thou hast forsaken manhood, and art
become a by-word in the world.' The king replied, 'Henceforth, advice profits me not; lo, begone.' Quoth the vezir,
'O king, if God most high took pity on thee and brought
the boy to life, wouldst thou forgive his fault? and what
wouldst thou give to him who brought thee news thereof?'
The king said, 'O would that it could be so! all the wealth
that I have in my treasury would I give to him who brought
me news thereof, and my kingdom would I give to the boy;
and I should be content to look from time to time on the

boy's face.' Then the vezir beckoned to the boy and he came in, and went and kissed the king's hand. As soon as the king saw the boy his senses forsook him, and the vezir sprinkled rose-water on the king's face and withdrew. When the king's senses returned he saw the boy beside him and he thought that his soul had gone and returned.

"When it was morning the vezir came before the king, and the king said, 'As thou hast brought the boy to me whole, go, all that is in my treasury is thine.' The vezir answered, 'O king of the world, rather is the wealth which is in my treasury thine; we are both of us the meanest of the king's slaves. May God (glorified and exalted be he!) grant fortune to our king and long life! We too shall live in thy felicity.' The king was glad at the words of the vezir, and bestowed many towns and villages on the son of the vezir, and offered up many sacrifices, and gave away much alms.

"O king, I have told this story for that the king may take profit and not do a deed without reflection, that he be not afterward repentant, like that king, and suffer not bitter regret and remorse. That king suffered so great regret and remorse for a vezir's son, yet this one is the darling of thine own heart. The rest the king knows. Beware, O king, slay not the prince on the woman's word." And he kissed the ground and made intercession for the prince for that day. So the king sent the youth to the prison and went himself to the chase.

When it was evening the king returned from the chase and came to the palace, and the lady rose to greet him, and they sat down. After the repast the lady commenced to speak about the youth. The king said, "Today, too, such an one of my vezirs made intercession for him and I sent him to the prison." The lady said, "O king, three things are the signs of folly; the first is to put off today's business till tomorrow, the second is to speak words foolishly, and the third is to act upon senseless words. O king, whatsoever thy vezirs say, that thou believest straightway and actest upon. Satan is of a surety entered into these thy vezirs and into thy boy; in whose heart soever he plants the love of office or of wealth, him in the end does he leave without the faith. Mayhap the king has not heard the story of the King and the Weaver." The king said, "Relate it, let us hear." Quoth the lady:

The King and the Weaver

"Of old time there was a great king. One day a man came before him and said, 'My king, I shall weave a turban such that one born in wedlock will see it, while the bastard will see it not.' The king marvelled and ordered that that weaver should weave that turban; and the weaver received an allowance from the king and tarried a long while. One day he folded up this side and that side of a paper and brought it and laid it before the king and said, 'O king, I have woven that turban.' So the king opened the paper and saw that there was nothing; and all the vezirs and nobles who stood there looked on the paper and saw nothing. Then the king said in his heart, 'Dost thou see? I am then a bastard'; and he was sad. And he thought, 'Now, the remedy is this, that I say it is a goodly turban and admire it, else will I be put to shame before the folk.' And he said, 'Blessed be God! O master, it is a goodly turban, I like it much.'

"Then that weaver youth said, 'O king, let them bring a cap that I may wind the turban for the king.' They brought a cap, and the weaver youth laid that paper before him and moved his hands as though he wound the turban, and he put it on the king's head. All the nobles who were standing there said, 'Blessed be it! O king, how fair, how beautiful a turban!' and they applauded it much. Then the king rose and went with two vezirs into a private room and said, 'O vezirs, I am then a bastard; I see not the turban.' Quoth the vezirs, 'O king, we too see it not.' At length they knew of a surety that the turban had no existence, and that that weaver had thus played a trick for the sake of money.

"O king, thou too sayest, 'On the morrow will I kill him; I will do this and I will do that'; and yet there is nothing. O king, I had that dream this night, there is no doubt that it is as I have interpreted. O king, if the king's life and throne go, who knows what they will do to hapless me?" And she began to weep. When the king saw the lady thus weeping his heart was pained and he said, "On the morrow I will indeed refuse the words of whichsoever of my vezirs makes intercession for him, and I will indeed kill the youth; for, according to the dream thou hast had, this is no light affair."

When it was morning the king came and sat upon his

throne, and he caused the youth to be brought and commanded the executioner, "Smite off his head." Whereupon the thirteenth vezir came forward and sought to make intercession, but the king was wroth and said, "Be silent, speak not." Thereupon the vezir drew a paper from his breast and said, "For God's sake read this paper, then thou wilt know." Then the king looked at the paper and saw that there was written thereon, "O king, yesterday I looked at the astrolabe; for forty days is the prince's ruling star in very evil aspect, such that the prince may even lose his head." Then all the forty vezirs came forward at once and said, "O king, for the love of God and the honor of Muhammed Mustafa, for the forty days have patience and slay not the prince; thereafter it is certain that this affair will be made clear, and when its origin is known must each one receive his due." Then said the vezir, "There is a story suitable to this; if the king grant leave I will tell it." The king said, "Tell on, let us hear." Quoth the vezir:

The Vicissitudes of Life

"There was in the palace of the world a great king and he ruled over the Seven Climes. But he had neither son nor daughter, and he was ever offering sacrifices in the way of God. One day God most high accepted his sacrifice and bestowed on him from his bounty a fair son who was in his time a second Joseph. So the king was glad, and that day he held a high feast, and at that feast he gave robes of honor and money to many men. After that he assembled the astrologers and made them cast the prince's horoscope; and the astrologers looked the one at the other and were bewildered and confounded. Then the king said, 'What see ye that ye stand looking the one at the other?' The astrologers replied, 'O king of the world, we have cast the prince's horoscope; and in the astrolabe and the Jāmesb-Nāma they thus rule, that from his thirtieth year to his sixtieth the prince's ruling star is afflicted so that he shall wander in strange lands, with tribulation and pain for his companions: "None . . . knoweth the unseen save God." [1] After the king had heard these things from the astrologers, at times his heart would be sad and at times he would plunge into the ocean of deliberation. Saying, 'God knows the end of the boy,' he began to train up the prince. When

[1] Koran, xxvii. 66.

the latter entered his seventh year he appointed him a
teacher, and he passed some years in acquiring reading
and writing. When he was become a young man his father
got for him a king's daughter; and after a time the prince
had two sons. These children, too, in a little time acquired
knowledge; and from time to time they would go out
a-pleasuring with their father.

"One day the prince's heart desired a sea voyage, and he
commanded that they prepare a ship, and with his children
and forty slaves and attendants he entered the ship. For
many days they sailed the sea full pleasantly. But there
was there a Frankish corsair filled with infidels, and they
encountered the prince's ship and straightway flung their
grappling irons, and took captive the prince and his two
sons and forty servants, and went off. They took the prince
and the forty men and sold them to the cannibal Negroes;
but the two boys they sold not, but kept them. The Negroes
fed up the prince and the men with delicate and delicious
foods, and every day they took one of them to their king's
kitchen and cut his throat, and cooked him at the fire and
ate him. When they had eaten the forty men, the prince's
turn came, him too they took and brought to the kitchen
that they might cut his throat. The prince perceived that
plight, and he entreated God in his heart to give him
strength, and he burst the fetters that were round his wrists
and, striking about with the chains that were in his hands,
he slipped through them and rushed out.

"While he was running on, a vast forest appeared before
him; he entered it, and although the Negroes searched for
him they could not find him. Then he came out thence
and fared on many stages till one day he came to a great
city. The people crying, 'He is an enemy,' rushed upon
him. And the prince exclaimed, 'O Lord, what tribulation
is this!' and fought with them. Word was brought to their
king, and he came and saw that the prince was fighting
like a dragon. When the king saw the prince's valor he
admired it, and said to his soldiers who were there, 'Let no
one attack the stranger.' Then the soldiers dispersed, and
the king took the prince and went to the palace. He prepared a suit of clothes, and sent him to the bath, and
caused his head to be shaven and made him put on those
clothes, and brought him back to the palace. The king said,
'Come, remain by me, I have a daughter, I will give her
thee.' The prince consented; so they gave him the king's
daughter; and he remained there two years and his lot was
right pleasant. One day the prince's wife died; now this was

their custom, they had a great deep pit, and if a man died they put his wife with him alive into that pit, and if a woman died they did the same with her husband; and they let down along with them a loaf of bread and a pitcher of water, and covered over the pit with a great stone.

"So they brought the prince and his wife with a loaf of bread and a pitcher of water to that pit, and, saying, 'It is our custom,' lowered both of them into the pit and placed that great stone over them. When the prince saw himself in such case he was bewildered and said, 'My God! what plight is this!' and he prayed to God. And he searched the inside of the pit carefully and saw a fair girl seated there, and he asked her, 'What manner of girl art thou?' She replied, 'I am a young bride; they have put me into this pit with my husband.' And the prince examined the pit, and saw it to be all full of the bodies of men, some of which were decayed and some of which were writhing in the agonies of death; and dread overcame the prince. Of a sudden, while he was seated, a rustling sound came from one part of the pit; the prince knew that it was some beast, and he arose and went with the girl straight to that place, and he found the passage through which that beast had come in. They went for a time through that passage, and at length came out on the skirt of a mountain on the bank of a great river. And they were glad thereat, and thanked God much.

"And there they found a boat, and they gathered fruit from that mountain and filled the boat, and they both entered the boat and went along with the current of the river. That river grew wider day by day; but it passed underneath a great mountain. When they came near to the tunnel under that mountain they could not govern the boat, and the water took the boat and bore it under the mountain. When the prince saw this he exclaimed, 'My God! O Lord! what tribulation is this too! how shall we escape from this!' Helpless they sat in the boat; now the water dashed the boat against the rocks, now it made it fly down precipices, and now the mountain became low and pushed the boat under the water; and they, never ceasing, emptied the water out of the boat. They knew not at all whither the boat was going, neither did they know whether it was night or day. For a long time they were a prey to that anguish; and scarce a spark of life remained in their bodies when, at length, after a hundred thousand perils, their boat came out from under the mountain onto the surface of the earth.

"They were glad, and they drew their boat to the shore and got out of it, and took fruits from the trees that were there, and ate them. While standing there they saw a great white vaulted building, the dome whereof was of crystal. The prince and the girl went up to it, and they saw that it was a great castle, and that the domed building was within the castle, and on the door of the castle was written, 'O thou who wouldst open this door, O thou who desirest to overcome this talisman, bring a five-footed animal and kill it before here, that the bolts of this talisman may be opened thereby.' The prince marvelled and said, 'Is there in the world a five-footed animal?' and he wondered. And they sat by the gate of the castle and lice tormented them, and they began to louse themselves. The prince killed a louse, and straightway the bolts of the castle fell, and they knew that the said five-footed animal was the louse. Then they both entered by a door, and they saw a garden, such that of every tree which is in the world there was therein; and ripe fruits were hanging there and running streams were flowing.

"And the prince felt a longing for those fruits and he went to pluck one of them that he might eat it, when he saw that those trees were of gold and their fruits of silver and jewels, and that precious stones were lying at the foot of the trees, scattered like pebbles in a brook. They passed through and came to that dome; it was fashioned of crystal. They entered by a silver door and saw that within that dome was another dome all of pure gold. It too they entered and saw yet another dome, all the walls and the top of which were of ruby, built after the fashion of paradise. They entered it and saw a throne upon which was a coffin made of jewels, and at the head of the coffin was a tablet whereon was written: 'O son of Adam, who comest hither and seest me, know thou that I was a king, and that all the world was in my hands, and my wealth was beyond bounds or computation. Men and demons and fairies and jinn were my warriors; and I lived in the world for a thousand years, and I never said, "I shall die"; and I made not any preparation against death. One day, of a sudden, I fell sick, and I knew of a surety that I was about to die, and I commanded that this dome be built in three days, and I made it a sepulchre for myself. And by my head are two fountains; drink, and pray for me.'

"And the prince saw those two fountains and drank; and from one of them flowed sugared sherbet and from the other milk. And they drank of both of them and remained a long while by that grave, and they nourished themselves on the milk and drank of the sherbet. At length they found some vases, and they took of the milk and the sherbet and the jewels and the gold, and filled their boat with them, and again set forth on their voyage. After they had gone for a time the wind drove their boat upon an island, and they went forth from the boat to look for fruit on the mountain that they might eat. Of a sudden a body of men came and seized them; and the prince saw these that they had no heads, their mouths were in their breasts and their eyes in their shoulders, and their speech, when they spake together, was as the chirping of birds. And they took the two and brought them to their king; and they remained there prisoners a long time.

"At length one day they found an opportunity and escaped, and again they entered their boat and sailed for a long time upon the sea. In brief, the prince wandered for thirty years upon the seas, sometimes happening among nine-headed men, and sometimes among bird-headed, and sometimes falling among elephant-headed folk, and sometimes among ox-headed, and then escaping; and each of them inflicted different torments on the prince. Still God most high opened a way and he escaped. And he saw these strange and wondrous creatures, and he marvelled. At length, through the grace of God (glorified and exalted be he!), the wind drove the prince's ship before a city, and he saw that the inhabitants of that country were all men, and he came out. When these saw the prince they cried, 'He is a spy,' and seized him and bound his arms behind his back, and tied a rope round his neck, and took him alongside a horse, and said, 'Our lord has put down: when ships come from the sea and touch at our country, seize their spies and take them to our king.' And the prince exclaimed, 'What tribulation is this too! how to go alongside a horse!' And while he was praying in his heart they reached the city. And they took the prince in this plight to their king.

"When the king saw the prince he asked, 'What manner of man art thou?' The prince said, 'Many marvellous things have befallen me'; and he related his adventures from their beginning to their end. When the king heard his story he loosed the prince's bands and took him to his side and clad him in sumptuous robes of honor. The prince asked for the jewels that were in his ship. The king bade bring them and said, 'O prince, I know thy kingdom, and I heard that the Franks had taken thee; and I know thy father too.

Come, go not away, stay; I have a daughter, I will give her thee, and we shall live pleasantly together.' The prince replied, 'O king, when I was born of my mother, my father caused my horoscope to be cast, and the astrologers thus ruled that my life was afflicted for thirty years; mayhap if I took the king's daughter, some evil might befall the king's daughter by reason of my affliction; I may not consent.' Then the king brought the astrologers and made them cast the prince's horoscope. The astrologers gave good news, saying, 'Glad tidings be to thee, those thirty afflicted years have passed, now his ruling star has entered the sign of good fortune.' The prince was exceeding glad and joyful.

"Thereupon the king commanded that they make ready a festival, and he gave his daughter to the prince, and he greatly honored and reverenced him. After some time the king died, and the prince became king in his stead. One day when he was seated on his throne they said, 'O king, a Frank has come with much merchandise; if the king grant leave, he will bring his merchandise.' The king replied, 'There is leave, let him bring it.' And the Frank brought his merchandise before the king. The king saw his two sons at the Frank's side, then the blood of love boiled, and the affection of paternity yearned for them; and he asked that Frank, 'Are these youths thine?' The Frank answered, 'They are my slaves.' The king said, 'I will buy them.' And he took the youths to a place apart and said, 'Where did this Frank get you?' Then they related their adventures from their beginning to their end; and the king knew of a certainty that they were his own sons, and he pressed them to his heart and kissed each of them on the eyes, and said, 'I am thy father.' Then the king arose; and they killed the Frank with a thousand torments.

"O king, I have told this story for that the king may know that haps such as this often befall princes. Their happy fortune passes into the sign of inauspiciousness, and they become a prey to a thousand tribulations and distresses, so that even gold turns into black earth in their hands, and all their friends become enemies to them. Afterward the malefic aspect gives place to prosperity and auspiciousness, then everyone is their friend. O king, this youth's ruling star is likewise afflicted for a few days. Beware, O king, until the days of the malefic aspect be fulfilled, slay not the youth, else afterward thou wilt be repentant, and too late repentance profits not. The rest the king knows." When the king heard this story from the vezir he asked for the youth's governor, but he could not be found. So again he sent the youth to the prison and went himself to the chase.

When it was evening the king returned from the chase and came to the palace, and the lady rose to greet him, and they sat down. After the repast the lady again began to speak about the youth. The king said, "Today, also, such an one of my vezirs made intercession for him and I sent him to the prison." And he related to the lady that story which the vezir had told. Then said the lady, "O king, the reason of these vezirs stirring up trouble is that they wish to sow enmity between thee and me. Beware, O king, go not by the words of these, but follow well my words, that thy present state and thy hereafter may be happy. When God most high decrees good between husband and wife he gives mildness and accord. And, moreover, O king, be it good news to thee, a week ago did I conceive by thee; till now I have not told thee, but now I have told thee and do thou believe it true." And the king believed it. Then she continued, "O king, lo, these vezirs say that this youth's star has fallen into a malefic aspect. His star became afflicted what time he made for thy life and thy kingdom and for me. God most high aided us and afflicted his star and brought down his head." And the lady was glad and said, "Thy true son is he that is in my womb; that youth is without doubt baseborn. Mayhap the king has not heard the story of him who had no sons." The king said, "Tell on, let us hear." Quoth the lady:

The King and the Sheykh

"There was in the palace of the world a great king, and he had neither son nor daughter. And there was in his country a sheykh whose prayers were answered. One day the king, while conversing with the sheykh, said, 'O sheykh, God most high has given me no son; do thou strive in prayer that God most high give me a son.' The sheykh replied, 'Send an offering to the convent that the dervishes may eat, and we shall pray for thee; God most high is a gracious king, he will give thee a son.' Now the king had a golden-ankleted fat ram that was valiant in fight; and he sent that ram to the sheykh's convent with some loads of rice and honey and oil. That night the dervishes ate and were pleased; and the sheykh sent of that meat in an earthen bowl to the king, saying, 'Let him desire a son and eat of the dervishes' portion.' Then the dervishes danced, after which they prayed and besought of God a son for the king. By the divine decree the king's wife conceived that night, and in a short time she brought forth a moonfaced boy.

"The king was delighted, and called the people of the country to the feast; and he took the prince and laid him on the sheykh's skirt, and he bestowed many gifts on the sheykh's convent. One day, some time after that, when the king was conversing with the sheykh, he said, 'O sheykh, what if thou were to pray and beseech of God another son for me?' The sheykh replied, 'The favors of God are many; to pray is ours, to give is his; send then an offering to the dervishes.' Now the king had a favorite plump horse, that sent he forthwith to the convent. The devotees cut its throat and roasted it, and again sent an earthen bowl of it to the king. They ate the rest themselves, and prayed and besought of God a son for the king. By the divine decree the lady again conceived, and in a short time she brought forth a moonfaced boy. And the king was delighted and sent many gifts to the dervishes. Sometime afterward the king requested the sheykh to beg of God yet another son. The sheykh said, 'To pray is ours, to give is God's; send again an offering to the devotees.' Now the king had a good mule, that sent he to the convent. The devotees sold that mule and took its price and therewith prepared a confection. And they sent a bowl of that, too, to the king. After the dance they prayed and besought of God a son for the king.

"Again the king's wife conceived and gave birth to a moonfaced boy. And the king was glad and sent many gifts to the dervishes. When the king's sons grew up, the eldest turned out very valiant; the second proved swift of foot and accomplished and possessed of understanding and sagacity; but the youngest was ill-omened and ill-natured, and oppressed men, and wounded and wasted the hearts of many poor creatures with the sword of his tongue. And the king was sore-grieved because of him. One day while conversing with the sheykh he complained of his youngest son and said, 'O sheykh, would that we had not besought of God that youngest boy.' The sheykh replied, 'O king, why art thou grieved? thou art thyself the cause of that youth being thus.' The king asked, 'How am I the cause?' The sheykh answered, 'First thou gavest in the cause of God a ram among beasts, and God most high hath given thee a son of courage among men; then thou gavest in the

cause of God a courser of the plain of earth among beasts,
and God most high hath given thee a courser of the plain
of glory and fortune and understanding and accomplishments among men; and after that thou gavest in the cause
of God an ill-omened and baseborn brute among beasts,
and God hath given thee such an one among men. O king,
he who sows barley reaps not wheat.' In the end the king
got no rest until he had killed the youth.

"Now, O king, I have told this story for that the king
may know that from this ill-omened, baseborn one no good
will come. They have said that the baseborn are of two
classes: the one the fruit of adultery, the other the fruit of
illicit union. This thy son is without doubt of one of these
two sets; lo, thy trueborn offspring is about to come into
existence." When the king heard these beguiling words of
the lady he said, "On the morrow will I kill the youth, be
not sad."

When it was morning the king came and sat upon his
throne and ordered the executioner that he bring the youth,
and he said, "Smite off his head." The fifteenth vezir came
forward and said, "O king of the world, it is not seemly to
kill the prince in compliance with the woman's word, for
the angels that are in heaven are not safe against woman's
wiles. Hast thou heard the story of the King's Remorse?"
The king said, "Tell on, let us hear."

TRANSLATED BY E. WILSON

MIRZA GHALIB: FOURTEEN POEMS

[from *Dīvān-i Ghālib*, Ghalib's Poetical Works]

The poet Ghalib (pen name of Asad Allah Beg Khan, who lived from 1797 to 1869) was the peerless master of modern Urdu poetry, resident poet at the late Mughal court, and one of those literary figures who, had he not existed, would almost have had to be invented.

In a relatively arid and unpromising literary era for Islam, Ghalib's brilliance is all the more impressive. Taking many themes and forms from older masterpieces and tradition, he especially excelled in the couplet and ghazal, the finest Mughal genres. Ghalib's poetry is truly the turning point of modern Urdu literature.

A Word

For whose masterly stroke
Does each creation so stand in prayer,
Clad in robes of paper,
Supplicant in the universe, everywhere?

Ask not of love's anguish when all alone,
To pass eve till morn, like cutting canal through stone.
See how my love for death does as a magnet serve
Even to the sword, which outside its sheath does curve;

Try howsoever much you may,
You shall never get a word of what I say:
Even in prison Ghalib is burnt with that desire,
And his chains turn like hair-coil in a fire.

Her Indifference

I love her indifference;
For broader my outlook be
When I find the joy of my heart
So hid from me.

Flasks full of wine in the Tavern show,
Few with love of wine to it did ever go;
So the more men in the world you find,
The fewer there are firm of will or mind.

A Lullaby

Like lullaby to a child
Is Holy Jesus' word
To lovers by love cut deep
To put them to sounder sleep.

Anew

Everything in the garden
Today is arranged anew,
Even the outer gate like dove's shelter,
To keep the world out of view.

Each breath of mine today
Brings forth a piece of broken heart,
Effect ensnared by sighs;
For my love, 'tis but a new start!

Clear out all ye cares
And love for joy and rest,
To drown the walls and doors
With tears today I am set.

I Fear

I fear lest my love for ye make me proud,
Cut my life, and my thoughts with enmity shroud;
Ghalib, unless flowers cover the whole view,
Take not spring in its prime, 'tis not yet new.

Love Aflame

The looking glass, but for its coating,
Would be afire
With the dazzling reflection
Of her blazing looks;

Lovers have flaming beauty
As their heart's desire,
As candle a burning wick
In its stride, with cheer does take.

Tongue of Love

Tongue of love
Lies in eyes;
In silence it talks,
In quiet it prays.

Like a musical instrument
Out of order,
Are plaints of lovers
With love in disorder;

With gratitude to Majnu[1]
For the miracle wrought,
A garden out of wilderness
By his blood tears is brought.

TRANSLATED BY R. K. KULDIP

And irrespective
Of whether I am good or bad,
My surroundings do not seem
To agree with me.
Neither the evil
Nor the good in me
Does seem to get a natural,
Unrestricted play wherein
The evil itself, in recoil,
Might lead to virtue.

[1]"Possessed, bedevilled," the classic figure of the lover; cf.
Anthology of Islamic Literature, pages 219–223.

If I am a flower,
I am smothered in thorns
And stinging nettles:
But if no more than an obnoxious
Weed, I find myself
Growing in a garden—
Out of place,
Unwanted in any case.
But what's the good
Of feeling bitter
Over things I cannot help?

I am like the mute lamp
That burnt out lies on some lonely,
Half-forgotten grave,
Where the mournful daylight
Seems to hang like a heavy
Oppressive veil, to deaden life;
And the brooding silence
Tells a tale of the end of futile,
Vain desire—of a thousand
Hopes which died ere born,
And rapturous dreams
Slashed and rent!

Thousands of deep
And desperate desires,
Clutching at the heart
With an intensity and fierceness
That chokes the breath!
And many a time, though,
Fulfilment too has come my way,
But always such as only
Adds to the torture
Of tantalising hopes—Oh God!
Never enough to soothe
These smouldering fires!

When there was nothing
There was God. Had there
Been nothing at all,
The Almighty God, even then,
Would have existed.
Then why for me
This slow but ceaseless
Grinding of the wheels—

Of wheels within wheels of grief?
My ruin proceeds
From this state of being—
From my life itself!
Oh God! Had I not existed
At all, what then?

In the wandering world
Of limitless depths,
In the deadly sweep
Of every wave,
A thousand dangers
Lie in wait,
A thousand perils
Watch their chance—
For a poor drop of rain.
What a life of long,
Relentless rigours
Before it changes into a pearl!

My race is run,
And the end has come
Of the mighty trail I blazed:
There lies ahead a darkening sea.
I hear the breakers roar below;
And curling mists, and a numbing
Cold are creeping up, steady
And sure of their helpless prey,
As from here there is no going back!

TRANSLATED BY A. Q. NIAZ

TWO OTTOMAN POETS

*Modern Turkish poetry began in 1859 with the pub-
lication of Shinasi Efendi's translations of French
fables, chiefly from Racine and Lamartine rather than
from La Fontaine. "In them breathes for the first
time that spirit which is to vitalise and inspire the
future. They are the earliest verses in the Turkish
language to exhibit any indication that such a thing
as European poetry is known to exist."[1] Shinasi spent
most of his life commuting between Istanbul and
Paris, associated often with newspapers and magazines
as was the vogue, and rising to and falling from public
office and the Court's esteem in the truest Ottoman
fashion. The fables in verse included here are
Shinasi's own imitations of La Fontaine, a distinct
advance in his poetic development, which calls to
mind the Kalīla wa-Dimna of Ibn al-Muqaffa at the
very beginning of Islamic secular literature.[2]*

The Ass and the Fox

From a vineyard once an aged ass was slowly toiling
    down
With a load of "beauty's faces"[3] he was bearing to the
    town.
Lo behold, just then a hungry fox before his eyes
    appeared,—
Eager longing for the luscious grapes had all his vitals
    seared.
Kicked a bit at first the donkey when the other came him
    nigh,
But his waywardness and coyness were not long in
    passing by.

[1] E. J. W. Gibb, *A History of Ottoman Poetry*, Vol. V, edited by
E. G. Browne (London, 1907), page 33.

[2] Cf. *Anthology of Islamic Literature*, pages 73–78.

[3] Rú-yi Nigár, "beauty's face," is the name of a variety of grape
of a light pink color.

The Fox:—

"Oh my lion, brave and mighty, may not I approach to
  thee,
"So that I may see thee near? Thy loveliness dumb-
  founders me!
"May the shadow of the favour of my lord abide for
  aye!
"Wheresoe'er yon blessed feet have trodden, blossom
  roses gay.
"Yonder tail so sweetly scented all would rarest musk
  suppose;
"Fain I'd smell it, if my master would not kick me on
  the nose.
"In those speaking eyes thine inward virtues and thy
  culture shine;
"Words poetic and melodious well beseem that mouth of
  thine!"

Hereupon the donkey mightily delighted brayed a deal
Just as though he'd seen a tender thistle or a melon peel.[4]

The Fox:—

"Ah, that charming voice hath reached e'en to the very
  heart of me;
"While if thou art silent, lo, another lovesome joy have
  we;
"For the nightingale hath heard thee, and to steal thy
  notes is fain,
"Singing so that to the listener comes a gentle sense of
  pain."

Thus the fox went on a-prattling, laughing slyly at his
  fere,
Till that he had brought the donkey where a well was
  deep and clear.

---

[4] In Turkey donkeys are often given melon peel, of which they
are very fond. "Like an ass that has seen a melon skin," is popularly
said of one who is taken up with a trifle, the figure being derived
from the donkey's habit of making for any piece of peel on the
roadside.

The Fox:—

"Down there is a lovely stable where are feeds in goodly
store;
"But alack! one cannot enter laden, narrow is the door.
"Pleasures many such as sleeping and as resting still are
there;
"Eating feeds and drinking water are the only toil and
care.
"Then the lady donkeys dwelling there have quite a
special grace;
"Just look in, but see thou be not smitten by some pretty
face."

Then the ass went near and gazed down on the liquid
mirror bright,
Saw his face therein reflected,—watered then his mouth
forthright.

The Ass:—

"Yes, indeed, a face all lovely and all gracious there I
see."

The Fox:—

"Call her then to come beside thee that thy playmate
she may be."

All excited, loudly bellowed out the donkey's "Come thou
here!"
From the well his words re-echoed fell upon his wildered
ear.

Shinasi also wrote a great many occasional poems. The
following one may reflect an early Islamic reaction to the
theories of Charles Darwin.

A Tale of Transmigration

A sham philosopher of scant esteem
Was wont himself Pythagoras to deem.

The transmigration of the soul his creed,
Disintegration of the frame his rede.
He said: "The beast that sticketh up his tail
"Will come in human form withouten fail."
A wise man heard the words that ox did say,
And with this answer stopped his mouth with hay:
"How can I question this religion's truth
"With thee thyself alive to prove its sooth?"

Ziya Pasha (1829–1880), the second of our poets, was
a contemporary of Shinasi Efendi and, like him, a sometime favorite at the Ottoman Court. He had been a brilliant
student of classical Islamic literature and, after assuming
a position at Court, devoted himself especially to the
translation of the French classics. Exiled in 1867, he lived
in the great cities of Europe; he returned to Turkey in
1871, and in 1876 was made Vizier. *Terji-bend*, his best-
known long poem, was written at Court. "Although the
pervading spirit is Western, the imagery remains Oriental,"
the translator says of it.[5] A short portion of it is given here,
followed by one of Ziya's famous shorter poems.

Of old time beauty, wisdom, love were all as gods
    revered;
For many a year in every land were idols served alone.
At length the season came wherein God's Unity was
    learned,
But e'en through that a thousand strifes, disputes and
    feuds were sown.
The mind now thought Creator and Created one, now
    two,
Believed now endless difference, now final union.
Some held the Substance manifold, the Attributes as one.
Then in one Origin did many an origin depone.
Each one desires to shape a God conformable unto
Those thoughts and aspirations which in truth are all his
    own.
As different as mind and matter each from other is,
So different the varied faiths and creeds the world hath
    known.
How passing strange that every folk holds others' creeds
    in scorn,

[5]Gibb, *op. cit.*, page 66.

And deems the way of righteousness belongs to it alone,
While yet with all this difference the aim of every sect
Is but with true devotion one Creator's rule to own!
  "Glory to Him before whose work all intellect is dazed!
  "Glory to Him before whose might the wisest stand
    amazed!"

The roses smile, the nightingale breathes out his life in
    sighs,
His fee is all the leech's thought the while the sick man
    dies.
The corpse of him who riches had is e'en as carrion,
Like vultures are the lavers and the heirs with greedy
    eyes.
Upon the couch of luxury the city lord reclines,
The stranger starves within the dust of scorn in woful
    guise.
The smiling taper sheddeth radiance o'er the joyous
    feast,
Amidst its flame, with crippled wing, the moth unheeded
    dies.
Garlic and onion freely smile like tulip or narcisse,
While prisoned close in narrow vial sweetest perfume lies.
The sordid fool reposeth glad on cushions of delight,
While in the stoke-hole of contempt croucheth the good
    and wise.
Earthly prosperity is oft the lot of ignorance,
What time the world a crust for wisdom's evening meal
    denies.
The banquet of society receives the false and vile,
The spirit of the world doth oft the true and leal despise.
The gifted poet many a time becomes the jest of fools,
The wise and learned many a time the idiot's mirth
    supplies.
The feeble and opprest must often want for daily bread
What while a cruel tyrant's deeds to fame and glory rise.
  "Glory to Him before whose work all intellect is dazed!
  "Glory to Him before whose might the wisest stand
    amazed!"

O Lord, how comes it every man of learning here below
Must through the curse of knowledge ever rest and peace
    forgo?
O Lord, why is it that with every wise man here on earth
The measure of his gifts is still the measure of his woe?

His peace of mind is gone, whatever side he turn his
glance;
His understanding is abased, wher'er his thoughts may
go.
With knowledge as the only weight for understanding's
scales
Is't possible the utmost truth of things to weigh and
know?
Thus impotent may any vision ever win to see
The final verity of all the things and haps that show?
And then, as though the burden of this sorrow were too
light,
From fools' o'erbearing tyranny in blood his vitals flow.
I know not; is it ordered in the canon of the world
That ever upon earth the brutish folk shall prosper so?
Since e'er the world hath been the world this rule hath
still prevailed,
Before the vilest lout the man of heart is humbled low.
The dullard prosperous and courted lifts on high his
head
Contemned and destitute the sage must ever humbly
bow.
Fair Fortune doth caress the fool, crowning his every
hope,
While fickle Fate the wise and good to beggary doth
throw.
   "Glory to Him before whose work all intellect is dazed!
   "Glory to Him before whose might the wisest stand
   amazed!"

Gazel

A tavern which each moment takes a life as pleasure's
pay is earth;
A glass which for a thousand souls doth sell
each drop of spray is earth.
The world's a Magian that adores the flame of power
and fortune high;
If thou should brightly shine, a moth about thy taper's
ray is earth.
Anon one is, anon is not—thus ever runs the
course of time;
From end to end a warning-fraught, a strange,
romantic lay is earth,

'Twixt sense and frenzy 'tis indeed right hard to draw
  the sund'ring line,
Ah me! If understanding's wise, demented sooth
  alway is earth.
The desolation of the world beside its weal is
  truth itself;
Just as prosperity it seems, so ruin and
  decay is earth.
How many Khusrevs and Jemshids have come,
  and from its bower have passed!
A theatre that vieweth many and many an act and
  play is earth.
Ziya, a thousand caravans of wise men through
  its realms have passed;
But yet no one can tell its tale, and all unknown
  this day is earth.

NASIR AL-DIN SHAH: THE SHAH VISITS PARIS

[from *Safar-nāmeh*, Book of Travels]

A most important influence on the creation of modern Persian prose came from an improbable and yet obvious source: the very embodiment of Iran and her traditions, the Shah himself. It had once been common for the shahs of Iran to engage in literary composition; and, in a sense, no one could be considered freer to break through the confining conventions of the past and originate a new style than he.

That is precisely what Nasir al-Din Shah did in diaries of his visits to Europe. He wrote them in a simple, intimate style entirely devoid of unnecessary baggage, and full, instead, of novelty and enthusiasm. They were widely read in the Teheran Gazette *and were quickly republished, translated, and imitated.*

Sunday, the 10th of Jumāda al-ūla (6th July), 1873

Today we noticed a singular frame of mind in the French. First of all, they still keep up the state of mourning that followed the German war, and they are all, young or old, sorrowful and melancholy. The dresses of the women, ladies, and men, are all dresses used for mourning, with little ornamentation, and very plain. Now and then some of the people shouted: "Vive le Maréchal," "Vive le Schah de Perse"; from another one I heard, as I strolled about by night, a loud voice saying: "May his reign and rule be firm and enduring." From the whole of these (circumstances) it becomes evident that there are at present in France numerous parties who desire a monarchy; but they are in three sections, one desiring the son of Napoleon, another the dynasty of Louis-Philippe, and the third Henry the Fifth, who is of the Bourbon family; and although this and the family of Louis-Philippe are really one race, they have distinctions. The wishers for a republic, on the other hand, have great power; but they are not all of one mind. Some are for a Red Republic, which is a fundamental commonweal. Others are for a moderate republic, in which monarchical institutions shall be found, without a monarch's existing. Others again wish otherwise. Among all these diversities of opinion it is now a very difficult matter to govern, and the consequences of these incidents will surely eventuate in many difficulties, unless that all combine on one plan and establish either a pure monarchy or a pure republic. Then, France is the most powerful of States, and all must take her into their calculations; whereas, with all these dissidences it is a difficult matter for her to preserve her institutions.

Well; the troops drawn up today in line were nearly twenty thousand in number. This edifice, which is allotted to us as our residence, was formerly the Council-House, *i.e.*, the House for the meeting of the Deputies of the nation. Since the expulsion of the third Napoleon from the sovereignty, and the establishment of a republic in France, the Deputies and the Government have all gone to Versailles, and have left the city of Paris entirely void of the governmental administrations. The city of Paris is now in reality the property of the peasantry and common people, who do whatever they like, as the Government has no adequate means of repression. The palace of the Tuileries, which was the finest building in the world, is now a mass of ruins, as the men of the Commune set fire to it. Nothing remains of the palace but its walls. We were sadly grieved for this; but, thanks be to God, the palace of the Louvre, which adjoins that of the Tuileries, has been saved and is not destroyed.

The Hôtel-de-Ville, one of the fine buildings of the world, and the Palace of the Legion of Honour, were entirely burnt. The column of the Place Vendôme, which the first Napoleon cast out of the materials of the enemy's guns, and on which he set up his own statue, portraying all his wars around the same, has been broken up by the Commune, and carried away, so that nothing of it remains but the block that was the base of the column.

Paris is a beautiful and graceful city, with a delicious climate. It generally enjoys sunshine, thus much resembling the climate of Persia.

In the evening we mounted a carriage and drove about the city with the Muʿtamadu-ʾl-Mulk and General Arture. We passed through the Rue de Rivoli and the Boulevard

Sébastopol—well-known thoroughfares, through the Place
Vendôme, and by the palace of the Tuileries, near to
certain bazaars and the like. The lamps of the city are all
illuminated with gas, so that it is a very bright, beautiful,
and charming city. Numbers of people were seated in
carriages and driving about; or, seated in the cafés and
similar places, were enjoying themselves.

The river Seine is not like the river Thames. It has less
width and less water. Large ships cannot navigate it.

Within our palace there is a pretty little garden, with a
basin of water and a fountain of porphyry in three stages.
A tent, too, has been erected there. From here one can
go to the Ministry of Foreign Affairs, which has been
assigned as quarters for our princes. It is a grand and beautiful building, where formerly the department of the Minister for Foreign Affairs was located. It has a very pretty
flower garden, and a small fountain throws up its water.
The upper floor of our palace possesses a handsome bath-
room, which I admired exceedingly, and which is supplied
with hot and cold water, so that in whichever way one
wishes to have it, there is no difficulty.

Monday, the 11th (7th July)

After breakfast we mounted our carriage and set out for
a drive about town. We passed along a street named Parc-
Monceau—a very beautiful street, by a very pretty flower
garden, and arrived at the Arc de Triomphe, going from
thence towards the Bois de Boulogne, where we first visited
the Jardin d'Acclimatisation. Here we alighted and entered
the garden. There were some flowers, and there was a place
built up of rocks, like a natural mountain. Passing by
these, we came to the park for wild animals and for birds.
They had prepared nettings of wire around rooms, and
within these they had set up trees and introduced water
for the use of the animals and birds. We here saw various
kinds of birds and parrots from the New World, Africa,
India, and Australia. There were also monkeys and other
things. There is an animal called the kangaroo that is found
in Australia—very similiar to the jerboa. It is a singular
thing; it jumps swiftly, but cannot walk. Its forelegs are
short, its hindlegs long. It must jump always. It is of
the size of a large jackal. The female has a pouch on the
lower part of her belly where she puts her young after

they are born and so jumps and runs about. They are very swift runners.

There were some very curious pheasants, with beautiful plumage, of all colours, that we saw also. There were likewise two elephants on which litters were arranged, and so women and children rode about on them. There was also a droshka in which a man was seated, harnessed to an ostrich, which drew it about easily, having the strength of a small horse.

It is extremely difficult to write up our diary in Paris day by day and in detail. Our strolls about the beautiful promenades by night as well as by day leave no chance for us to carry on the diary. However, all that is needful shall be entered in a succinct manner.

One day after breakfast we went to the palace and park of Versailles. The weather was very sultry. We went in state. There were great crowds on both sides of the road. We passed along the Champs Élysées, by the Arc de Triomphe, through the Bois de Boulogne, and across the river Seine. The prefect and other authorities of the Department of Seine et Oise, a separate department on the other side of the river, came to an audience and delivered an address, to which we replied. We then proceeded through the town of Sèvres—famous for its manufactory of porcelain, the village of Chaville, and the village of Ville-D'Avray, so reaching Versailles. Troops of cavalry and infantry were drawn out, and stood in a line on either side of our road. Great crowds were also collected.

We went to a mansion that was the residence of M. Buffet, the President of the National Assembly, and one of the palaces built by Louis XIV; that is to say, the whole of Versailles, palace and park, was called into existence by him. I saw some beautiful paintings and portraits in these few rooms. The whole palace is of stone, and very solidly built. It is the first building of the Franks in point of sculptures, paintings and architecture.

M. Buffet came to meet us at the bottom of the stairs, the other Ministers of the Government being present. We went upstairs into a room, and sat down on a chair. The wife of M. Buffet came into our presence. We then rose; and by the same route through which we had arrived, we returned; until, at about half way, we came to a place where Marshal MacMahon has his quarters. Alighting there, the Marshal, with other commanders, met us, and we went upstairs, taking a seat in a room. That place was also an imposing, handsome, and highly decorated palace, being part of the pile of Versailles. The wife of the Marshal was received in our presence. She is a very noble woman. The Marshal has one son, grown up, apparently of about seventeen or eighteen years of age; also two daughters. They came into the room. The Duc de Broglie—Minister of Foreign Affairs—was also there.

We now descended; we and the Marshal took seats in a carriage, went into the gardens of Versailles, and drove about. They have many basins and fountains of water, the source of which, like that of the fountains at the Crystal Palace of London, is derived from a steam-engine. They had opened the sources and let the water on in the fountains. There was a lake below the basins and fountains, very beautiful and spacious avenues, forest trees, the heads of which were all intertwined so as to form a kind of roof, with every here and there a circular open space of grass with trees around, having in the centre a large basin with a fountain of great altitude. It is a very charming place.

One spot was formed into a kind of artificial mountain, with a cascade falling from the mountain. Several marble statues were placed behind the cascade—one, a group named Apollo, who was the specific deity of manly beauty, of light, and of poetry. He is adorning himself, the others round him are holding a mirror, flowers, or implements of the toilet. It was so beautiful a piece of statuary that one could not even imagine it. I formed the desire to go up near to these statues under the cascade. The Marshal and General Arture said it would be very difficult to go there, as the path was altogether precipitous—of rocks and steep. I said I would go; I alighted from the carriage, and went up. It is true that the way was disagreeable; but to us, who had seen and traversed much worse paths in the hunting-grounds of Persia, it offered no difficulty. When we had arrived near the statues, General Arture came also; but, meeting with a fall, all his clothes were bemired, and his sword was either bent or broken. The Marshal likewise came up, but with great difficulty, and with the assistance of several persons. But this manner of getting up there by a Marshal and a general of France is in no way derogatory to their firmness and courage. Well; the statues were very beautiful, though somewhat soiled, and covered with cobwebs.

Coming down from there, we went to another place made like a circus. In the middle of it were a basin of water and a fountain, and all round it two rows of stone columns. Between these columns was a tall stone basin on a pedestal, from the middle of which a very lofty fountain spouted. There were about eighty or ninety basins of water, from each one of which a fountain sprang, the whole of the columns, fountains, and floor, &c., being of stone.

In like manner, in other parts of the garden, there are numerous fountains, marble statues, and other adornments, with many spacious and beautiful avenues, to do full justice to which, in writing their description, is an impossibility: what is requisite is that a person should see the whole for himself. Women and men, spectators, had formed a rare crush; they uttered cries, they shouted hurrahs.

We turned back and went upstairs in the palace, strolling about for a while through the apartments. Marshal Canrobert, and Palikao—who commanded the expedition to China—were received in audience, and conversed with. Palikao is now unemployed. He said that from want of something to do, he was engaged in writing a diary of his expedition to China. Canrobert is also out of employ, but is a very able commander, possessing judgment and firmness. In the Sebastopol war he commanded in chief, and at the siege of Metz was under the command of Marshal Bazaine. At the surrender of that fortress to the Germans he was among the captives, and was greatly mortified at being under Bazaine's command.

We next saw the sons of Louis-Philippe. In the time of Napoleon they were expelled from France and went to England, returning to the French territory after the republic had been proclaimed. They have a claim to the sovereignty of France, up to the point which God may ordain.

Well; after a while Marshal MacMahon came, and we went to the room in which is the bedstead, with the bedding, of Louis XIV. After seeing these we went to table to dinner. The table was very long, the dinner very good. The most part of those present were military commanders and officers, deputies, and the like. On our right was seated M. Buffet, the President of the Assembly; to our left, the Minister of Foreign Affairs. Opposite to us was Marshal MacMahon, with the Grand Vazīr to his right. In like manner, the princes of Persia, with the others, were seated along the two sides. The Sanī‹u-›d-Dawla stood behind our chair and acted as interpreter. It passed off very pleasantly.

The dining hall was a long apartment, very handsome, and highly decorated, with numerous chandeliers.

After dinner we came downstairs, and I, with the Marshal, took my seat in a carriage, proceeding to witness the illuminations of the palace and gardens. Armour-wearing cavalry, each man holding a flambeau in his hand, preceded us; and the crowds were very great. Afterwards we turned in another direction of the gardens, where there was a lake. The further side of this was arranged in stages, over which water flowed as in a cascade, while fountains spouted from the basins. Great numbers of commanders and grandees, the members of the Diplomatic Body, nobles, notables, deputies, and others, were present. They had placed a chair, and on it we took our seat. Then all sat down, and a very beautiful display of fireworks took place. It was moonlight; the weather, too, was extremely beautiful and pleasant.

At the conclusion of the fireworks we mounted our carriage, and went past St. Cloud—which was a noble royal palace, but took fire, and was burnt in the German war, though its avenues and park are still left—through the Bois de Boulogne, to the city, and home. On our road we everywhere conversed with General Arture.

One day we went to the Invalides, where are seen the tomb of the first Napoleon, those of his commanders and brothers, together with others of older commanders of the days of Louis XIV, &c. At our quarters, which were formerly the Palace of the National Assembly, i.e., at the Palais de Bourbon, there is a vast area fronting the Invalides, with avenues full of trees. We arrived there. The aged veteran soldiers, wounded, some without arms or legs, and some blind, were drawn up in line, and did us military honour, we returning their salute. In the court of the Invalides are some large old cannon, mortars, and the like. The Governor of the Invalides, a very aged personage, and palsied, was present, whose name was Martinprai. He came to meet us with his aides-de-camp and other officers. He was formerly a Governor in Algeria, and Chief of the Staff in the Crimean and Italian campaigns.

We entered the chapel, where was a handsome altar of stone, with giltwork, which Louis-Philippe, the former King of the French, had set up. It is a grand structure. On the other side of the altar, under a dome, is the tomb of the first Napoleon, whose body was brought from the island of St. Helena by Louis-Philippe, and buried here. The stone that covers the tomb, of a pea-green colour, was brought from the island of Corsica; while the stone above that, a most beautiful Siberian stone, with a ruddy tint, was sent by the Russian Emperor Nicholas. The general structure of this chapel of the Invalides is of the time of Louis XIV; but the altar and some other of its arrangements were constructed by Louis-Philippe. It was the latter who excavated the interior of the dome, in which the sarcophagus of the tomb is placed. Around it, above, is a walk to which people come to visit the tomb. The palace of the Invalides is a very noble pile, the dome of which was gilt by Napoleon.

We saw there a few veterans who had been in the battles of Waterloo, Friedland, or Jena, who were still hale and hearty, and who gave descriptions of those battles.

On the other side of the tomb was a place where, in a glass case, they had placed the hat worn in his battles by the first Napoleon. We lifted the hat and examined it long. We held in our hands the hat of a very great monarch and commander. It was evident from the hat itself that Napoleon had always worn this very hat, which was a plain hat. The sword of Napoleon that was by his side on the field of Austerlitz was also there. We took it up, and examined it. The sword was small and straight; its hilt was of gold, but the sword was rusted and could not be drawn from the scabbard. With the utmost veneration did we replace both articles, and came away.

We now proceeded to the museum, in which they have collected and arranged specimens of ancient and modern cannon, with inventions relating thereto, ancient weapons of commanders and champions of old, quantities of armour for man and horse, all ticketed with a number and with the names of their owners. There were also other places used as armories, &c., but, as we were somewhat fatigued, we deferred to another day a visit to them, and returned home.

The present number of inmates of the Invalides, officers and men, is five hundred and ninety souls. Of these, thirty-five are from the days of the first Napoleon, the rest from later times. The palace was founded in A.D. 1670 by order of Louis XIV, Louvois being then the Minister of War and its builder.

There are thirty-two pieces of artillery at the gates of the Invalides, which are fired when any event of importance occurs, such as a great victory or the like. On our arrival in Paris, too, these guns of the Invalides were fired.

The flags taken from the enemy in battle in the time

of the first Napoleon, and since, are kept at the Invalides, as are also those taken in the days of Louis XIV, downwards. Around the tomb of Napoleon forty-six flags are disposed, taken by himself in battles; while within the chapel, another two hundred and forty-five flags are seen, taken at earlier periods, or later.

Three days before our arrival in France, two trains came into collision on the Cherbourg Railway, when a number of people were killed or wounded.

M. Crémieux, one of the French national deputies, and a Jew, who was always in opposition to Napoleon III, and is a marvellous orator, came to an audience. He is an old man, and very short. He still speaks in the Assembly and is in opposition to the Government.

The celebrated Rothschild, a Jew also, who is exceedingly rich, came to an audience, and we conversed with him. He greatly advocated the cause of the Jews, mentioned the Jews of Persia, and claimed tranquillity for them. I said to him: "I have heard that you, brothers, possess a thousand crores of money. I consider the best thing to do would be that you should pay fifty crores to some large or small State, and buy a territory in which you could collect all the Jews of the whole world, you becoming their chiefs, and leading them on their way in peace, so that you should no longer be thus scattered and dispersed." We laughed heartily, and he made no reply. I gave him an assurance that I do protect every alien nationality that is in Persia.

M. Lesseps, so well known, who has joined the Mediterranean to the Red Sea—i.e., a large company having been formed—has, through the exertions of this personage, opened that road, and by this means shortened for commerce the passage to India, Persia, China, &c., from Europe, by about two thousand leagues—came to an audience, together with his son, a youth. He has now a fresh scheme in his head—that of making a railway from the town of Orenburg in Russia to the city of Samarqand, and thence on to Peshawur in British India. But this is a notion very remote from reason and distant from practicability.

TRANSLATED BY J. W. REDHOUSE

MUHAMMAD ABDUH: RELIGIONS AND HUMAN PROGRESS

[from *Risālat al-Tawḥīd*, Treatise on Unity]

Muhammad Abduh started life as an Egyptian fellah, a poor peasant's son, and ended as the most unsettling Arab Moslem thinker of at least two generations. In his view, Islamic thought had gone fearfully wrong in disregarding modern problems, and he blazed wide and sometimes wild trails through the Islamic traditions and Koranic exegesis in search of compatible answers to them.

Mastering the formidable obstacles of the Azhar in Cairo, he impressed his lines of thought through massive inertias into the cold light of modern day. Nourished equally by his Sufi ascetic past and his religio-nationalist present, he encountered the challenges of the non-Islamic world with optimism and success. He became Grand Mufti, and had made permanent his school of interpretation before his death in 1905.

When religions first began, men understood their well-being, whether general or particular, only in a most rudimentary way, rather like infants lately born, who know only what comes within their senses and distinguish only with difficulty between the present and the past. Only what they can manually touch do they really cognize, and they have no inner awareness by which to "sympathize" with family or fellow, being concerned simply with self-preservation and too preoccupied for the implications of their relationships with others, unless it be a hand to feed them or to steady them on their feet. Religions in this sort of context could not intelligibly relate themselves to men on subtle aspects of consciousness or "extend" them with rational proofs. On the contrary, the great grace of God is seen in their handling the peoples as children, in just the way that a parent treats his child—with the utmost simplicity and within the senses of hearing and sight. The religions took men and gave them straight commands and firm restraints, to which they required obedience to the utmost possible degree. Though the meaning and purpose were there to be known, obedience was irrespective of actual comprehension and intelligent knowledge. Religions came with astonishing and impressive miracles and laid upon men the forms of worship consonant with their condition.

During the centuries that followed peoples flourished and declined, waxed and waned. They quarrelled and agreed. The times brought sufferings and there were endless vicissitudes of prosperity and adversity, through which they were prompted to finer sensitivity and deeper self-awareness, which may not unworthily be compared to what goes on in women's hearts or belongs with growing youth. A religion came which spoke to these feelings and, tenderly confiding to these compassions, made its appeal to the gentle arts of the heart. It laid down for men sacred laws of asceticism, drawing them away from the world altogether and turning them towards the higher life. It taught men not to press even their undoubted rights, and barred the doors of heaven to the rich. Similar attitudes characterizing it are well enough known. It ordained patterns of Divine worship consistent with its understanding of man and in line with its message, and had deep effect in breaking the ills and retrieving the evils of the souls that hearkened to it. But in the course of a few generations the resolve of men grew weak and weary of it. Men lapsed from its provisions and precepts as being more than they could sustain. They took to assuming that there was an inherent impracticability in its commands. Its very custodians themselves began to rival kings for their authority and to vie in wealth with the idle rich. The great mass of people declined sadly from its noble quality through "reinterpretation," and in their vain fancies imported all kinds of false accretions.

So things went, in respect of actions and disposition. Purity was forgotten and integrity bartered. As for dogmas, these were compromised by schism and heresy. The custodians abandoned all its principles, except one they mistakenly supposed to be its strongest pillar and chief ground, namely the veto on intellectual enquiry into faith, or indeed into the details of the universe and on the pursuit of the secret things of the mind. They promulgated the principle that reason and religion had nothing in common, but that, rather, religion was the inveterate enemy of science. It was not simply that this view could be taken by anyone for himself: rather they strenuously imposed it as the proper thing for all. They pressed the doctrine with such force as to provoke the most shameful of all conflicts in human history, namely, civil war within the household of religion for the imposition of religious decrees. And thus the very foundations were broken up and communal relationships destroyed. Concord, co-operation and peace were ousted; schism, contention and strife reigned in their place. And so men continued until the advent of Islam.

At length, human society reached a point at which man came to his full stature, helped by the moral of the earlier vicissitudes. Islam supervened, to present its case to reason, to call on mind and intelligence for action, to take emotion and feeling into partnership for man's guidance to both earthly and heavenly blessedness. It clarified the things that provoked human discords and demonstrated that religion with God was one in all generations, that there was a single Divine purpose for their reform without and their cleansing within. Islam taught that the sole aim of outward forms of worship was to renew the inward recollection of God and that God looks not on the form but on the heart. It required the devotee to care as well for his body as for the soul, enjoining outward as well as inward integrity, both of which it made mandatory. Sincerity was made the very heart of worship, and rites were only laid down in so far as they conduced to the hallowing of moral character. "Verily prayer preserves men from foul and evil things." (Surah 29.45.) "Man is created restless. When evil befalls him he despairs, but touched with good fortune he becomes niggardly—though not those who pray." (Surah 79. 19–22.) The rich man who remembers to be grateful is raised by Islam to the same level as the poor man who endures patiently. Perhaps Islam even esteems him higher. Islam deals with man in its exhortations as a wise and sober counsellor would deal with a mature person summoning him to the full harnessing of his powers, both outward and inward, and affirmed this quite unequivocally to be the way of pleasing God and showing thankfulness for His grace. This world is the seed plot of the world to come. Men will not come by ultimate good, save as they endeavour a present well-doing.

Islam confronts the obdurate with the words: "Say: bring your evidence if you are speaking the truth." (Surah 2. 111 and 27.64.) It was round with controversialists and partisans, for undermining the bases of assurance and declared that separatism was a crime, parting company as it does with manifest truth. Islam was not content with mere verbal exhortation, counsel and argument, but built concord into the fabric of law and action. It allowed the Muslim to marry with the people of the Book and partake of their table and directed that in controversy they should always be high-minded.

It is a familiar fact that kinship spreads love and binds men in amity. Intermarriage happens only where there is mutual affection between the families of the parties and ties of concord—greater factors as these are than just the love of the particular husband for his wife of another faith. God said: "One of His signs is that He has created from among yourselves wives that you may find joy in them and He planted love and kindness in your hearts." (Surah 30.21.) Furthermore, it was made incumbent on Muslims to defend those who became their protégés (*dhimmah*) from other communities, just as they did themselves. Islam laid down that the rights and duties of these were no whit less than those of Muslims, though only a small tax was levied on them for their property, in respect of this protection. After payment of this tribute (*jizyah*) all compulsion relating to religion was forbidden. The hearts of the believers were gladdened with the words: "O believers, you are responsible for yourselves only: he who goes astray cannot harm you if you are on the right way." (Surah 5. 105.) Theirs was the duty to invite men to good by the better way. They had neither right nor duty to employ any kind of force to induce people into Islam. It was worthy to penetrate men's hearts by its own light. The verse quoted does not relate to well-doing as between Muslims, since it only speaks of "guidance" (into Islam) after the injunction to good relations has been performed. The whole purpose is to direct men to the fact that the Divine institution of religion is not for separatism but for men's guidance into every meaning of the good.

Islam removed all racial distinctions within humanity, in the common dignity of relationship with God, of participation in humankind, in race group and particular setting, as well as the dignity of being in the way of the highest attainments prepared of God for men. This universal dignity contrasts sharply with the exclusive claims of those who pretend to privileged status denied to others and consign allegedly inferior mortals to permanent subjection, thus strangling the very spirit of the peoples, or most of them, and reducing them to walking shadows.

Such is Islam, and the forms of Divine obedience accord-

ing to its Book and authentic tradition, as befits the majesty
of God and His transcendent glory behind all likeness, and
in accord with the mind and sound thinking. Prayer in-
cludes kneeling and prostration, movement and stillness,
petition and entreaty, praise and ascription of greatness—
all of which arise from that awareness of the Divine
authority which overwhelms men and claims every energy.
To Him the heart is bowed in awe and the soul brings
homage. In all there is nothing beyond reason's range,
except an abstruse question such as why the prescribed
number of ritual movements or the stone-throwing on
pilgrimage—about which one can readily defer to the wisdom of the all-knowing, the ever-aware, in the knowledge
that there is nothing evidently futile, or meaningless or
inconsistent with the principles of thought with which God
has furnished the mind.

Fasting is an abstinence which serves to impress on the
spirit the greatness of God's command and a means to
appreciate His gifts through forgoing them and, by exercise
in His loving-kindness, to know its quality in truth. "Fasting is prescribed for you, as it was for those before you,
perhaps you may truly fear Him." (Surah 2.183.)

As for the pilgrimage ceremonies, they recall to man his
most elemental needs and—if only once in his lifetime—
serve notice on him forcibly of the equality among all men,
in that there the distinction between rich and poor, pauper
and prince, is annulled. All are present in a common garb,
bareheaded, without adornment, and with the single aim
of worship before God, the Lord of all the worlds. By the
circumambulation of the *Ka⸱bah* and the "running" and
the "standing" and by the touching of the Stone they
perpetuate the memory of Abraham, father of faith. Yet
they are well aware that none of these material things, for
all their sanctity, have the power to harm or profit super-
stitiously. Each of the various parts of Islamic worship,
when men truly submit themselves to them, proclaim the
Divine transcendence and His holy separation from all that
man vainly associates with him.

When will anything comparable be found in the rites
of other nations, where reason goes awry and there is no
clear way to the pure secrets of the unity and transcendence
of God?

Islam dispelled the clouds of illusion which obscured
from the mind the realities of the macrocosm of this world
and the microcosm of man. It affirmed that the great
signs of God in the making of the world hinge on Divine

laws, laid down in the eternal knowledge of God and ever abiding unchanged. Yet God's part in them must never be overlooked. On the contrary, the remembrance of Him must be alive in every act of cognizance we make. In the Prophet's words: "The sun and the moon are signs of God: they do not suffer eclipse for anyone's death, nor for his birth. If you see an eclipse let it remind you of God, and wait for the reappearance of the light." This confirms that all earthly phenomena follow one pattern, within the agelong care of God for the laws on which He established the universe.

Islam also drew back the curtain that obscured the conditions of human well-being, whether of persons or peoples, and of the trials with which men are beset. It made the issue unmistakably clear in both respects. The good things which God gives some to enjoy in this life and the adversities they suffer—riches and honour, power, children, or poverty, indigence, frailty and bereavement—these may perhaps result from law-abiding integrity or intransigence and crookedness in the life of the individual concerned. But more frequently God bears with evil excesses or immoral living and leaves such people with life's pleasures here, and awaits their condign punishment in the life to come. And oftentimes He tries His faithful servants, commending their submissive acceptance of His judgements. These are they who in tribulation sincerely bow before Him and say: "We are God's and to Him do we return." (Surah 2.156.) Thus it is not men's anger, nor their docility, nor their inward sincerity, nor yet their active wrongdoing which affect their adversities nor yet their particular blessings, except in so far as there may be some direct causal connection in the ordinary way—poverty, for example, resulting from excessive indulgence, and humiliation from cowardice, and loss of authority from injustice, or like the obvious link generally obtaining between wealth and a wise disposal of affairs, and public esteem from a care for public interests. Such like sequences of cause and effect are well enough known and are not our subject here.

It is not this way, however, in respect of nations. There is a spirit from which the life of nations takes its rise, illuminating their true well-being in this world here and now, before the other world is reached. It is the spirit which God has implanted in His Divine laws for the right ordering of thought and reflection, the discipline of desire and the curbing of ambition and lust. It is the spirit which bids us assess every question on its proper merits and pursue all objectives soundly, keeping faith, holding brotherly affection and co-operating in right dealing, with mutual loyalty through thick and thin. "He who wishes his reward in this world, We will give him thereof." (Surah 3.145.) God will never deprive a nation of His favour as long as this spirit animates them. Rather He will multiply their blessings in proportion to its strength and diminish them when it is weak. Should the spirit no longer be found in the nation, happiness also takes its place and peace with it. God then turns its strength into decline and its wealth to poverty. Well-being then gives way to wretchedness and peace to trouble. While they slumber in neglect, they will be overpowered by others, either by tyrants or by just masters. "If We desire to bring a nation to destruction, We first warn those of them who live in comfort. But if they go on in sin, they bring down upon themselves a righteous judgement and We utterly destroy them." (Surah 17.16.) God has commanded righteousness, but they have perverted it to evil. In that event, wailing and weeping will bring them no help, nor will intercession avail, nor the surviving appearances of activity. Their only hope of staying the rot is to repair again to that gracious spirit and seek its renewed descent from the heaven of mercy upon their affairs, through the promptings of thought and recollection, of patience and thanksgiving. "Truly God does not change a people's condition until inwardly they change themselves." (Surah 13.11.) "This was the pattern of God's relationship to those who passed away before you: you will never find the way of God to vary." (Surah 33.62.) There is no finer word than that spoken by ʿAbbās ibn ʿAbd al-Mutṭalib when he prayed for rain: "O God, there is no distress that comes upon us without our having transgressed: and none is lifted off us save by repentance."

The earliest of the Islamic people lived by these laws. While the Muslim spirit was exalted by these noble beliefs and worked them out in worthy actions, other peoples supposed that by their prayers they could shake the earth and rend the heavens with their lamentations while they wallowed in their passions and persisted in extravagant ways, so that their idle hopes of intercession profited them nothing.

The Qurʾān urges instruction and right direction for the ordinary people and kindly dealing and vetoes evil-doing. It says: "A group from each community should stay behind to be well versed in religion, so as to admonish their people when they return, so that they may take heed."

(Surah 9.122.) It commands the same in the verse: "Be a people who invite men to goodness, who enjoin kindly dealing and forbid what is evil. These are the prosperous ones. Do not be like those who were divided and quarrelled among themselves after clear evidence had been given them. These incur sore punishment, on the day when some faces will be radiant and others sombre. To the blackened-face sinners God will say: Did you belie your faith after you believed? Then taste the punishment. For you are unbelievers. As for those whose faces are cheerful, these will abide forever in God's mercy. Such are the signs of God, which We recite to you in truth. God desires no injustice in His worlds. Unto Him are all things in the heavens and the earth." (Surah 3.104–109.)

After these admonitions, which bring disquiet to the transgressors and affirm the retribution of those who defy or fall short of the Divine commands, the Qurʾān sets out the happy case of those who are steady doers of good and who shun the evil, in the plainest terms: "You are the best people, raised up for mankind; you enjoin the good and forbid the evil and you believe in God." (Surah 3.110.) The mention of these two in this verse prior to the phrase about believing, despite the fact that faith is the source from which righteous dealing derives and the stock from which the branches of goodness spring, is to highlight that moral obligation and make it paramount. Indeed, we may say that the order of the verse witnesses to the fact that goodness is that which preserves faith and its guardian angel. The Qurʾān emphasizes its repudiation of those who neglect these things and of the religionaries who disregarded them. It says: "The unbelievers in Israel were cursed by David, Jesus and Mary, in that they rebelled and were transgressors. They did not forbid one another the evil they committed. Their deeds were verily deplorable." (Surah 5.78–79.) Such a malediction as was uttered against them is the most intense expression of God's wrath and abhorrence.

Islam laid down for the poor a well-defined right to the property of the rich, which the latter were freely to honour, in relieving the need of the destitute, healing the distress of the afflicted, emancipating the enslaved and helping "the sons of the way"—the homeless people. It held such expenditure in the pursuit of goodness the most urgent of all its exhortations, making it oftentimes the token of faith and a sign of having been guided into "the straight path." By this means it neutralized the grudges of the poor and cleansed their hearts from envy at the bounty with which God had blessed the well-to-do and thus conduced to a mutual charity of heart between the two. Compassion in the wealthy for the lot of the wretched brings tranquillity to all. Where is there a more salutary cure for the ills of society? "That is God's grace which He bestows on whomsoever He wills: For God is the Lord of great magnanimity." (Surah 57.21.)

Islam also barred the way to two evils and cut off two copious sources of wickedness in outlawing wine and gambling and usury—which it did absolutely and without compromise.

From all the foregoing, it is clear that Islam has not omitted to treat of any one of the basic virtues. There is no important aspect of good conduct in which it has not brought a new lease of life—nothing essential to the social fabric it has failed to enjoin. As we have shown, it brings together for mature man, freedom of thought, intellectual independence of action, and thus integrity of character, enhancement of capacity and a general quickening of intention and achievement. Whoever reads the Qur²ān rightly will find new impulse and initiative and unfailing treasure.

When one has sound training, does one need a mentor, or a guardian when one's mind is fully ripe? Hardly! for the true has been distinguished from the false and all that remains is to follow the guidance and from the hands of mercy take the way that brings one to happiness here and hereafter.

For this reason, Muhammad's prophethood brought prophecy itself to an end. His message terminated the work of messengers, as the Book affirms and the authentic tradition corroborates. The fact is evidenced by the collapse of all pretensions to prophethood since Muhammad, as well as by the world's contentment with the truth that has come to it from him. The world knows that there is no acceptability now in claims made by pretenders after mission with laws and revelation from God. It acknowledges the heavenly word which says: "Muhammad is not the father of any man among you. He is the messenger of God and the seal of the prophets. God truly knows all things." (Surah 33.40.)

TRANSLATED BY ISHAQ MUSA²AD AND KENNETH CRAGG

ABD AL-RAHMAN AL-KAWAKIBI: THE VIRTUES OF THE ARABS

[from *Umm al-Qura*, Mother of Communities]

A more pointed and powerful analysis of the state of Islam at the turn of the century, with a ready remedy, was that provided by the Syrian Abd al-Rahman al-Kawakibi (1849–1902), whose thinking fused Pan-Arabism with Pan-Islamism. His notions, derived to some extent from the Englishman W. S. Blunt, offered a far more coherent and revolutionary system than those which had preceded them.

Al-Kawakibi envisioned the restoration of the Arab caliphate headquartered (an innovation) at Mecca as the necessary prerequisite and leadership for the revitalization and resurgence of Islam. In doing so, one authority says, he "may be considered as the first true intellectual precursor of modern secular Pan-Arabism. . . . He was the first to declare himself, without ambiguity, as the champion of the Arabs against the Turks. Moreover, in his praise and condemnation there were no half tones, no reticences: the Arabs were better people than the Turks and ought to have the primacy. And by launching, in Arabic, the idea of a merely spiritual caliphate he took the first step toward a purely secular politics. Traditionally, the well-known European distinction between the spiritual and temporal has no place in Islam, and those who wanted to reform Islam, toward the end of the nineteenth century, were never really prepared to envisage a political system in which the temporal would be divorced from the spiritual. For all his preoccupation with the state of Islam, al-Kawakibi, once he introduced the idea of a spiritual caliph, was led to consider politics as an autonomous activity divorced from divine prescription, and fully subject to the will of men. Such an idea is an essential prerequisite of nationalism."[1]

[1]Sylvia G. Haim, *Arab Nationalism: An Anthology* (Berkeley and Los Angeles, 1962), page 27.

Because the society [of Umm al-qura][2] is concerned only with the religious renaissance, it has found it necessary to pin its hopes on the Arabian Peninsula and its dependencies, and on its people and their neighbors, and to lay before the eyes of the Muslim nation the characteristics of the peninsula, of its people and of the Arabs in general, in order to eliminate political and racial fanaticism as well as to explain why the society has shown preference for the Arabs. We therefore say:

The peninsula is the place from which the light of Islam originated.

It contains the exalted Kaaba.

In it is found the Prophet's Mosque and the holy ground of his house, pulpit, and grave.

The peninsula is the most suitable center for religious policy, since it lies halfway between the Far East of Asia and the Far West of Africa.

Of all countries it is the most free of racial, religious, or sectarian intermixture.

It is the most removed of all the Muslim countries from the vicinage of foreigners.

The peninsula is most worthy to be a land of free men, owing to its remoteness and natural poverty which preserve it from the greedy and the ambitious.

The Arabs of the peninsula have Islamic unity because religion appeared among them.

The habit of religion has become ingrained in them because religion is more compatible with their social customs than with those of others.

Of all Muslims they are the most knowledgeable in the principles of Islam as they are the oldest to practice it; many hadiths give witness to the strength of their faith.

The Arabs of the peninsula are the most zealous of all Muslims in preserving religion, in supporting it, and in glorying in it, especially as that zeal for the Prophet's cause is still alive among them in the Hijaz, in the Yemen, in Aman, in Hadramaut, in Iraq, and in Africa.

The religion of the peninsula Arabs is still governed by the right example of the ancients, free of excess and confusion.

Of all other Muslims, the peninsula Arabs possess the strongest *esprit de corps* and are the most proud because of the Bedouin characteristics which they possess.

[2]Another name for Mecca, and by extension, in the author's view, the whole community of Arabs under the order of Islam and Moslems under the order of an Arab caliphate. [Ed.]

The princes of the peninsula Arabs descend from noble fathers and mothers and are married to noble consorts of good birth; their honor remains untainted.

The peninsula Arabs are the most ancient of nations in having a polished civilization, as is shown by the proliferation and the excellence of their wisdom and their literature.

Of all Muslims, the peninsula Arabs are the best able to bear hardships in order to attain their aims, and to undertake travel and residence abroad, because they have not succumbed to the servile habits of luxury.

The peninsula Arabs preserve better than all other peoples their race and customs, for though they mingle with others they do not mix with them.

The peninsula Arabs are, of all the Muslim nations, the most jealous of their freedom and independence and those who most reject oppression.

Of the Arabs in general, their language, of all the languages of the Muslins, takes greatest care of knowledge; it is preserved from extinction by the noble Koran.

The language of the Arabs is the language common to all the Muslims, who number 300 million souls.

The language of the Arabs is the native language of 100 million people, Muslim and non-Muslim.

The Arabs are the oldest of nations in following the principles of equality in rights and in eschewing great disparities in society.

The Arabs are the oldest peoples to practice the principle of consultation in public matters.

The Arabs know best, of all people, the principles of socialist living.

The Arabs are amongst the most noble of people in respecting treaties, and the most humane in keeping faith, and the most chivalrous in respecting the rights of vicinage, and the most generous in the doing of good deeds.

The Arabs are of all nations the most suitable to be an authority in religion and an example to the Muslims; the other nations have followed their guidance at the start and will not refuse to follow them now.

TRANSLATED BY SYLVIA G. HAIM

ZIYA GÖKALP: THE IDEAL OF NATIONALISM

One of the most creative and influential thinkers on the then all-important subject of nationalism was Ziya Gökalp (1876–1924). It was he, more than anyone else, who influenced two generations of Turkish writers. His main preoccupations were how the Turks should adopt Western civilization and how this effort should be harmonized with their Turkish and Islamic backgrounds.

Youth is asking: "If we believe that ideals are the product of historical disturbance and social crises, will it not then be necessary to assume that another ideal, one which may be born from the impulse of different circumstances, will succeed the ideal of nationalism? Will not, for example, the idea of socialism supersede the sentiment of nationality in the near or distant future?"

My answer to this question is as follows. Essentially an ideal is the actualization of the existence of a social group by its members. The rays of the sun do not have the power to burn unless they are intensified through a lens. Similarly, the group is unable by itself to manifest its "sacredness" unless it reaches a state of social combustion. This sacredness, even before it has reached consciousness, exists in an unconscious state in the psychological unity of the social group. So far it has remained a hidden treasure (*al-kanz al-makhfī*), with all its halo of sanctity. The function of the crowd situation is to make this reality manifest to the members of the group by transforming the latter amorphous existence into a clear-cut form. Social agitation becomes a source of ideals by its capacity to transform the group, which until now has been in a loose state, into a compact body. The emergence of an ideal means its rise from the subconscious to the conscious level.

Before the rise of the ideals of Ottomanism, Islamism, and Turkism, the Ottoman state, the Islamic *ümmet,* and the Turkish nationality all existed. The working class existed in a scattered state before the ideal of socialism was born, the latter emerging as a consequence of the concentration of workers, which itself was a result of the development of large-scale industry in Europe.

Therefore, a social group must have an existence, an organized form and institutions, in order to assert its existence in the consciousness of its members in a crowd situation. Its institutions—political, religious, or linguistic —must certainly have an existence. No crowd situation or condition of social agitation can create a group from nothing. Not only do ideals not emerge from a crowd situation that has no organizational basis, but such a crowd is itself inconceivable. Only something which exists in a state of laxity may be transformed into a state of solidity.

It follows from what has been said that any major social emergence taking place in the future must have its basis in already existing conditions. In order for an ideal to arise in the future, it must spring from the intensification of one of the existing groups. Therefore, a great ideal should be born out of the intensification of only that group which, in addition to being the richest and most powerfully organized, is in a position to bring together and assimilate all other groups in its own organization.

Which, then, is this inclusive group? Among the existing ones it is the language group—that is, the nationality group —which is most capable of fulfilling such a function.

First, those who speak the same language are usually descendants of the same stock, and thus a nation also means an ethnic unity. . . . Secondly, language is the carrier of ideas and sentiments, the transmitter of customs and tradition; hence, those who speak the same language share the same aspirations, the same consciousness, and the same mentality. Individuals thus sharing common and homogeneous sentiments are also naturally prone to profess the same faith. It is because of this that language groups in many cases are of the same religion. Even if in the beginning certain conditions interfered somewhat with this religious homogeneity, historical events show that peoples of the same language groups do tend to embrace the same faith. Thus, the Latins have been inclined to Roman Catholicism, the Germanic peoples to Protestantism, and the Slavonic peoples to Eastern Orthodoxy. Of the Ural-Altai group, the Mongols adopted Buddhism, the Manchurians Confucianism, and the Finno-Ugrians Christianity. Various sections of the Turks, in the beginning, had accepted Buddhism, Manichaeism, Judaism, and Christianity; but with the conversion of the majority to Islam, all became Muslims with the exception of the Shamanist Yakuts, who constitute only some two hundred thousand people. The main reason why the latter remained outside Islam is that their home lies far out of the Turkish lands. They will either embrace Islam and remain Turks or become Russified by accepting Christianity.

As language plays a part in deciding religious affiliation, so religion plays a part in determining membership in a nationality. The Protestant French became Germanized when they were expelled from France and settled in Germany. The Turkish aristocracy of the old Bulgars became Slavicized following their conversion to Christianity. And today, the non-Turkish Muslims migrating to Turkey in a scattered way are becoming Turkified because of their religious affiliation. We may conclude, therefore, that there is a close relationship between linguistic and religious association.

Thirdly, when universal military service and sovereignty of the people were introduced, national defence ceased to be the monopoly of a trained and privileged *sipahi* order, and administration of the government was no longer the privilege of a ruling class directly responsible only to the ruler. The peasants who previously had no arms except their ploughs, and the townsfolk who were used to staying at home, now became soldiers; the people, who had no notion of administration, came to the point where they could control the government. It became necessary to instil in them a sense of patriotism and to teach them how to assume the responsibilities of voting. When the needs of adult and universal education became apparent, conflicts arose among the different ethnic groups in the state over the question of which language should be spoken in the schools. The government began to insist on the dissemination of an official language, but each ethnic group demanded that its own language become the main channel of education and instruction. Thus, in the last century it came to be realized that confining the state and the country to a single language was no longer possible, and, as in the case of Austria-Hungary, the state adopted two main languages. Today in Europe only those states which are based on a single-language group are believed to have a future. Every national group is demonstrating the kind of future to which it aspires by voicing its wishes for a national home, with or without an historical basis.

Today all of us realize that the idea of a state or homeland supposedly common to diverse nationalities is nothing but a mere concept, devoid of any zeal, enthusiasm, and devotion. Just as it is inconceivable for more than one person to win the love of one individual, so there can be no real common home and fatherland for diverse peoples. A state that is not based on a united spirit can be only a common source of subsistence and nothing more. A land that is not the home of a nation is like a public kitchen where everyone merely feeds himself.

The institutions of state and fatherland achieve permanent life only when based on a national ideal, but they are destined to fall if they are based only on individual interests. Men without ideals are egoistic, self-seeking, pessimistic, faithless, and cowardly; they are lost souls. A state must be founded on national ideals, a country has to be the home of a nationality if it is to have permanent existence.

We see, therefore, that the concept of the language group encompasses the concept of state as well as that of national home. Smaller units, such as family, class, corporation, village, tribe, and religious community, exist within the confines of the national unit. The family is composed of individuals of the same faith. They speak the language of a single nation. Other groups share a common religion and language. They are all, therefore, but smaller, constituent organs of the nation.

In short, all ideals connected with the ethnic unit (*kavm*), religion, state, national home, family, class, corporation, etc., are auxiliary to the national ideals. As long as social evolution substitutes intellectual and sentimental for material factors, the value and effectiveness of the national language as a means of expressing these ideals will increase, and in this way the sentiment of nationality will become a permanent ideal.

It is true that, as large-scale industry grows in Turkey, the ideal of socialism will arise here too. But this ideal is destined to remain auxiliary to the national ideal, as have all other secondary ideals. Although socialism in Europe is constantly gaining strength, we see clearly that it gives way to the national ideal in times of war. Not only during political wars, but even in economic competition, class ideals are subordinated to national ideals.

Furthermore, we can easily detect that the substance of all aspects of social life—such as religion, morality, law, politics, economics, science, and fine arts—is language. Any increase in the importance of these spheres of social life means an increase in the importance of language. Language is the basis of social life, the texture of morality, the substratum of culture and civilization. All future social movements—with respect to any group or activity—will always solidify language groups directly or indirectly, and out of every crisis the ideal of nationalism will effervesce, each time more powerful and with increasing vitality.

TRANSLATED BY NIYAZI BERKES

MOHAMMED IQBAL: SECRETS OF THE SELF

[from *Asrār-ī Khūdī,* Secrets of the Self; *Bāng-i Darā,* The Call of the Road; *Bāl-i Jibrīl,* Gabriel's Wing; and *Darb-i Kalīm,* The Rod of Moses]

> *Born in 1877 in the Punjab, Mohammed Iqbal was one of the most erudite and deepest Moslem thinkers in modern times. He is considered by many the father of the State of Pakistan,[1] where he is widely venerated.*
>
> *Philosopher and lawyer, Iqbal was also a very gifted poet. He was at home in many languages. He wrote his early poems in Urdu, but chose Persian for many of the later ones. He wrote in all of the classical poetic forms and seemed to prefer them to the newer forms. He propounded a vigorous philosophy of "self-hood" in which elements of Hegel and the Neo-Hegelians were ingeniously commingled with the wisdom of the Sufis. Asrār-i Khūdī was one of his brilliant poetic collections. In it, the translator writes, "Iqbal's philosophy of thought and phrase presents itself under a different aspect. Its audacity of thought and phrase is less apparent, its logical brilliancy dissolves in the glow of feeling and imagination, and it wins the heart before taking possession of the mind."*

My being was an unfinished statue,
Uncomely, worthless, good for nothing.
Love chiselled me: I became a man
And gained knowledge of the nature of the universe.

I have seen the movement of the sinews of the sky,
And the blood coursing in the veins of the moon.
Many a night I wept for Man's sake

---

[1] See the excellent studies of S. A. Vahid, *Iqbal: His Art and Thought* (London, 1959); and Annemarie Schimmel, *Gabriel's Wing* (Leiden, 1963).

That I might tear the veil from Life's mysteries,
And extract the secret of Life's constitution
From the laboratory of phenomena.

I who gave beauty to this night, like the moon,
Am as dust in devotion to the pure Faith—
A Faith renowned in hill and dale.
Which kindles in men's hearts a flame of undying
    song:
It sowed an atom and reaped a sun,
It harvested a hundred poets like Rumi and Attar.

I am a sigh: I will mount to the heavens;
I am but smoke, yet am I sprung of fire.
Driven onward by high thoughts, my pen
Cast abroad the secret behind this veil,
That the drop may become co-equal with the sea
And the grain of sand grow into a Sahara.

Poetising is not the aim of this *masnavi*,[2]
Beauty-worshipping and love-making is not its aim.
I am of India: Persian is not my native tongue;
I am like the crescent moon: my cup is not full.
Do not seek from me charm of style in exposition,
Do not seek from me Khansar[3] and Isfahan.

Although the language of Hind is sweet as sugar,
Yet sweeter is the fashion of Persian speech.
My mind was enchanted by its loveliness,
My pen became as a twig of the Burning Bush.
Because of the loftiness of my thoughts,
Persian alone is suitable to them.

O Reader! do not find fault with the wine-cup,
But consider attentively the taste of the wine.

TRANSLATED BY R. A NICHOLSON

Man and Nature

Watching at daybreak the bright sun come forth
I asked the assembled host of heaven and earth—

---

[2] The poetic form in which the poem was expressed, strongly associated with Sufi tradition. [Ed.]
[3] Khansar, which lies about a hundred miles northwest of Isfahan, was the birthplace of several Persian poets.

Your radiant looks are kindled by that glowing orb's
    warm beams
  That turn to rippling silver your flowing streams;
That sun it is that clothes you in these ornaments of light,
  And whose torch burns to keep your concourse bright.
Your roses and rose-gardens are pictures of Paradise
  Where the Scripture of *The Sun*[4] paints its device;
Scarlet the mantle of the flower, and emerald of the tree,
  Green and red sylphs of your consistory;
Your tall pavilion, the blue sky, is fringed with tasselled
    gold
  When round the horizon ruddy clouds are rolled,
And when into evening's goblet your rose-tinted nectar
    flows
  How lovely the twilight's soft vermilion glows!
Your station is exalted, and your splendour: over all
  Your creatures light lies thick, a dazzling pall;
To your magnificence the dawn is one high hymn of
    praise,
  No rag of night lurks on in that sun's blaze.
And I—I too inhabit this abode of light; but why
  Is the star burned out that rules *my* destiny?
Why chained in the dark, past reach of any ray,
Ill-faring and ill-fated and ill-doing must I stay?

  Speaking, I heard a voice from somewhere sound,
  From heaven's balcony or near the ground—

You are creation's gardener, flowers live only in your
    seeing,
  By your light hangs my being or not-being;
All beauty is in you; I am the tapestry of your soul;
  I am its key, but you are Love's own scroll.
The load that would not leave me you have lifted from
    my shoulder,
  You are all my chaotic work's re-moulder.
If I exist, it is only as a pensioner of the sun,
  Needing no aid from whom your spark burns on;
My gardens would turn wildernesses if the sun should
    fail,
  This sojourn of delight a prison's pale.
Oh you entangled in the snare of longing and unrest,
  Still ignorant of a thing so manifest—
Dullard, who should be proud, and still by self-contempt
    enslaved

[4] Koran 91.

Bear in your brain illusion deep-engraved—
If you would weigh your worth at its true rate,
No longer would ill-faring or ill-doing be your fate!

Ghazal

Each atom pants for glory: greed
Of self-fruition earth's whole creed!
Life that thirsts for no flowering—death:
Self-creation—a godlike deed;
Through Self the mustard seed becomes
A hill: without, the hill a seed.
The stars wander and do not meet,
To all things severance is decreed;
Pale is the moon of night's last hour
No whispered things of friendship speed.
Your own heart is your candle, your
Own self is all the light you need;
You are this world's sole truth, all else
Illusion such as sorceries breed.
—These desert thorns prick many a doubt:
Do not complain if bare feet bleed.

Reason and Love

Reason once said to me:
    Moonstruck is Passion!
Passion once said to me:
    Reason would fashion
Mere worms in her book,
    Men bloodless and pale!
—Passion, a look;
    Reason, a veil.

Passion, hot breeze on
    The world-strife's fervescence—
The attribute Reason
    Shows, Passion the essence!
She is peace and long-during,
    Life, death, the reply
In her silence immuring
    To Reason's shrill cry.

She moulds on her wheel
    The king's oath, the priest's vows,

Her poor thrall with the seal
    And the sceptre endows;
She is dweller and dwelling,
    And country and hour,
And victory-compelling
    Faith is her dower.

By the path Love has branded
    Hearth-welcome is hidden,
The storm-wave commanded,
    The hugged shore forbidden;
No fruits in her season,
    But lightnings above—
The Book's offspring is Reason,
    Its parent is Love.

Dazzled by Europe

Your light is only Europe's light reflected:
You are four walls her architects have built,
A shell of dry mud with no tenant soul,
An empty scabbard chased with flowery gilt.

To your mind God's existence seems unproved:
Your own existence seems not proved to mine.
He whose Self shines like a gem, alone exists;
Take heed to it! I do not see yours shine.

A Student

God bring you acquainted with some storm!
No billows in your sea break in foam,
And never from books can you be weaned
Which you declaim, not comprehend.

TRANSLATED BY V. G. KIERNAN

TEWFIK AL-HAKIM: INSTANT JUSTICE

[from *Yawmiyyāt Nāʾib fī al-Aryāf*, Journals of a Deputy
in the Country]

> *Tewfik al-Hakim, one of the most versatile and prolific
> of modern Arab writers, was born in 1902 in Alex-
> andria. He studied law in Cairo and later in Paris,
> and has carried on his literary career simultaneously
> with a career in law and government.*
>
> *Although he has written in other forms, Al-Hakim
> is most famous for his novels and plays. His thorough
> mastery of dialogue and sensitivity to scene have
> lent a dramatic quality even to his fiction. There was
> a persistent note of social criticism in his earlier works.
> The following portrayal of a judge, framed in the form
> of a diary of a local public prosecutor, represents one
> of his most biting satires.*

I went to sleep shortly after nightfall, for on the following day there was to be a session of the court, presided
over by our brisk judge, and I had instructed my assistant
to be present, with myself by his side, to train him in
court procedure and the formalities which are observed
on these occasions. When morning came, I went to the
court, where I found my assistant in the conference room
holding under his arm the envelope containing his official
sash. He was waiting for the judge, who soon arrived from
his journey on the Cairo train, followed by Shaʿban the
court usher. They were striding along, and the judge was
pulling money out of his pocket and handing it to Shaʿban.

"It must be real country meat, ribbed cutlets. And be
careful about the eggs, Shaʿban Effendi; and butter and
cheese as you always get. Pack it all nicely in the basket,
and wait for me at the station for the eleven o'clock train,
as usual. You go off to the market—the attendant will do
your work for you."

The usher went off briskly and the judge came in, greeting us hurriedly: "I think we'll go in now."

He clapped his hands.

"Usher, call the court to order. Hurry up!"

He threw his white linen travelling coat on a chair, produced his red sash from his case and donned it instantly. The office boy brought some coffee, which the judge swallowed in a couple of gulps, without sitting down. He then charged into the courtroom, with us on his heels.

"Court in session!" yelled the usher.

The judge examined the list of cases.

"Misdemeanours! Mohammed Abdal Rahim al-Danaf . . . Failed to remove the cotton worm. Absent—fifty piastres fine. Tuhami al Sayyid Uneiba . . . Failed to bring his son for inoculation. Absent—fifty piastres. Mahmud Mohammed Qindil . . . In possession of a rifle without a permit. Absent—fifty piastres and gun confiscated. Absent —fifty piastres . . . Absent—fifty piastres. . . ."

The judge shot out his sentences like arrows. Nothing gave him pause. The usher only had time to call out each name once if he wished to keep up with the judge. If someone did not hear his name, he was considered absent and sentenced *in absentia*. If someone happened to hear his case called, he would come rushing forward, only to be anticipated by the judge.

"You, sir, let your sheep graze in your neighbour's pasture."

"The fact is, your Honour——"

"I've no time to listen to stories. Defendant present. Fifty piastres . . . Abd al Rahman Ibrahim Abu Ahmed," etc., etc.

The misdemeanours were dealt with in a flash. Next came the turn of the felonies, which involve the hearing of witnesses and the submission of counsel, and thus require a certain amount of deliberation. The judge produced his watch and put it down in front of him.

"Hurry up with the first case!" he shouted at the usher.

"Salim Abd al Mejid Shaqraf!" called the usher.

The judge glanced at the case-list, ascertained the charge and turned to the defendant. Before the man had crossed the threshold of the court room he shouted to him:

"Did you hit the woman? Yes or no? Tell me at once!"

"Your Honour, does a gentleman strike a woman?"

"No philosophy here! One word—that's all. Did you hit her: Yes or No?"

"No."

The judge addressed the usher: "Pleads not guilty. Fetch the witness."

The woman who had been struck hobbled up in her long black dress. The judge yelled at her without waiting for her to come in: "Did he hit you?"

"The point is, your Honour, God bless you——"

"There's no point. Did he hit you or did he not? One word is enough."

"He hit me."

"That's enough. The Court dispenses with further witnesses. What have you got to say, defendant?"

The man coughed and began a speech of defence. The judge ignored him, being busy writing the evidence and judgment in the case-list with a pencil. When he had finished, he lifted his head and pronounced his sentence without looking at the defendant or waiting to hear the remainder of his defence.

"Month with hard labour. Next case . . ."

"Your Honour! I've still got witnesses. I didn't strike her at all. It's an injustice. Listen, everybody, it's unjust!"

"Be quiet! Take him away, constable!"

The man was removed, and the next case was called. A decrepit bent-backed man with a white beard came forward, hobbling on a stick. The judge pounced on him with a question.

"You expended reserved wheat?"

"It was my wheat, your Honour, and I ate it with my family."

"Pleads guilty. One month with hard labour!"

"A month! Do you hear, Muslims! My own wheat, my own crop, my own property! . . ."

The policeman dragged him away. As he went, he stared at those in court with goggling eyes, as though he could not believe that he had heard the sentence aright. Surely his ears must have deceived him and the spectators must have heard the truth. For he had stolen no man's wheat. It is true that the usher had visited him and "reserved" his wheat, appointing him as its trustee until such time as he paid the Government tax. But the pangs of hunger had seized him violently—him and his family; so he had eaten his own wheat. But who could possibly regard him as a thief on that account and punish him for stealing? It was impossible for this old fellow to understand a law which called him a thief for eating his own harvest, sown with his own hands. These were crimes invented by the law to protect the money of the Government or of private creditors; but they were not natural crimes in the eyes of the poor farmer whose simple instinct could not find any sin in them. He knows well that assault is a crime, and murder is a crime, and theft is a crime, for all these involve an obvious aggression against somebody else and reveal clear and evident moral turpitude. But "expending reserved property"—this was something whose principle and definition he could not grasp. For him it was purely a formal, legalistic crime, whose impact he must go on enduring without believing in it at all.

So the old man resigned himself to his Creator, and he was taken into custody, muttering, "There is no power and no might save in God!"

The next case was called. Before the usher could pronounce the name of the accused the judge had weighed the file in his hand and found it heavy with the testimony of many witnesses. He glanced at his watch, and then looked at the advocate's bench, where he saw no counsel for the accused. I understood that he intended to adjourn the case, and my expectation proved correct, for he turned to the Prosecution and asked: "Does the Prosecution wish for an adjournment?"

My assistant turned to me in embarrassment. I replied hastily: "On the contrary, sir. The Prosecution objects to any adjournment."

The judge smothered his disapproval and mumbled: "Oh, well, let us hear it. Call the witnesses!"

Suddenly, however, he remembered that this case was an appeal against a previous sentence pronounced *in absentia*, and that such an appeal should be presented within three days. He briskly read out the relevant dates, and immediately addressed the accused with a sigh of relief:

"The case is rejected on technical grounds, as the appeal was presented too late!"

The wretched peasant understood nothing of this pronouncement.

"So what do I do, your Honour?"

"The previous sentence of imprisonment must be carried out. Take him into custody, constable!"

"But it's unjust imprisonment, your Honour. I've been wronged! No judge has heard my case, no Court has asked me any questions to this very day!"

"Be quiet. Your appeal was presented too late!"

"So what?"

"The law provides that you are limited to three days."

"But—your Honour—I'm a poor man. I can't read or

write. Who is there to explain the law to me and read out
the dates?"

"It seems that I've been too patient with you. You silly
animal, you are supposed to know the law. Take him into
custody, constable."

The man was put amongst the prisoners; as he went, he
looked left and right to see if he was the only one to whom
the whole process was incomprehensible. And I began to
ponder for a moment on the misery of the creature who
was "presumed to understand" the Napoleonic code.

Finally, the session came to an end. The judge leapt up
and rushed back to the conference room, hastily removing
his sash. There were only seven minutes to go before the
departure of the return train, but the judge was quite accustomed to last-minute embarkations, and, for all his
haste, lost nothing of his inner certainty and quiet confidence. He seized his white travelling coat, draped it over
his arm, bade us farewell, and went off to the station at a
trot. Suddenly the clerk of the court rushed in with some
files, closely followed by a policeman dragging a prisoner.

"Has the judge gone?" he panted. "We've got an appeal
against imprisonment to be submitted to his Honour."

"Catch the judge at the station before he leaves," I
replied.

The clerk screamed at the policeman: "Bring the
prisoner, the sergeant, and come along to the station."

Everybody hurried off—the clerk, the sergeant, and the
prisoner running behind his guard, tied onto a chain, as
though he were a dog. They all rushed after the trotting
judge. This was a familiar spectacle to the villagers on the
days of these sessions, for late appeals and renewals of
imprisonment orders were always examined and signed in
the station buffet two minutes before the departure of the
train. The train would start moving while the judge had
one foot on the platform and the other in the rear com-
partment, and pronounced judgment.

"Appeal rejected and imprisonment of defendant to continue."

The clerk would record this judgment on the marble
table of the buffet while the judge received the basket of
eggs, butter and meat from Shaʿban, who came sprinting
behind the moving train, shouting at the top of his
voice:

"Good meat, sir—ribs and kidneys!"

TRANSLATED BY A. S. EBAN

MAHMUD TAYMUR: UNCLE MITWALLI

[from *Ammī Mitwallī*]

Mahmud Taymur was born in Cairo in 1894 into a
prominent family of Turkish origin. His father and
brother were also writers of distinction. He himself
excelled in the short story, a bold new form in Islamic
literature. "Uncle Mitwalli" is one of his earlier stories,
first published in 1925 but revised in 1942. In this
story Taymur refers to the Islamic belief in the
"mahdi," a messianic figure who will be sent by God
to inaugurate a new era of justice and "purified" Islam.
Many persons in Islamic history have claimed the
title, including the famous Muhammad Ahmad,
Mahdi of the Sudan, whose state was destroyed by
forces under Lord Kitchener in 1898.

Taymur has often acknowledged the influence of
Guy de Maupassant on his style. In this story he
combines his remarkable powers of characterization
(here by means of semianonymous characters) with
his customary decisive, antiseptic style, which proved
new and delightful to modern Arab readers, and a
subtle note, subtler than most, of social criticism.

ʿAmm Mitwallī was a hawker of peanuts, melon seeds
and sweets, well known to the inhabitants of Hilmīya and
the neighbouring districts. He went about in a long white
turban and a broad-sleeved *gallabīya*,[1] with a dignified
demeanour, and cried his wares to the children with a
Sudanese accent, in a faltering voice weakened by poverty
and infirmity, yet still retaining something of the ring of
command.

The man had grown up in the Sudan and had fought in
the armies of the Mahdī with the rank of Divisional Commander. He had lived all his life alone, with neither wife

[1]A long, white garment worn by the poorer classes in Egypt.

nor child; and occupied a small, dark room in the alley of
ʿAbdallah Bey, furnished only with an old trunk and a
straw mat with a tattered cushion and blanket. Yet despite
his obvious and abject poverty, cleanliness encompassed
him and all he possessed.

He used to return to his room overwhelmed with weariness. When he had recited the evening prayer he would
light his pallid oil lamp, sit by his trunk and take out an old
sword. He would rest it across his knees and sink into long
reveries, going over the memories of his past life; and
when the memory of the Mahdī passed through his mind
he would lift up his eyes and pray to God to hasten the
days of Return, the days of the awaited reappearance of
the Mahdī—the Flagbearer of the Faith—when he would
descend upon the world and cleanse it of its corruptions.
Then he would lower his eyes, stroke his tear-stained beard,
and take the old sword and kiss it with great passion.

So he would rise for his evening meal and prayer, and
when he had completed them he would go to bed, to sink
before long into a restful sleep, and to dream of his proud
past and of his future made splendid by the Mahdī's return. At dawn he would rise to recite the morning prayer
and read the Litanies of Sīdī Gulshānī[2] and the Praises of
the Prophet until, with the first warm shafts of sunlight
coming through his narrow window, he would rise slowly,
put his basket on his back, and turn towards Hilmīya to
begin his daily round.

This had been his way since he had come to Cairo fifteen
years earlier, and he had changed nothing in the order of
his life. Buildings had fallen and others had risen, men
had died and children had grown up, but ʿAmm Mitwallī
knew nothing of Cairo and its outskirts but his accustomed
round. He had his resting places on the way, places where
he ate and sat awhile. There were two especially where he
spent most of his moments of repose. The first was a
small mosque, by the door of which he would take his midday meal, and when he had finished, he would praise God
at length and go into the mosque to pray and sleep. His
second halt was before the house of Nūr ad-Dīn Bey in
Suyūfīya, which he always sought after the sunset prayer.
There by the palace gate the doorkeepers of the neighbouring houses and the servants of Nūr ad-Dīn would gather
around him and converse of Islam in its former glory and
of how it had fallen on evil times. Thereupon ʿAmm

[2] Ibrāhīm al-Gulshānī, a famous Persian mystic who died in Cairo
in A.D. 1533–34.

Mitwallī would rise with radiant eyes and tell them tales of the Return that is to come, with measured and awe-inspiring accents and a powerful and captivating eloquence that won all their hearts. They would all sit reverent and contented, listening with rapt attention to this great saint, as he spoke of the appearance of the Mahdī and the cleansing of the world of its corruptions and the return of Islam to its former greatness. At that time Nūr ad-Dīn Bey would come out of the door of his house leaning on his expensive walking stick. He would walk towards ʿAmm Mitwallī and greet him courteously, bestow his gift upon him, and leave him, emitting a haughty and pompous cough.

Ibrāhīm Bey, the son of Nūr ad-Dīn Bey, would come too—a merry and playful youth in his sixteenth year. He would approach ʿAmm Mitwallī, crying: "Are you still telling of the battles and adventures of the Mahdī and his army?"

"I tell them and I glory in them. I was in command of a thousand warriors."

Ibrāhīm Bey would roar with laughter and, affecting a posture of reverence, would button his jacket, straighten his fez and raise his right hand to his head in a military salute. Then he would take a piastre from his pocket and give it to ʿAmm Mitwallī, saying: "Please give me a piastre's worth of melon seeds and monkey nuts . . . O General!"

One day at noon ʿAmm Mitwallī went to the house of Nūr ad-Dīn Bey and sat near the gate, as was his custom. The children began to run to him as usual to buy his wares; the servants thronged to him from all sides. When they had settled down in a circle to listen, ʿAmm Mitwallī rose and spoke to them in his accustomed manner. But as they listened enraptured to his enchanting words, Ibrāhīm Bey appeared, and cried: "General Mitwallī . . ."

The preacher paused and the people turned their eyes in anger and enquiry towards the merry youngster. Without paying any attention to them, Ibrāhīm came forward and continued: "My father wishes to see you. Would you please follow me?"

The gathering deplored this interruption. ʿAmm Mitwallī left the circle with his basket on his back and walked calmly towards the door, giving his faithful followers a look of affection and apology. He followed Ibrāhīm Bey into the garden of the palace, and they walked together for some time along a path leading to the

entrance of the visitors' quarters, where Nūr ad-Dīn Bey
was waiting for them on a broad seat. He welcomed ᶜAmm
Mitwallī, and, dismissing his son, bade the old man sit
by him on the ground.

A brief silence reigned, during which ᶜAmm Mitwallī
repeated in a low voice his thanks to God and his prayers
for the Prophet. Then Nūr ad-Dīn spoke, and informed
ᶜAmm Mitwallī, after a brief introduction, that the
venerable lady his mother had heard much of him and of
his qualities, and desired to meet him and hear his noble
religious tales and his wonderful stories of Islam. ᶜAmm
Mitwallī's heart quivered with joy that his fame had
penetrated the outer walls of houses and reached the ears
of secluded ladies.

Nūr ad-Dīn Bey rose and walked towards the women's
quarters of the house, ᶜAmm Mitwallī following behind
him. They passed through a wide corridor and a huge
doorway leading into the garden of the women's quarters.
Then they walked up the stairs of a dark terrace, and into
a hall so vast that hardly had ᶜAmm Mitwallī crossed the
threshold when he was overcome by its magnificence and
his heart was filled with awe and wonderment. Never had
he seen—not even in the castle of the Mahdī—so vast and
magnificent a chamber.

ᶜAmm Mitwallī was still lost in wonderment when a
weak, female voice came to his ears. He turned towards
the voice and found the lady of the palace sitting on a
large divan not far from him and smoking. He walked
towards her until he was near enough to see her clearly.
She was a Turkish lady with bent back and wrinkled skin,
wearing gold-rimmed spectacles and dark clothes.

ᶜAmm Mitwallī advanced towards her, kissed her thin
hand and wished her long life and good fortune. Introduc-
tions were completed, and Nūr ad-Dīn Bey left them and
went his way. The lady spoke and expressed her joy at
his coming and her desire to hear some of his tales. He
lowered his eyes and began to gather his tales and traditions
in his mind. Then he raised his head and began to tell his
story with a fluency and with moving accents that
fascinated the lady. When he had finished his story she gave
him a present—a sum greater than any he had dreamt of,
and overwhelmed him with expressions of admiration that
embarrassed and confused him. Then he left, repeating
words of gratitude and loyalty to her and to her family.
No sooner had he reached the garden than a crowd of
maidservants began to cluster round him, seeking blessings

from him and stroking his sleeves with their hands. They asked him to sell something of his wares, and he sat happily on the ground, opened his old basket, and began to sell until he had no more. And so left and went straight to the mosque, where he prayed with forty prostrations, thanking God for His bounteous gift.

From that day ʿAmm Mitwallī went often to the house of Nūr ad-Dīn Bey, where he was welcomed with respect and esteem and showered with favours. His condition changed, and he began to bear himself upright, always speaking with a firm voice. He rented a better-situated room, with new furniture, and changed his diet from cheese, leeks and radishes to rice and vegetables every day and meat twice a week. He was able to make his turban bigger and longer, to broaden the sleeves of his gallabīya, to wrap a cheap cashmere shawl around his shoulders, and to wear bright red slippers and a silk sash with a long fringe. He gradually gave up hawking, freeing himself from his weary round. He enjoyed long and pleasant slumbers, and began to give alms to the poor and became known among them as a sustainer of the needy. He could go to the mosque at his leisure to attend the sermons of preaching and admonition, which he could repeat later to the lady, the mother of Nūr ad-Dīn Bey.

So his fame began to spread in the neighbourhood and men began to whisper to one another and to exchange news concerning him, and the image of ʿAmm Mitwallī, the hawker of melon seeds and monkey nuts, the man of poverty and infirmity, faded before that of a great dervish.

A group of his followers were sitting by the door of Nūr ad-Dīn Bey, awaiting his appearance, when one of them said: "Do you think, my friends, that ʿAmm Mitwallī is merely a righteous man, who can speak well and eloquently of Islam?"

Another asked him: "What do you think he is?"

The man replied in a whisper: "He is one of the Saints of God, one of the Great ones of the Faith."

"Who told you?"

"Look into his eyes awhile, you will see a strange light shining from them. This is a sign that he is a saint. . . ."

"I had an adventure with him which I fear to tell you, lest you disbelieve me! . . ."

The gathering drew nearer to him, saying: "Tell us! Tell us!"

"I was walking with him once in Sīdī Shāwīsh Street

and the time was evening. The street was lit only by two oil lamps, giving a weak, pale light. . . . Suddenly a strong gust of wind put them both out, leaving us in pitch darkness. A sudden fear came over me, and I seized ʿAmm Mitwallī's hand and pressed it, and he murmured: 'Fear nothing, we are in God's keeping!' "

While they were listening to his words, another man began to speak: "Now that I have heard your story it is easier for me to tell you what I know about this righteous saint, with whom we have associated much, though we knew but little of his true character."

The group turned their eyes towards him, and one of them said, with avid interest: "And what do you know of his character?"

The man spoke with a constrained voice and a tense face: "He is the Mahdī, the awaited Mahdī!"

They craned their necks forward and whispered to one another: "The Mahdī? . . . The awaited Mahdī? . . ."

The speaker went on in the same tone, his voice trembling with emotion: "I have seen the sword of Prophecy in his trunk, and when I touched it with my hand I was able to heal my son, my son whom the doctors could not cure, who was on the point of death! . . ."

They vied with one another in questioning the man, and he answered them willingly, with much detail. The clamour grew, and the circle was increased by others who came to ask what was afoot, and to listen to the man who was speaking of the sword of Prophecy and the generosity of the Mahdī, whom God had sent a second time to guide mankind.

At that moment ʿAmm Mitwallī appeared from afar. The gathering saw him, and the tumult died away. They hastened to open a path for him between their serried ranks.

ʿAmm Mitwallī came with his deliberate tread, grave and dignified, giving a calm and sweet smile to those who welcomed him. The people gathered reverently around him, thronging to him and kissing his fingers and the hems of his sash. The man who had touched the sword of Prophecy stepped forward and said: "My Master . . . my Lord, saviour of my son from death! We know you in spite of your concealment. You are the servant of God whom He has sent to guide mankind; you are the vicar of the Prophet; you are the awaited Mahdī. . . ."

ʿAmm Mitwallī stared at the man in astonishment, and said, "What are you saying? Are you raving?"

"You can no longer hide your noble character from us. Yes, you are the Mahdī, the vicar of the Prophet, the bearer of the sword of truth amid men!"

"Be silent! Be silent! For I have not this tremendous honour!"

"Did you not save my son from death?"

"I?"

The man who had told the tale of the dark street slipped forward, and said: "Did you not light up the street with your resplendent face?"

"I? I?"

The man who had spoken previously said: "The righteous Abū Bakr[3]—may God be pleased with him—visited me in a dream and revealed your character to me."

ʿAmm Mitwallī murmured in a low voice and leant on the man standing by him.

"The righteous Abū Bakr revealed my character to you?"

He took refuge in silence awhile, staring about him. Then he began to speak, as if to himself: "My children! The Mahdī is a mighty man, mightier and greater than I. I am but a faithful servant of God. . . ."

He did not sit long with them, but returned home early, sunk in dreams.

ʿAmm Mitwallī was scarcely awake next morning when he heard a knock on his door. He got up to find out what the matter was, and saw a man with a bandaged head and an emaciated body approaching him, clinging to his garments, moaning and supplicating.

"Let me touch the sword of Prophecy from your pure hand."

"The sword of Prophecy?"

"Save me from my sufferings, O my master. Have pity on the wretched who seek you, O mighty vicar of the Prophet!"

ʿAmm Mitwallī let him into his room, and tended him all day. He recited a section of the Litanies over his head. When evening approached, he put him to bed by his side, with the "sword of Prophecy" under his head.

The next day the sun rose on the sick man, and he declared himself to be full of happiness and energy, in a state of health such as he had never known before. He went up to ʿAmm Mitwallī and pounced on his hands, smother-

---

[3]The father-in-law of Muhammad, and the first Caliph in Islam (reg. A.D. 632–34).

ing them with kisses. His voice bellowed thanks and prayers.

The days passed, and the dwelling of ʿAmm Mitwallī became a place of pilgrimage for men from every part, who came to seek a cure for the ills of their bodies and the whisperings of their souls. ʿAmm Mitwallī left home rarely, spending all his time straying amid endless dreams. If he awoke from these dreams, he would take out his sword, place it on his knees, and stare at it in bewilderment.

One day ʿAmm Mitwallī saw the noble lady, the mother of Nūr ad-Dīn Bey, come to visit him amid a crowd of his followers. As soon as she saw him she knelt before him reverently, took the skirt of his robe and began to kiss it, saying: "O mighty vicar of the Prophet! I have come to you, submissive and humble, to seek your grace! . . ."

From that day ʿAmm Mitwallī confined himself to his room, never leaving it. Sometimes he received visitors, and sometimes he locked the door of his room and let none come near him. He would sit leaning his back on the wall, with lowered eyelids, and would spend long hours in this manner. Then suddenly he would start out of his reverie, agitated and feverish, draw his sword from the scabbard, and thrust at the air this way and that, leaping around the room and shouting, bidding the devils avaunt . . . until he fell senseless to the floor.

The neighbours heard much of this shouting, and they knew that the righteous saint in his hours of retreat was meditating his mighty mysteries. They gathered around his door with intent ears, with souls full of awe and veneration. ʿAmm Mitwallī remained so for a few weeks.

One day he was seen to rush out of his room with dishevelled hair and eyes that blazed like burning coals, brandishing his sword right and left. . . . He hurried to the nearby coffee house and began to strike with the sword at those who were sitting there, shouting, "Away, O rebels, O evildoers" . . . and people gathered around him to stop him.

At last he fell into the hands of the police, screaming in a weak voice: "Praise be to God! I have accomplished my mission. I have completed my holy war."

And his strength failed. . . .

TRANSLATED BY BERNARD LEWIS

ÖMER SEYFETTİN: LOVE'S WAVE

[from *Aşk Dalgası*]

Seyfettin's life was as brilliant in achievement as it was brief in span. With the success of the Young Turk movement he emerged as a major young writer, and participated during the crucial decade around the First World War in the nationalistic and (if you like) "liberal" aspects of the literary revival in Turkey. He died in 1920.

The subject matter of his writings ranged over nearly the whole extent of latter-day Ottoman society, from European-educated intellectuals to ignorant Ottoman bureaucrats, from backward ulema to self-styled atheists, from secluded Turkish women to the loose-living wives of foreigners. Yet certain themes are repeatedly emphasized, particularly the rise of the new nationalism and the return to literary realism; and Seyfettin's style never failed to reflect his goals.

Love's Wave is, as anyone can plainly see, the immature work of a gifted young man. It was chosen for inclusion precisely for that reason, and because we are suddenly so far away from those (not so by-gone) years when it was honestly important that bright young men deliver impassioned sermons on the close connection between love and the unveiling of women.

The steamer was full as an egg.

The last whistle blew and the two wheels on either side began to move, emitting a shrill sound as if huge sea stallions had suddenly been awakened within their narrow cages. The whole steamer shook slightly. It was a delightful day. We were going to Kadiköy.

Great, white-bordered clouds, like frothy waves that have separated, were slowly increasing in number, dispersing and coming together again, on the long, undisturbed horizon. Outlined by the domes and minarets of the Marmara, the horizon was melting at its extremities into a lilac-colored mist, the fusion of deep blues and purples gathered in the hollows and in the high hills. The burning June sun fell upon the awnings of the steamer, now turned brown from smoke and rain. The wind, irresolute, remaining still yet at the same time beginning to blow, seemed like a drunkard who was trying to grasp something lively that had attracted him.

Milk-white gulls, which looked as if they had come from distant and unknown mythical islands, were flying around us. With their sweet and deep cries, they were calling to those unfortunate urban dwellers who suffocated from crowds, from struggles, from anger and anxiety. They were calling them to come to their own country, to quiet and solitary places which were faraway from there, to taste a little of love and poetry. Kizkülesi, which in the dark-blue waves resembled a fairy-tale castle, set off my imagination: though its light white walls bored me, they erased from my mind all awareness of my surroundings. I nearly forgot that I was on a steamer. I was corrupting myself with that strange and morbid addiction of a man who reads a little poetry every day of his life: he sees nothing—neither the houses nor the domes nor the minarets nor even the old Tibbiye Mektebi. In place of these, I was creating virgin forests of fir and beech, and in their clearings silver and diamond waterfalls were flowing, and in their cool shadows rosy, naked couples were kissing each other.

Looking at this picture which I had brought into my mind and which, of course, did not exist at all, I saw it as a great lofty vision, and I said, "This is the place for love— oh, what a place for love!" To the gulls I said, "Come, to faraway lands, to the other side of this lilac-colored fog. There you have white flowers, there are maidens waiting in eternally green springs, come, come—" and my imagination, hearing sounds which were coming quickly from very far away, became confused, and I turned my head. Just above Kizkülesi, I saw a flock of fairies, a thousand or so, flying together. So close were their transparent wings that one could have reached out and caught them by hand as they flew.

Suddenly a hand touched my shoulder. I turned around.

"Hey there, what's this?"

"Nothing—"

"Don't I know you?"

"Possibly—"

"Wake up! Come, let me see your hand."

Suddenly, I felt a warm and powerful hand squeeze my cold hand which was extended to it. But I was hardly aware of what was taking place, for I was not yet able to escape from my pleasant sleepy feeling.

"It *is* you!"

"Yes, of course, it's me."

It was one of my favorite school friends, and we had not seen each other for twelve years.

Twelve years—Aman Yarabbim! It seemed like yesterday. There is nothing, besides a movie, which comes to an end quicker than the long events of life and reality. At school my genial, good-natured friend had known everyone, made fun of everyone, and made everyone laugh. He had changed much since then. Above his red lips an awkward, light-brown mustache jutted out, and the hair that was on his temples had become completely white; he was, moreover, a little fat. But the eyes, these small and brilliant members of our body without which we would know nothing, our spirits would extinguish in darkness, and human intelligence would be forever closed off—they had not changed at all. They still radiated a blue gaiety which seemed to smile at the events of the last twelve years. Our coincidental meeting, as it lengthened our friendship, made me happy. I was very pleased. And with all my might I grasped his warm hand.

We were on the upper deck of the steamer. Behind us, under the canopies, there was no place to sit down, nor was there any lady to be seen on the deck. The steamer was blowing its whistle rapidly at barges which were passing in front of it. Old men, at times dozing, were reading their newspapers and smoking cigars. If they were not speaking in short phrases to those who were sitting next to them, they listened attentively to the gurgling noise of the wheels. Youths, dressed in the latest style, remained very close together in order not to drop the monocles which each was wearing. They were showing off the colored socks they wore beneath ironed pants coming down to slightly above the knees. All of them would have wished others to think they had grown old, tired, and a little foolish. They wore a sour expression on their hairless, clean-shaven faces, as if their stomachs were aching, and they made their eyebrows and lips appear wrinkled from the wind.

We were leaning on the white railing of the steamer, and my friend said: "What's your problem? I saw you over here, so immersed in thought that you didn't even notice me. What goes with you, old man?"

"Nothing, really . . . I was just passing through a wave."

"What sort of wave?"

Smiling, I answered: "The wave of love . . . Love's wave."

"Are you still a bachelor?"

"Yep."

The old twinkle that had characterized my friend's blue eyes faded. As I was looking at him from the third step of the deck, it seemed to me that he could not have appeared more aggrieved and resigned had he been attending a sick man to whom he was trying to give every possible consolation without himself catching his disease. He was like a mother taking pity on one of her children. He lifted his hand, which had been resting on the banister, and thrust it into his pocket. Turning a little, he fixed his suddenly serious eyes on mine.

"If you're still a bachelor, and if you're passing through the wave of love," he said, "beware, my friend. We don't come to understand such things by going in and out of a library. Suppose some ladies passed in front of us right now. Even if you were *expecting* to enter a wave of love, you wouldn't be able to understand it. As long as you refuse to face reality, you can never be happy."

"What reality?" I asked, smiling.

"What reality! *Social* reality!" he answered. "If you can't see that reality, you won't be able to contend with *real* love."

I looked him straight in the face and asked, "Why is that?"

"In every country," he went on, "there's a principal, inclusive social conscience which, in spite of all the differences between the arts, logic, knowledge, and philosophy, prevails in an absolute and oppressive manner. In our environment, in our Turkish surroundings, there is a prohibition *against* love. It's the devil's machine, a prohibition worse than a bomb or a dynamite explosion! A Turk fourteen years of age still hasn't seen any woman's face except his mother's, his sisters', or his aunts'. Who will *he* fall in love with? No one. The power, the terror of this environment and this social conscience! Some philosopher whose name I've forgotten, when he was discussing the effect of God on man, on man's relations with his fellow man, and on morals, said, 'Oh, if there was nothing but social environment!' I find these words very true. The ancient holy books and Almighty God have crushed by means other than the use of social environment those who have been devoid of religion and who have opposed them in every way at every turn. Yet the power which scourged Galilee in ancient times is ignoring the millions of school children who are reading and repeating that great and terrible offense of Galilee! If the bullets which pierced the head of Fere in Spain were able to be exploded in France, only senile men and women would remain. Thus, in the view of this philosopher, each society, in order to make the eternal law of God work, must teach that it is just for each environment to use its own social conscience. For, in fact, one eternal and indisputable law does not exist in every place, in every country, in every continent; rather, it varies according to each village and each city.

"The superiority of the system here is offset by its crime there; the usefulness of it there is offset by its evil here: the holy books, opposing all nature, organism, and evolution, remain unchanged, even in those matters where change is necessary; thus, in a sense, they cause embarrassment everywhere. Their primary assumptions are that Christianity exists only in Europe, America, and Africa—Islam is limited in that way too. Where is it other than in Hindustan, Liverpool, Bukhara, and Turkey? If you go to Arabia and Persia, you find it there too, but *only* there, only in *those* places—that's all.

"So, the uncontradictable law of our God who is in Turkey, that is, social conscience, forbids us to love. No one can love in Turkey. And from now on, forever more, no one will be able to love in Turkey—because you have to see before you can love. One is supposed to make a home with a young girl, to live happily with her until death, and yet not to speak to her or understand her or love her! It is even impossible to see her face for a short time! Those who are opposed to this powerful prohibition struggle against the conclusion reached by the anarchists and the nihilists, those irreligious ones who have entered into this affair.

"Though both anarchists and nihilists continue to be extinguished in a tragic, social death, they remain shrewd, skilled smugglers of a forbidden love, exactly like outlaws, whether they are old and bold tobacco smugglers or Greek pickpockets; and they are not disgusted by what they do. They live within the palpitation of every heart. At night they wait for hours in deserted streets, in suspicious corners of dark gardens, through wind, cold and dampness, and at last out of fear and confusion come two meaningless words, a quick, hurried kiss whose flavor was never tasted—and

that's it! The love stories, poems, and accounts which came
from Persia in ancient literature and are coming from
France in modern literature brought these smugglers into
full existence. Like an incurably sick European, they are
always looking for an adventure. Since their women appear
uncovered in public, they wish to thrust the customs of their
opposite, foreign environments, for instance the hoax of
falling in love, upon an environment which strongly pro-
hibits these customs. They project themselves as the heroes
of imaginary novels who are passing through distant,
foreign countries.

"You have, of course, read many of their poems in the
literary collections. The invariable subject: night and
women. . . . However, in Turkey, the two do not also go
hand in hand. The Turkish custom is that all the curtains
go down after one o'clock and that all the streets are deserted in the evening *alaturka*. Darkness spreads from house
to house, from town to town, even into the mouse's hole
which has not yet become his house.

"Casinos, ballrooms, theaters, and so on. . . . The new
district of Beyoglu is not and never will be Turk. Foreigners
live there in their own environments, after their own
customs. In restaurants, in public gardens, they travel
around, talk, joke, and laugh with their women, arm in
arm. Some Turks mix among them. They doze at the head
of their tables; they look ruefully at the foreign women, at
foreign beauties, foreign breasts. There is no such thing as
an evening for Turks!

"Moreover, in these new poems lakes are understood
as being measured lengthwise. Which lakes? I don't know
any lake other than Terkos in Istanbul, nor, my friend,
have any of *their* poets gone *there* either. In fact, there is
not a night lodge anywhere in the neighborhood of Terkos.
Those who love one another, those beloved who are
lauded in hundreds of lines of poetry, it's all a lie! There
is a beloved of the poet, but where? The poet is talking
with and kissing his beloved, but where? Ah, barely in his
mind!

"To love in reality, to be able to talk three or four
minutes with a young girl in the Turkish society of today
is as impossible as for fish to leave water and fly in flocks
through the air and perch on the branches of thin poplars
in gardens! There is no such thing in Istanbul and its vicini-
ty as a young Turkish lad going around on evenings, arm in
arm with his girl, listening to nightingales and saying words
of love to each other. It is even considered dangerous to

ride in a carriage with our mothers, who might possibly seem, in the absence of daylight, a little like a young girl!

"Think!—Even in excursion spots, in these unfortunate, painful, and ridiculous places, love is also impossible. Young men and women are never able to approach one another to fall in love. There is always at least a few hundred feet between them, and a few dozen policemen! These latter are supposed to enforce the social conscience of the environs, that is, the wish of the notorious giant of fanaticism and ignorance. They perform their duties as if their authorities were extended to those of an eternal king without deputies. They are the ones who see to it that if you say a word in the street to your daughter, it creates a scandal. Always to the police station! And it is your good fortune if you are not thrashed around a little to prove that it *was* your sister or your mother or whoever it may have been that you were talking to.

"And you know who it is that wants this prohibition of love more than the religion, the traditions, the customs, the ulema, the old men, the reactionaries, and the government police of our society? *Women* themselves. Turkish women. They are the worst enemies of love and beauty! They do not reveal their faces or look at the men in their own homes, who, for their part, cannot see the face of any woman *outside* their family. More terrible than the police outside are the women inside!

"What do they do when taking on a new servant? They find the ugliest one, a filthy, corrupt man with a big mouth, thick lips, and a crooked nose; then they have special skills, a sinister genius for making him even uglier. Further, they wear very loose clothes, so that you do not see see their protruding hips. Over their hair they put a very tight colored handkerchief, on the pretext that their hair is too full. They turn their unfortunate husband into a true orangutan.

" 'You should not look into the face of any man,' they think to themselves, 'you should not speak while at his side; you should not answer when he asks you anything; you should keep your arms free; you should not walk with him while having stockings on, and so on.' And they do not hesitate to give forewarnings. When they hold a grudge against one of the servants, they say, 'An industrious, clean, quick girl, but her mouth is where her nose should be.' That is the most unpardonable sin for them!

"Since it is never possible for boys and girls to see one another or to fall in love, mothers resolve the question of marrying so as to keep matters in their own hands. Their first hope is to buy an ugly girl for their sons. The visiting mothers go to houses they have not seen. Not knowing most of the girls, they look for an ugly rather than a beautiful bride—and they succeed! If a beautiful girl is bought, she causes the mother to go so mad because the woman thinks that her sons and daughters will like the newcomer, that they might listen to her words; that afterwards mother herself might be shifted to a small house. She starts with fear of beauty. Ninety out of a hundred of those who aren't finding a husband in Istanbul are the most beautiful, the friendliest, and the most lovable.

"Visiting mothers don't like those unfortunate, beautiful Turkish girls. 'Ah, the child is very beautiful but she is widely recognized as a devil,' they say. 'We didn't want an evil spirit for our son; we want a lady.' Their objects are as small as they are puny, malicious, and *alafranka*. They resemble nothing more than a plump, whitish, meek, weak, imbecile, ignorant, and wet chicken. The mothers come straight up to a girl and exclaim, 'Oh, what an angel!' and they begin to converse, bearing in mind the exaggeration they will tender to their sons and brothers. The unfortunate male trusts that luck will send him a beautiful person; but upon raising the veil on the eve of his wedding night, he sees opposite him only a white, shapeless, confused lump which is unable to reply to his question, 'What is your name, lady?'

"Women who are waiting for males, deprived from seeing beauty or love and unable to fall in love, do not miss an opportunity for inflicting the same cruelty on their own sex. By chance an event passes concerning a woman they know. For example, one finds a book on love, or another is divorced from her husband, and they all scold her at once and pardon her with difficulty. Long years pass in between; they change paths when they see that woman on the street; some go so far as to spit in her face. The fairest sympathize a little: 'Ah, the unfortunate thing has come to bad times; that is her destiny,' they say. Knowing to what extent the saying 'The first duty of a woman is to become beautiful' has become a dangerous lie, mothers forbid beauty, liveliness, luxury, and freedom to their daughters as much as possible. When the daughters of these mothers exit to the street, the unchanging piece of advice they whisper to their ears is: 'My daughter! Drop your veil. Keep your hands inside your dress. Don't raise your head that high. They will call you a "fast" woman! Look ahead

of you! Don't walk fast like European women. Slowly,
slowly. . . . Don't heave your breast! . . . they will ridicule
us behind our backs! They will speak nastily of you. Your
name will come up. If you will only stay at home—'

"It happens that each family which knows one another
and sees one another becomes after a while like an inspector of one another. You certainly don't pass through
a small love affair within one family. Gossip immediately
appears to its members as a scandal: everyone speaks ill
publicly of heroes. They scold all those mothers and their
associates who don't pay attention to the fact that their sons
and daughters are seeing each other and writing letters
secretly. They become disgusted, saying, 'Oh, at this point
the woman has exceeded herself!'

"As for the great, famous world that some new novels
depict to be in Turkey—this world, in every respect, is the
product of a daydream. There never has been and is not
today a privileged class among the Turks. The fact is that
the families of some Turks, such as those of officials on the
rise or of pashas who remain from the old days, are
striving to make the world big and artificial. Denying their
origins, they are becoming Western and European. But
for what? All society is their enemy. Thus, in a certain
quarter of town, the first family that appears to their relatives offering their daughters in marriage is given the
nickname 'The Bad Ones'; then their neighbors begin a
boycott. All their happiness is extinguished amid sounds
of disgust and wrongdoing which mount from the side of
their relatives. They find it necessary to abandon homes
and native lands and go to solitary villas in a faraway
desert. Yes, the women of the new novels who go to their
relatives or to friends of their spouses in preparing for
their wedding—these women are as big a lie as the lakes,
the evenings, the loves that take place in the new poetry.
They are not *real*! These novels are nothing more than
shadows, repetitions, and translations of European novels.
Show me a Turkish family in Istanbul whose daughters
ever see a stranger or even the men they are going to
marry, and I am prepared to give you everything I have
earned in five years. The Europeanized families who are
described in these novels are as opposed to true Turkdom
as the private, unpublished plays of Kel Hasan and Abdi,
our famous playwrights. In the theaters men pass frequently
to the side of ladies; grannies squeeze milk from their
breasts saying, 'Oh, cream.' This is impossible among Turkish families! These scandals are untrue to the last letter.

The women who are pressing the hands of their spouses in the new novels, who are talking in the presence of their husbands with foreigners, sometimes unveiled, always immodest—these woman are false, misplaced specters, coarse and unseemly to the point that they invert reality.

"Don't let me go on; now there is an answer for you. In this society, love is forbidden to both the man and the woman who are planning to get married. What forbids it? Religion, tradition, custom, law, government, the police, the family organization, and even the women. Yet, isn't there a certain vagabondage, a persistency to seek love and to be loved, even in this society? And what could be more insane or mad than to come up against the social conscience of a country, to raise anarchy against the most powerful and glorified government?

"I was bothered to see that you, whom I had thought so intelligent, were struggling with this impossible daydream. Ah, my unfortunate friend, you must endure the lottery; you must accept the crowd, drifting to its destiny; and the soldiers, you must help them to reach their camp over the arable field. Only then will you be barely happy. But love's wave is passing over you now; you are running through an endless desert to the precipice of hell. Yes, you are running to a distant image, false and deceiving, behind which hidden volcanoes are gushing forth fire. . . . If—if you only knew how much I pity you! . . ."

The steamer arrived at Kadiköy. While I was listening to my friend, I had remained standing on my boot heels, lightly leaning on the railing. I straightened up. My right foot had fallen asleep. I was unable to walk.

"Wait a little, my friend," I said. "My foot is numb. We will leave last."

He smiled and said, "It's not your foot but your brain which has gone numb."

The steamer heeled to the quay. From the top and the bottom levels men were getting off. The sun was lost amid thick clouds. The air took on a brownish iron color; it became sad, like a pale and angry eye which dampens as it begins to weep.

I looked at those who were leaving. What had been a simple wave for me half an hour ago had turned into a raging storm. Thinking about what my friend had said, I wondered what would become of a nation and a people which, by imprisoning mothers, wives, and daughters, by causing them to look on love and being loved as forbidden, by separating them into a different group from men, continued to remain in a dreamless and granitelike sleep. Those who were passing quickly with a timid preciseness along the narrow boards reminded me of a flock of timid animals dispersing. There was no woman among them. All, old and young, rich and poor, were men. Rubbing my knee with my hand, I said, "Weren't there any women on the steamer at all?"

My friend smiled again and answered, "Be patient. They're forbidden to mix with the men. They leave last."

The steamer was completely emptied. We were still on the paddle box, leaning against the white railing. The numbness in my leg had not yet passed. Limping to my friend's side, I began to walk to the quay.

Almost at the same time the women emerged. As they trembled and staggered forward, they appeared like sick, mute specters who had been cursed from life and sentenced to carry forever the chains of slavery and oppression. So wrapped up in cotton were they, with veils on every side, that they seemed to be deaf to the gurglings of the steamer. In unison, they inclined their heads before them, striving to see the deck through their thick, black veils, fearing that they might fall, or touch something, or strike one another, or take a false step.

TRANSLATED BY BRUCE LAWRENCE

TEWFIK AL-HAKIM: SHEHERAZADE REVISITED

[from *Shahrazād*]

This scene from Shahrazād, *a play in seven acts, shows how far the Arabic theater came, in a relatively short time, from rudimentary theatrical forms to highly sophisticated drama. Tewfik al-Hakim, who has already been introduced for his fiction, also proved himself many, many times over as a master playwright.*

[ISIS: "I am all that has been, all that is, all that will be. No one has ever lifted my mask."]

SHAHRAZAD: ... Has sorcery or science explained a single one of those secrets you are burning to understand?

SHAHRAYAR: Be quiet, woman.

SHAHRAZAD: Am I torturing you?

SHAHRAYAR: For God's sake, leave me alone.

SHAHRAZAD: Look what happens when you mix with magicians and priests:—you get into wild states like this.

SHAHRAYAR: What do you want me to do? I despair of you.

SHAHRAZAD: Do you still want me to reveal myself to you?

SHAHRAYAR: Shahrazad!

SHAHRAZAD: Why do you look at me like that?

SHAHRAYAR: Don't mock me.

SHAHRAZAD (*looking hard at him and whispering*): You don't deserve even to be mocked at.

SHAHRAYAR: What do you say?

SHAHRAZAD: What is it you want to know about me?

SHAHRAYAR: You know what I want.

SHAHRAZAD: You want to know who I am?

SHAHRAYAR: Yes.

SHAHRAZAD (*smiling*): I am a beautiful body. Am I anything but a beautiful body?

SHAHRAYAR (*shouting*): Blast the beautiful body.

SHAHRAZAD: I am a great heart. Am I anything but a great heart?

SHAHRAYAR: Blast your heart.

SHAHRAZAD: Can you deny that you loved my body once? And loved me with your heart once, too?

SHAHRAYAR: All that has gone. Gone! (*speaking to himself*) Today I am a miserable man.

SHAHRAZAD (*going towards him*): Don't despair, Shahrayar, my darling.

SHAHRAYAR: Go away, you hypocrite. You care for no one but yourself.

SHAHRAZAD: Do you think that?

SHAHRAYAR: A deceitful woman.

SHAHRAZAD (*smiling*): Why do you keep me alive then?

SHAHRAYAR: What devil has brought you here now?

SHAHRAZAD: You let me live because you don't know me.

SHAHRAYAR (*wearily turns his face away from her*): I no longer mind about you or anything else.

SHAHRAZAD: You turn your face away, blind man. If you could see just a little!

SHAHRAYAR: I have seen more than I should.

SHAHRAZAD: On the contrary, you miss everything.

SHAHRAYAR (*wearily*): There's only one thing I ask for.

SHAHRAZAD: What is it?

SHAHRAYAR: To die.

SHAHRAZAD: Why? What's distressing you?

SHAHRAYAR: There's nothing new in life. I've exhausted everything.

SHAHRAZAD: Isn't there a joy in the way of nature that makes you want to stay with her?

SHAHRAYAR: Nature's only a dumb captive with a stranglehold tightening round her throat.

SHAHRAZAD: You have gone mad, racking your mind till it's unhinged. What mystery are you driving after, stupid? Are you going to spend the rest of your life struggling and striving with a fallacious curiosity riddled with illusions?

SHAHRAYAR: What value is there in living any longer? I have tried everything and dwelled on everything to excess.

SHAHRAZAD: And do you think you have gone the right way to what you're seeking? Whose word have you that what you are seeking exists? Look in the water of this pool. What do you see? Clarity. The same clarity you may see in my eyes. Can't you read any of the great secrets there?

SHAHRAYAR: Curse clarity and everything that's clear. This clear water terrifies me. The man who drowns in clear water is damned.

SHAHRAZAD: You are damned.

SHAHRAYAH: Clarity! Clarity is her mask!

SHAHRAZAD: Whose?

SHAHRAYAR: *Her* mask! Hers! Hers!

SHAHRAZAD: I am afraid for you.

SHAHRAYAR: Her mask is woven of clarity; of the clear sky, clear eyes, clear water, the air, the void, all that's clear. What is beyond clarity? The thickest curtains are more transparent than clarity.

SHAHRAZAD: The whole trouble is, Shahrayar, that you are an unhappy king who has lost his humanity and forfeited his heart.

SHAHRAYAR: I have finished with humanity. I have finished with the heart. I no longer want to feel, I want to know.

SHAHRAZAD: Know what? There is nothing worth knowing.

SHAHRAYAR: A lie and deceit. Give me the answer to what I'm always asking you. That's all I want from life now.

SHAHRAZAD: Ask whatever you like.

SHAHRAYAR: Who are you?

SHAHRAZAD (*smiling*): Shahrazad.

SHAHRAYAR: Stop going round in the same circle. I know you are called Shahrazad—but who is Shahrazad?

SHAHRAZAD: The daughter of your ex-Minister.

SHAHRAYAR: I know my ex-Minister fathered Shahrazad. Just as God created nature—so that Shahrazad might not be thought a bastard or nature be imagined the child of accident. But you know these explanations won't satisfy me.

SHAHRAZAD: Why? Why aren't you willing to see me as a woman like other women, with father and mother and the usual way of coming into the world?

SHAHRAYAR: Because you are not a woman like the others. For all I know you may not be a woman at all.

SHAHRAZAD: See how far your madness has gone.

SHAHRAYAR: Perhaps she is not a woman. How could she be? I ask you, who is she? She has been imprisoned in a boudoir all her life, yet she knows about everything on the earth as if she were the earth herself. She never went further than the summerhouse in her garden, yet she knows Egypt and India and China. While she was a virgin she knew man like a woman who had lived among men for a thousand years. She knows the whole character of men, from the sublime to the sordid in them. She is young, but she climbed, unsatisfied with the knowledge of earth, to the skies and can tell of their designs and hidden things as if she were the adopted child of angels. And she went down to the depths of the globe to tell of its giants and demons and their strange underground kingdoms, as if she were the daughter of the djinns. Who could she be, who spent her twenty years, and no more, in rooms with drawn curtains, and yet—? What is her secret? Is she twenty, or is she ageless? Is she limited to one place or does she belong to all places? My mind is like a boiling kettle. It wants to know. . . . Can she be a woman when she knows everything in nature as if she were nature herself?

SHAHRAZAD: Stop it, Shahrayar. Your hands are trembling. Your face is marked with a terrible fatigue.

SHAHRAYAR: Yes, I feel exhausted. But my mind will not be quiet till I know.

SHAHRAZAD: I told you not to think of all that. Leave things alone.

SHAHRAYAR: You are my wife whom I love. Aren't you my wife? How long do you suppose I can bear to have this curtain keeping us apart?

SHAHRAZAD (*to herself, almost*): Do you imagine that if this curtain were drawn aside you could bear to look at me for a moment's duration?

SHAHRAYAR: What do you say?

SHAHRAZAD: Nothing. Go off to bed now. You need rest.

SHAHRAYAR (*shouting*): I won't go. I must know now. I've waited long enough.

SHAHRAZAD: Don't be childish, Shahrayar. You know that if you persisted twenty centuries you wouldn't get another word out of me. Because it's not mine to give away. You are asking something impossible. And you are a sick man.

SHAHRAYAR: You know. You know everything. What a mystery you are. You do nothing and say nothing that is not planned beforehand. Nothing happens by accident. Nothing comes by caprice. You live according to an exact calculation which is never out so much as a hair's breadth. It is as exact as the sun and moon and stars. You are only a tremendous mind.

SHAHRAZAD (*smiling*): You are describing me in your own image, Shahrayar.

SHAHRAYAR: I am describing the truth.

SHAHRAZAD (*mysteriously*): Always the truth!

SHAHRAYAR: Won't you tell me it?

SHAHRAZAD: You should go and sleep and rest. And if you won't do that, go back to torturing your mind or to the magicians and priests.

SHAHRAYAR (*under his breath and staring hard*): The curse of God!

SHAHRAZAD: Why are you looking at me like that?

SHAHRAYAR: Come here. . . .

SHAHRAZAD: What do you want?

SHAHRAYAR: To kiss you.

(*He takes her head between his hands, lifts the black hair away from her neck, and draws his dagger.*)

SHAHRAZAD: God help you, what are you doing?

SHAHRAYAR (*in a queer voice*): I see a grey hair, like the thread of dawn in a beautiful night.

SHAHRAZAD (*struggling from his grip, then bending down to look at her reflection in the pool*): Where is it? (*She pulls the grey hair out.*)

SHAHRAYAR: Why have you taken it out?

SHAHRAZAD (*coming back to him*): What made you act like that? I shall begin to think your madness really dangerous. How could you have endured my loss?

(*She arranges her hair and exhibits the beauty of her body. Shahrayar stares at her.*)

Why do you keep looking at me like that?—as if you had never seen me before.

SHAHRAYAR: No. No. I don't want to see you like that.

SHAHRAZAD: What do you mean?

SHAHRAYAR: She does that, too—always exhibiting her beauty and hiding her secret.

SHAHRAZAD: Who is she?

SHAHRAYAR: Nature.

SHAHRAZAD (*pityingly*): You poor thing.

SHAHRAYAR: You hypocrite.

SHAHRAZAD (*taking his head in her hands*): I pity this fatigued head and this pale forehead and these twisted lips. . . .

SHAHRAYAR: My face is pale like the faces of the dead.

SHAHRAZAD; Don't say that.

SHAHRAYAR: Yes, Shahrazad. I shall die.

SHAHRAZAD: No, don't let weariness and despair have the better of you. No. Shahrayar, you will live.

SHAHRAYAR: I don't want to.

SHAHRAZAD: You are not old (*caressing his hair*). Look, your hair is as black as night.

SHAHRAYAR: Stroke my hair as you used to. Let me hear your soft, compassionate voice. . . . I never realised you were so beautiful. Is this your mouth, Shahrazad? It's like a cup of pearls. Is this your hair? It's like clusters of grapes.

SHAHRAZAD: Come and rest your body a little while.

SHAHRAYAR: Let me put my head in your lap, as if I were your child or your husband. Am I really your husband? Sometimes the thought seems quaint and false. Tell me it's true. Put your arms round my neck. They are silver arms, Shahrazad. I want to know that all these treasures are mine. Talk to me about your love for me, if you have ever loved me a little. . . . But you have no feeling for me. . . .

SHAHRAZAD (*slightly mocking*): So you are coming back to love and the heart.

SHAHRAYAR (*in a sleepy voice*): Shahrazad, I feel now as if I were a happy man. I want to know what place you have for me in your heart. Sometimes I become anxious. . . . I feel that you are great . . . very great . . . and could never descend to the love of a person like me . . . an ordinary man. . . .

SHAHRAZAD (*slyly*): Don't you still want to know who I am?

SHAHRAYAR: I want to kiss your beautiful silver body.

SHAHRAZAD: So you are coming back to the body, I see.

SHAHRAYAR (*struggling with sleep*): I want you to recite poetry to me . . . Shahrazad . . . tell me one of your stories . . .

SHAHRAZAD (*looking towards the door*): Play something, slaves. Some music.

SHAHRAYAR (*asleep*): . . . sing me a song . . .

SHAHRAZAD: Shahrayar . . .

SHAHRAYAR: . . . .

SHAHRAZAD: Shall I sing for you? . . .

SHAHRAYAR: . . . .

SHAHRAZAD (*half to herself*): Sleep . . . sleep . . . sleep . . . Child whom playing has exhausted.

TRANSLATED BY HERBERT HOWARTH AND IBRAHIM
SHUKRALLAH

REŞAT NURI GÜNTEKIN: THE CONVENT SCHOOL

[from *Çalıkuşu*, The Wren]

*The son of an army doctor, educated at the Lycée
Français in Izmir and at the University of Istanbul,
Reşat Nuri Güntekin spent much of his life in teach-
ing. He was at one time Inspector General of the
Turkish Ministry of Education, member of Parliament,
and Turkish Representative to UNESCO.*

*He began his literary career as a playwright and
critic. In 1922 he published* The Wren, *"which
revolutionized the novel in Turkey," its translator
states, "and made him the most widely read Turkish
novelist. Until then, Turkish novels had for the most
part been too artificial in style to interest a wide
public.* The Wren *was the first Turkish novel about
ordinary and real people, written in straightforward
spoken Turkish, without any claim to literary effect. It
broke all records for Turkish best sellers, and its
author afterwards concentrated on this genre, publish-
ing other novels . . . with the same blend of romantic
story and realistic observation."*

A novel will describe a grief-stricken person as dumb and
inert, with bent shoulders and unseeing eyes; someone, in
fact, who's in a really bad way. I was always exactly the
opposite. When I am really worried my eyes sparkle, my
whole attitude is lively, and I feel as pleased as possible
with myself; I am convulsed with laughter, as though the
world meant nothing to me, and I talk inconsequently and
do every kind of mad thing. All the same, I think this is
better, if you have no one near you in whom you can
confide. After parting with Hüseyin I remember I did the
craziest things, and used to bully my cousins, whom they
brought in the hopes of amusing me.

With a lack of constancy that would have shocked a
stranger, I quickly forgot all about Hüseyin. I don't feel

very sure, but it's probable that I really was angry with him. If his name was mentioned in my presence, I would make a face, and say (in the Turkish words I had just begun to learn) "Dirty Hüseyin! ugly Hüseyin! bad-mannered Hüseyin!" and spit on the ground. At the same time, a box of dates which the poor unfortunate, dirty and ugly Hüseyin sent me the moment he got to Beirut seems to have assuaged my wrath. Although I looked on their coming to an end as a disaster, I cleared the whole lot off at a sitting. Fortunately the stones remained, and with them I played for weeks. I mixed them with some of my lucky beads, strung them on a thread, and hung them round my neck like a splendid cannibal necklace. The others I planted here and there in the garden, and for months I used to water them every morning with a small bucket, awaiting the growth of a clump of date palms.

My poor grandmother was sorely troubled. It was impossible to do anything with me. I would wake before it was light in the morning, and until I gave in exhausted at night I spent all my time in making disturbances and getting into mischief. If my voice was stilled for a time everyone in the house became anxious, because this meant either that I had cut myself somewhere, and was trying to stop the bleeding without saying a word, or that I had fallen down from somewhere and was doing my best not to howl, or else that I was doing some kind of damage, such as sawing off the legs of the chairs, or painting the coverings of the divans.

One day I climbed to the top of some trees to make nests for the birds with pieces of linen and little bits of wood. Another day I climbed to the top of the roof in order to throw stones down the chimney of the kitchen fireplace, and frighten the cook. Now and again a doctor used to come to the house: one day I jumped into the empty carriage which was waiting for him at the door, and whipped up the horses; and another day I rolled a big wooden washing tub down to the sea and let myself go with the current. I don't know whether it's the same with others, but in our family it was considered a sin to lay hands on an orphan. When I reached the limit, the punishment they chose was to take me by the arm and lock me up in a room.

We had a strange relative whom all the children called "Uncle Whiskers." This uncle used to call my hands "the railings round a saint's tomb"; for my fingers were never free of wounds and scratches; they looked as if they had been dipped in henna and tied up afterwards.

I couldn't get on at all with my companions. I even used to frighten the cousins who were older than I was. If by an out-of-the-way chance a wave of affection swelled within me, that proved another misfortune. I couldn't learn how to love like a human being, or to treat those I did love with kindness. I would throw myself like a little wild animal upon the ones I felt most for; I would bite their ears, scratch their faces, and thoroughly torment them. It was only with one of my cousins that I had an inexplicable feeling of hesitation and want of courage—Kâmran, the son of my aunt Besimé. But it would not be right to call him a child. In the first place, he was older than I was, and he was very well-behaved and serious. He didn't care to bother with other children. He used to walk about alone with his hands in his pockets along the seashore, or read a book under the trees.

Kâmran had curly fair hair, and a pale, delicate, bright complexion. So bright was his skin that I felt that if I had had the courage to seize him by the ears and put my face close to his cheeks, I should see myself reflected there, as if in a mirror.

All the same, in spite of my backwardness, I had a row with Kâmran, too, one day. I had a piece of rock which I had put in a basket and was carrying up from the sea, and I dropped it on his foot. Was it that the stone was very heavy or that he was particularly sensitive? I don't know. But suddenly there was a yell and a howl of lamentation. I was alarmed. With the agility of a monkey, I climbed a big plane tree which stood in the garden; and neither scoldings nor threats nor even supplications would make me come down again. In the end they sent the gardener up after me. But the higher he climbed, the further up I went. So much so that the poor man perceived that if he went on, I shouldn't hesitate to climb onto the thinnest branches, which would not bear me, and that there would then be an accident. So he came down again. In the end, I roosted on the branch of the tree that night until it got dark.

I gave my poor grandmother no chance to sleep. The good woman had lavished all her love upon me. Some mornings, before she had recovered from her tiredness of the day before, she would be wakened by the noise I was making; thereupon she would sit up in bed and hold me by my arms, and shake me, scolding my mother as she did so, saying: "Why did she go and die, and leave me in my old age at the mercy of this wild animal?" But this much was certain, that if at such moments my mother had

appeared before her and had said: "Will you have this wild
animal or me?" my grandmother would have had no
hesitation in choosing me, and sending my mother back to
the place she had come from.

Yes; it's hard on a delicate old lady in poor health to be
roused from her sleep before she has recovered from her
previous day's fatigue. But we must remember, too, what
it is to wake with a rested body, a brief memory, and a
soul thirsting for further trouble. In a word, in spite of all
the trouble I gave, I am sure that my grandmother found
me a consolation to her, and was, in her heart, contented.

I was in my ninth year when we lost her. My father
happened to be in Istanbul as well. They had transferred
the poor man from Tripoli to Albania, and he could only
stay one week in Istanbul. My grandmother's death left
him in a difficult situation. An officer who was also a
widower could not have dragged around with him a nine-
year-old little girl. But for some reason or other he did
not fancy leaving me with my aunts. He probably feared
that I should fall into a position of dependence on them.
However that may be, he took me by the hand one morning, onto the steamer, and across to Istanbul. At the bridge
we got into another carriage, and climbed endless hills passing through the bazaars until we came to a halt at last
before the door of a big stone building.

This was a convent school, in which I was to be shut
up for ten years. They took us into a gloomy room near
the door, the windows and the shutters of which were all
closed.

Everything must have been discussed and arranged beforehand, because a woman dressed in black, who came in
soon after, bent over me and looked me closely in the face,
stroking my cheek, while the flaps of her white headdress
touched my hair like the wings of some strange bird. I
remember that my very first appearance at school began
with an accident and a bit of naughtiness on my part. While
my father was talking with the Mother Superior I began
to wander round the room and to finger one thing after
another. A vase, with coloured pictures above it that I
wanted to touch with my fingers, fell to the ground and was
smashed. My father leapt from his seat, his sword rattling,
and seized me by the arm, in a great state of concern. The
Mother Superior, on the other hand, who proved to be
the owner of the broken vase, simply laughed, and tried to
calm my father, waving him aside.

How many more things like this vase was I not to break at school? The untamable nature I had shown at home persisted here too. Either those Sisters were really angels, or else there must have been a pleasanter side to my nature. Or was it that there was no other way of putting up with me? I was always talkative in class and given to wandering all over the place. It was not for me to go up and down stairs as other people did. I would be sure to hide in a corner and wait for the others to come down, and then, jumping on to the banisters as if mounting a horse, I would let myself go from top to bottom. Or I would hop downstairs with my legs together. There was a withered tree in the garden; one of the teachers saw that whenever I got the opportunity I climbed up it, and heedless of warnings would jump from branch to branch till I had no breath left. She called out one day, "That child isn't a human being: she's a wren (Çalıkuşu)!" And from that day on my real name was forgotten, and everyone began to call me Çalıkuşu.

I don't know how it was, but thereafter this name caught on in the family, and my real name Feridé remained an official one, used on special occasions, like clothes that one wears on feast days.

I liked Çalıkuşu, and it served my purpose. When they complained about some impropriety, I would shrug my shoulders helplessly and say: "What can I do? What can you expect from a 'Çalıkuşu'?"

Now and again a spectacled priest with a small, goatlike beard round his chin used to come to and fro to the school. One day I cut a piece of my hair with the hand-work scissors, and fixed it to my chin with glue. When the priest looked in my direction I hid my chin in my palms, and when he turned his head in the other direction, I withdrew my hands and wagged my beard, mimicking the priest and making all the others laugh. The teacher couldn't make out what was amusing us, and began shouting at us all at the top of her voice, in a rage. I happened to turn my head for a moment towards the window of the classroom which opened onto the corridor. And what should I see but the Mother Superior looking at me through the glass? What do you think of that?—and what was I to do? I was horror-stricken. I bowed my head, put my finger to my lips to signify "silence," and then I blew her a little kiss with my hand. The Mother Superior was the senior Sister of the school. From the oldest teacher down, everyone treated her like a god. All the same, my inviting her to be

my accomplice against the priest tickled the good woman,
and as though afraid she would not be able to maintain her
composure if she came into the class, she laughed, shook
a warning finger at me, and disappeared in the darkness
of the corridor.

The Mother Superior caught me one day in the dining
room. I was busy putting the scraps from the table into a
paper basket I had stolen and brought along from the
classroom.

She called me to her rather severely: "Come here,
Feridé," she said, "what's that you're up to?"

I couldn't understand what harm there was in it, and
raising my eyes to her face, I asked: "Is it wrong to feed the
dogs, Mother?"

"Which dogs? and with what food?"

"The dogs in the ruins. Oh, Mother! if you only knew
how pleased they are when they see me! Last night they
came to meet me right from the street corner, and began to
go round and round my feet. . . . 'Steady, now. Hi! what are
you doing? I shan't give you a thing till you get back there!'
The creatures don't understand a word you say to them.
They pulled me down. . . . But I was obstinate, and hid
the basket in my skirts. They very nearly tore me to pieces,
but thank Heaven a street breadseller was passing by, and
he saved me."

The Mother Superior fixed her eyes on mine, and
listened.

"All right, then; but how did you get out of the school?"

Without any hesitation, I explained that I had jumped
over the wall at the back of the laundry.

The Mother Superior put her hand to her head, as though
she had had some very bad news.

"However did you dare?" she asked me.

With the same innocence, I said to her: "Don't worry,
Mother. . . . The wall is very low . . . and how do you
expect me to go out by the door? . . . Do you think the
porter would ever let me? The first time I went, I took
him in, by saying: 'Sister Thérèse is calling you,' and got
through that way. Please don't give me away . . . because
there's such a danger the dogs might starve. . . ."

What strange creatures those Sisters were! I imagine
that if I'd done the same in any other school, I should have
either have been shut up, or I should have got some other
punishment. But in order to avoid coming face to face
with me, the Mother Superior knelt down on the ground.

"My child, to care for animals is a good thing, but to be

disobedient is not. . . . Leave the basket with me . . . I will have the scraps taken to the dogs by the porter."

In all my life perhaps no one loved me as that woman did. Actions of this kind on the part of the Sisters seemed to make about as much impression on my behaviour and bad manners as the tide makes on the rocks. But with time they worked secretly within me, and I fear they have left indelible traces: an incurable weakness, and a sediment of pity.

Yes, I was indeed a strange child, difficult to understand. I had probed the weaknesses of my teachers, I had thoroughly explored what it was that would worry each one of them, and I prepared my tortures accordingly.

TRANSLATED BY WYNDHAM DEEDES

MARMADUKE PICKTHALL: THE KEFR AMMEH INCIDENT

[from *As Others See Us*]

Today Marmaduke Pickthall is perhaps best known as a translator of the Koran, a British convert to Islam who produced the nearest thing to an "author- ized" English version of its sacred book. But he once enjoyed widespread and deserved acclaim as a novelist, and was ranked among the best of his contemporaries in this art.

In Saïd the Fisherman, *his most famous novel, and* Knights of Araby, *his best, Pickthall re-created "the rich imaginative superstructure, the vivid por- traiture, the animated dialogue, and profusion of incident"[1] of classical Arabic storytelling, together with a powerful psychological insight.*

But there was another side to his art, a firm and sometimes fierce criticism of the British colonial presence in the Islamic world, which his experience and conversion to Islam enabled him to understand and depict with even greater subtlety than some of the best Moslem writers working within the Islamic world proper. Pickthall's Orient was not synthetic or senti- mentalized; nor was his Islam.

This is the true history of the Kefr Ammeh incident which greatly disconcerted some of the English governors of Egypt, though no notice of it found its way into the newspapers. A number of fellâhîn were tortured by the omdeh (headman) of a place of some importance out of sheer devotion, as it seemed, to Mr. Sandeman, the English inspector for the district. To the authorities the case ap- peared inexplicable. To me, who had been able to observe affairs at Kefr Ammeh from the Egyptian no less than the English point of view, the "incident," however startling,

---

[1]Anne Fremantle, *Loyal Enemy* (London, Hutchinson, 1938), p. 259.

appeared not unnatural, seeing the strange popularity which
Mr. Sandeman enjoyed there and the almost mystic awe
which he inspired in the inhabitants. He was, in fact, a kind
of fetish for the population, and that for reasons of which
he personally had no knowledge, reasons quite independent
of his rank as an official. The key to understanding of the
situation came into my possession quite by accident, three
months before George Sandeman's appointment to the
district, when I visited Kefr Ammeh for amusement at the
season of the Môlid of the local saint. On the first night
of the fair I chanced to stroll into a circus tent, where I was
privileged to witness a most strange performance.

The ring was lighted by the flare of five tall cressets set
at irregular intervals on its circumference. The large tent
was crowded. Men and women of the poorer sort, with
swarms of children, sat or sprawled upon the ground
around the ring. Behind them rose a mist of black robes,
white turbans, and brown faces, tier on tier, from which
there came the steadfast gleam of teeth and eyeballs. The
audience was hushed, devouring with its thousand eyes the
antics of some clever tumblers and a few conventional
displays of horsemanship. Then came the clown, and there
were murmurs of delight, since he was known to be the
pearl of all his time for drollery. After mimicking an
omdeh, a shawîsh and an Egyptian judge, oppressors of the
poor, amid much laughter, he put his hand into the placket
of his baggy trousers and fished up a wig of tow which he
adjusted to his head. He then rubbed some red dust upon
his face until it wore the colour of pomegranate-bloom, put
on a Frankish collar and an old pith helmet brought to him
by an attendant, took in his hand a cane and began to strut
up and down stiffly with elbows raised, opening his mouth
very wide and saying: "Wow! Wow!" at frequent intervals.
During his toilet you could have heard a pin drop in
the tent; but now as he marched to and fro with that strange
cry, a sigh arose: "What is he now? O Lord, inform us
quickly: What is this?" and someone cried in accents of
delight: "The name of God be round about us! He is
become a ghoul—a sinful ghoul!"
A doll was thrown into the ring. With a shout: "It is my
son!" the clown pounced on it and clasped it to his
breast. He laid it upon one of two chairs which had been
placed in readiness, while he himself took seat upon the
other, saying: "Rest thou there, my son, until they bring
thee meat and milk and vegetables, all duly stale from hav-

ing been enclosed in tins for many years!" And then the fun became so furious that those who witnessed the performance had no time to guess its meaning. Man after man came in, upon his feet, and the ghoul, with curses, made him go down on his hands and knees. "It is for your good," he cried. "We wish to see you all made equal under us. We teach you good behaviour. We are a just race."

At length three men came in at once. As fast as one of them went down obediently upon his hands and knees, his brothers rose up on their feet, until the ghoul grew so infuriated that his mind flew from him and he knew not where he stood. Retreating backwards to his seat wow-wowing loudly, he mistook the chair, sat down upon his child and squashed it flat.

"Wâh! Wâh! My son is dead!" he roared, holding up the doll for all to see. Then from the mighty crowd there came a shout of laughter with cries of "May our Lord have mercy upon him, O thou foolish monster!"

"Bring water!" cried the ghoul, beside himself. "Bring water, sprinkle and revive my son. No, no! It will do harm. It is not filtered. Hi, there, you doctors! Bring my son to life or I will cut your heads off!"

"O atheistic monster!" roared the crowd. "Canst thou not see that thy misfortune is from God?"

"Down on all fours, beasts that you are!" he cried. "Convey my son with honour to the hospital!"

They answered: "It is useless, O khawâgah! He is truly dead!"

The ghoul then seized a chair and killed the doctors with it, which done, he once more gave attention to his child. His brick-red face became convulsed with grief; he opened his great mouth and howled "Wow! Wow!" He stamped his feet and tore his wig of tow. Then the men who had been killed rose up and fetched an open coffin such as Muslims use. "No, no!" he bellowed on beholding it. "Go fetch a tin. All meat must be preserved in tins or it goes bad."

They changed the coffin for a kerosene tin into which they thrust the doll, then ran away with it, the ghoul pursuing them with shouts: "The lid! Where is the lid? My son will spoil!" Just as they were leaving the arena they flung away the tin, the doll fell out, the ghoul, with "Wow! Wow!" seized his child in one hand, the tin in the other, and ran out after them; the play was ended.

The audience drew a deep sigh of regret. There followed argument in whispers as to its significance. Someone said: "It was an Englishman." "No," came the answer, "it was nothing of the seed of Adam, but a cursed ghoul with some resemblance to an Englishman." A third exponent cried: "It was an atheist, and all the evil which befell him comically was from God."

Kefr Ammeh, as I learnt, had no acquaintance with the English, though but a stone's throw from the town there stood a government rest house where Englishmen occasionally came and spent a night. The sole exceptions were the omdeh, who had met with their inspectors, and the custodian of the rest house aforesaid, a pious sheykh devoid of curiosity, who told his beads and gave scant heed to men who came and went. The watchman had not seen the clown's performance, but the omdeh had; and when the crowd emerged at length into the street of tents, alight and noisy underneath the stars, the latter was beset with eager questions. Was the tow-haired, red-faced creature with the curious voice an Englishman, as some were saying, or a ghoul?

A ghoul, most certainly, the omdeh said, the English being men of regal bearing, remarkable above all things for self-restraint. Yet some of the visitors to the fair from distant places vowed that the clown had played the English to the life. The men of Kefr Ammeh took the omdeh's word for it. What they had seen had been a ghoul most certainly; and the inadvertent squashing of his offspring, the derision which he met with in the end, had been the due reward of tyranny and atheism. It had been a moral tale unfolded comically, in the true Egyptian manner; and the fact that all points of his application were not absolutely clear made it the more attractive to the rustic audience, most of whom revisited the circus on the second evening of the fair, to see it and learn from it.

The clown portrayed the omdeh, the shawîsh, the judge, exactly as before; but when the people clamoured, some for the ghoul and others for the Englishman, he ran away with shaking of the head. The clamour went on vainly for some time. At length a juggler sprang into the ring, playing with balls of light until their flying glitter attracted all those eyes, when murmurs ceased. Afterwards it was known that the Egyptian government official who had been sent to oversee the fair, informed of the performance of the previous night, had put a stop to it. This high-handed action fixed the clown's play permanently in the public memory. Men grieved for the suppression of a little drama which (as they said) combined amusement with religious teaching. They mourned their ghoul, and spoke much of him in the weeks which followed, laying stress upon the fact, as stated by the omdeh, that he had borne not the remotest likeness to an Englishman, to show the great injustice of suppressing him.

And then George Sandeman arrived at Kefr Ammeh.

Some children were at play one evening on the dust heaps which extend between the government rest house—a white, one-storied building in the open fields—and the little mud-built town adorned with palm trees, when a foreigner, emerging from the rest house, came upon them suddenly, exclaiming: "Where is the house of the omdeh?"

The children all with one accord fell down upon their hands and knees.

"Security, O khawâgah! Guarantee but my security and I will show thee," cried one braver than the rest.

"Be not afraid!" the Frank replied; on which the guide ran off as one who flees from danger. The children's game was at an end. They followed awestruck.

A man who passed the stranger in a narrow place stood staring after the tall, white-clad figure strutting along so stiff with elbows raised. He exclaimed: "I seek refuge in Allah from Satan the Stoned," and followed the weird apparition to the omdeh's house, which presently became a place of concourse. First one and then another of the village notables kept dropping in till the reception room was full; while at the doorway women, children and the poorer men gathered and stared intently at the foreigner. Was he, or was he not in truth their ghoul? He had removed his mushroom hat which had enforced the likeness, and laid it down on the divan beside him. His hair was not like tow in texture, but it was of a light colour, and, ruffled as it was just then, recalled the wig of tow the clown had worn. His face was very red, though in repose the eagerly desired resemblance almost vanished. But when he opened his great mouth and showed his teeth and laughed, their ghoul was present. The Englishman's "Ha! Ha!" which sent a shudder down the spine of every listener, was as near as could be to the mountebank's "Wow! Wow!" He bellowed every word as if his hearers had been deaf.

The omdeh used him with the greatest reverence, receiving with expressions of delight the information (conveyed in most peculiar Arabic) that he was English and had been commanded to reside at Kefr Ammeh for some months; but while making much of him as host to guest, he stole dismayed, inquiring glances at his face. Another laugh, "Wow! Wow!" rang forth, and meaning looks were interchanged all round the room. But it was when, in reply to a polite remark to the effect that English people were the lords of justice, he declared without the least demur that that was so, and added, "If we seem like tyrants sometimes it is for your good," that strong suspicion leapt to certainty and exultation reigned in every heart. A murmur of applause went up from the group of common people at the door, which group had now become a crowd that overflowed the little courtyard of the omdeh's house. On the hush which followed this betrayal of emotion came a child's cry: "O my mother, lift me up that I may see the ghoul!"

The Englishman at length took leave with loud expressions of good will, so loud as to seem menacing to all who heard them. A troop of little boys and girls adhered to him with no worse object than to gaze upon his wondrous face. He told them to be gone, and beat those nearest to him, when, seeing they annoyed His Grace, a village watchman dispersed them with his quarterstaff. The watchman wished to guard His Honour to the rest house, but the Englishman commanded him to go back whence he came and, when he tried remonstrance, used obscene expressions such as the worst of men in cities bandy, threatening, moreover, to chastise him to the point of death.

The town was thrilled and deeply interested, with the feeling one would have supposing some remembered dream come true in every detail. Inquiry of the cook at the rest house, when he came to do his shopping in the sûk next morning, elicited the fact that the khawâgah ate tinned foods and never drank a drop of water which had not been filtered. When this was known some women let their voices flutter forth in joy cries, as is usual on occasions of festivity. The Englishman was certainly their ghoul. From that day forth he was assured of popularity. Though he was seen to be uncouth, devoid of manners as of understanding, and likely to prove dangerous at unawares, the people loved him and would crowd to gaze on him, hugging to their hearts the blest assurance that they saw his whole significance more truly than he did himself.

The Englishman was as strong as a camel and less sensitive, for he would ride like mad upon his business in the heat of noon, would exert himself sometimes with scarce a break from the third hour till sunset; and when

he had by chance an idle day did not repose, but rode his
horse for pleasure for an hour or so, returning from which
pastime he would change his clothes and presently come
forth upon the dust heaps to fatigue himself still more.
Armed with some curious sticks, he would take stand with
legs apart and smite with all his strength a small white ball,
pursuing it from place to place until he lost it, when he
would proceed to search for it for hours beneath the
burning sun, assisted by the village youngsters, who were
accustomed to observe his labours from some spot of
shade, from which the offer of a coin alone could tempt
them. If they came too close he beat them with his club,
and cursed them in abominable language. They feared the
beatings, but the language interested them. Their dreamy,
serious eyes were always fixed upon his face, and in the
earnestness of their attention they would mimic all unconsciously the strange grimaces which he made when
bludgeoning the small white ball, which he seemed to look
on as a sinful thing, his enemy.

He had a small white dog with black ears and a stumpy
tail which attended him whenever he went out on foot,
adhering to him like his shadow, walking when he walked,
stopping when he stopped, always at his heel. This dog he
loved above all other living creatures. When walking with it
in the town, or out among the fields, he carried in his hand
a monstrous whip, wherewith he was prepared to flay the
pariah dogs if they attacked it. He spoke to it in gentle
tones as to his soul's beloved, and once, when boys began
to tease it and it gave a squeak, he beat and cursed the
culprits so unmercifully that all the children who beheld the
sight fell down before him.

"Whoso touches my dog," he roared, "I will hang him
and his parents and defile their graves."

The children thought: "His dog is as his son. Please
God, he will ere long sit down on it"—a contingency which
seemed the less remote because the dog invariably kept so
close behind him. All animals appeared to have his
sympathy, except the pariah dogs aforesaid, which he
persecuted. A boy had stuck a knife into a donkey to
accelerate its pace: he flew in a great rage, chastised the
boy and stole the knife. A man had lost his temper with
a sullen mule: he lost his temper with the man, and
threatened him with death and hell. Neither the mule nor
the ass was his property, nor could the manner of their
treatment, by any way of thinking, be esteemed his business. But it was apparent that he could not help himself.

At sight of beasts oppressed his mind flew from him, and
in his madness he oppressed the sons of Adam. The men
of Kefr Ammeh shrugged their shoulders, perceiving that
the illness was upon him from the hand of God. The wise
among them whispered that in regions where a beast is
king one must expect dumb beasts to be preferred to men.
The Berberine cook and butler at the rest house told how
the Englishman would take the small white dog upon his
knees and let it freely lick his face and hands; how it slept
in the same room with him and shared his meals.

The ghoul, the small white dog and the small white ball
had for the fellâhîn the charm of something magical, a
mystery whose true significance was known to God alone.
The children knew the ball, having all handled it, and
they believed it to be made of human bones and skin
pressed tight together. But a man, Selîm Ghandûr, who
happened to encounter it upon the dust heaps, declared
with oaths that it was made of solid and essential fire.
It had brought him near to death, but while he had said
the necessary prayers, writhing in awful anguish on the
ground, the ghoul came to him with his mouth wide open,
laughing "Wow! Wow!" and thrust a dollar on him. The
ghoul was not a miser, very certainly. He rewarded all who
did him service, and, having persecuted anyone, would,
when his wrath subsided, give him money. His intention,
it was clearly seen, was not iniquitous. He often visited the
omdeh's house, and honoured other houses when implored
to do so. His awful voice and his bloodcurdling laugh lost
something of their terrors as they grew familiar. The
omdeh, who had much to do with him as an official,
pronounced him very simple, even brutal, in his methods,
and very, very easy to deceive; though, while deceiving
him, a man well knew that, did he but suspect a fraud, his
vengeance would be terrible and all-destroying—a knowledge which imparted zest to the shy game. He was, upon
the whole, extremely popular, and thanks to his discerned
capacity for wholesale murder if enraged, respected. The
fellâhîn were circumspect in their behaviour towards him,
for none could tell beforehand what small thing would
raise his fury, or whether he might not go mad spontaneous-
ly.

One evening there arrived two other Englishmen upon a
visit to the rest house. The loud wow-wowing of their welcome could be heard afar. Thereafter, at the third hour of
the night, most frightful sounds alarmed the waking town.
A roaring as of wild beasts, in a solemn cadence, lasted

for several minutes at a time; then came a moment's hush, then a fresh outburst. The people thronged the roofs and listened, stiff with fright.

"Perhaps," the children whispered, "our ghoul has sat down on his son, the small white dog!" The sweet conjecture was passed on from roof to roof. The men said: "He could hardly make that noise alone—not even he! Two others of his kind arrived at sunset. The probability is that they have drunk strong drink until they have become intoxicated, and thus roar in madness."

"If they are drunk, then make fast every door; remove the women to a place of safety!" counselled one old man, a member of the omdeh's household, raising his hands in anguish to the stars. "They will presently break forth to slay and ravish. I remember, years ago when I was in the army, how the Circassian and Albanian officers would thus sit up and drink until their wits forsook them; then, rushing out, would chase us with their swords, calling us (saving your presence) Nile mud and the accursed dung of Pharaoh. They would even run into the streets abusing all they met."

"Merciful Allah!" cried the omdeh, who forthwith despatched a runner to the rest house to inquire if there was any danger of a massacre. The two Berberines, the cook and butler of the Englishman, assailed with such a question, laughed contemptuously. In the manner of experienced stablemen explaining to some nincompoop the ways of horses, they told the messenger that Englishmen were most benevolent when thus elated. The dreadful roaring was the mode of singing in their country. They would roar till there was no more voice left in them, and then betake themselves like lambs to bed. This information, carried straightway to the omdeh, somewhat relieved the apprehensions of the people; but few were they in Kefr Ammeh who deemed it safe to go to bed that night.

From the English point of view George Sandeman was not abnormal. He sported all the small inanities and irritating tricks of manner, varying with the mode from year to year, which mark the youthful Englishman of good society. A man with men, a gentleman with women, he dressed well without foppery, adorned his rather jerky conversation with the latest slang, and was in some demand for dances in the Cairo season.

He having failed in the initial step to various careers, one of his uncles, who was in the Cabinet, had forced him into the Egyptian Civil Service, much to the annoyance of the British lord of Egypt, who hated to submit to private influence. Sandeman was put into positions especially designed to prove his incapacity. But somehow he survived successive ordeals. He did not love his work; his whole delight was in field sports and in the pleasures of the town; yet he did not do badly. It had become apparent that the government would have to keep him after all, about the time when he was sent to Kefr Ammeh. Once there, his unexpected popularity, reported in high quarters, was set down to tact as an administrator, and his name was made.

"It's a rummy thing," he told me when I spent an evening with him at the rest house, "but I believe the beggars somehow take to me. And I like them too in a way. Can understand how a chap like you, who's read 'em up, can find them interesting, and all that. Do, myself, in a way. They're all right if you know how to handle 'em. I go in and call on 'em and have a talk—treat 'em like human beings; but they jolly well know I won't stand cheek or any nonsense from 'em. That's the way. They're tricky, though; you can't see into them."

As an example of their trickiness or their opacity, I know not which, he told me how the omdeh had sent round one night, when he and two other Englishmen were singing school songs after dinner, to ask if there was any danger of a massacre.

"Now was that innocence or was it cheek? I ask you. What? When the cook came in and told us, splitting his sides with laughter, I felt pretty small. Didn't sing much after that, I can assure you! We had, of course, been kicking up a most infernal row, enough to frighten people who had never heard that kind o' thing. But I'm not so sure that message wasn't meant for cheek. D—d cheek, if it really was sarcastic. What? Yet he's a dear old thing, and quite a pal o' mine. They're rummy beggars."

He sat in silence for a minute, stroking the fox terrier upon his lap, wrestling, it seemed, with some elusive thought.

"I tell you what, old man," he said at length. "I shall have to write a book about 'em someday. Started notes already. I come across some rummy things down here. I don't say I should ever print the stuff, but it'd be amusin' just to see what I could do. Keep me from going mad in this damned hole."

I praised the notion highly, being always eager to encourage the first shy movements of a mind in healthy flesh.

He added: "I believe I've got upon the track of something —pretty big discovery, it seems to me—about the beggars."

He seemed to be desirous to be plied with questions. I, therefore, begged him, with effusion, to confide in me.

"You won't crib my notion? You've got to promise that before I tell you. Well, it may be nothing really—just an accident, or some other feller may have spotted it before— but I believe these beggars aren't quite men like we are— a bit nearer to the monkeys, Darwin and all that. What put me on the track was this—a rummy thing! If you talk to any of their youngsters a bit sharply, raise a stick to them or anything of that sort, it's ten to one they'll go down on all fours. As if"—he puffed at his cigar with zeal, manifestly struggling with a tough abstraction—"as if they felt safer, more at home, once they could get their hands on the ground. As if—some instinct, don't you know?—and all that! I never saw a man do it but once, and then he may have done it for a purpose, for he tried to lick my boots. But the little kiddies do it nearly always—nearer to nature. What? It's a queer thing."

He went on talking of the "beggars," as he called them, till we went to bed, which did not happen until after midnight. We met at breakfast the next morning, and then said good-bye, Sandeman going to his daily work, while I set off upon my journey to another rest house.

I did not meet George Sandeman again until the following winter, when he was much in Cairo, having some relatives and hosts of friends among the fashionable visitors. Then, as it happened, we met rather often in attendance on a certain English family in which there was a very pretty girl. I may as well confess I offered marriage to the damsel, only to learn that she adored George Sandeman—a predilection which I cannot for my life explain except by the old adage about youth attracting youth. We remained good friends, however, and by her contrivance I was wheedled into something more than toleration for my favoured rival. In English society I must say that the said George appeared to great advantage, being evidently in his element, which I was not. I felt much more at home in Kefr Ammeh.

"How is your book getting on?" I asked one afternoon, when I found him having tea alone at one of the little tables in the hall of the club.

"Oh, that!" was the reply. "I still jot down a note occasionally. But I may tell you that I've chucked the great discovery—all rot! I bet you knew that at the time, you

secretive old beast—and wouldn't tell a feller!" He laughed
without a trace of animosity.

"Their dropping down like that was simply cheek. I
guess you twigged that—eh? I caught them grinning once
or twice. That was enough. I've put a stop to it for good
and all. God knows what made 'em take to it. The only
thing that I can think of's this: You know I'm devilish fond
of my small dog. The children started teasing just once. I
let 'em know that I'd jolly well hang, draw and quarter
the whole lot of 'em, with their fathers and grandfathers—
and so I would, by Jove—if anybody touched my dog
again. Well, to rag me in return for that, the beggars made
believe that I was only fond of beasts—a bit of a beast
myself, no doubt—and so dropped down like that for
mercy—kind of sarcastic business, don't you see? What first
gave me a hint that they were not so simple as I used to
think was the old omdeh sending round that night about
our singing. Made me feel exceeding small, that did. So
damned sarcastic! He's a dignified old boy. God knows
what they think of us, or what they see us like with those
queer eyes of theirs. I must say I should like to know for
once."

I told him that he seemed to me to be developing, however tardily, the faculty of abstract thought—beginning to
"take notice," as our nurses say. He flicked a crumb of
toast at me, and then continued: "They really are quite
decent in some ways. About my shooting, for instance.
There's good sport around the place. They give me leave
to go just where I like, and clear the ground of kids and
cattle for me. I have one really ripping gun, and always
make a point of cleaning it myself. You should see the
beggars eye it! They've got a legend that it kills with every
shot. I believe they think I worship that and my small dog.
I have to row them sometimes just to keep 'em in their
place, but on the whole I find 'em jolly decent. Only
don't go saying that to Joan or her mamma. They're always fishing for an invitation to come down and see me.
No place for women, as you know. Do put them off! I
shouldn't know what to do with 'em"—he blushed profuse-
ly—"should feel ashamed, an utter worm before the
beggars. Can't explain. You might come down and look
me up sometimes. Come the first week next month. Our
Môlid will be on, and if there's ever going to be fun in
Kefr Ammeh, you'll behold it then."

I could not reply definitely to the invitation on the spur
of the moment, but after a few days I wrote accepting it.

Alighting at Mastûrah station about ten o'clock one morning, I succeeded in procuring donkeys for my servant and myself and rode along the dykes to Kefr Ammeh. From afar I saw a line of tents much longer than the face the town presented, shining out against a palm grove to the southward; discerned the flutter of innumerable small red flags and heard the hivelike murmur of the fair. Sandeman seemed pleased to see me. We had luncheon and then sat and talked till four o'clock, when we went out to pay a call upon the chief official of the fair. The crowd within the canvas town was dense, and Snap, the small white dog, was at his master's heels. He ought not to have been there, but we did not discover his attendance until it was too late to send him home. I noticed children calling out "Isnâb!" alluringly, and saw some of them stoop to pet the dog. They belonged to Kefr Ammeh. Strangers, who knew not Snap, were less considerate. Twice he received a kick which sent him yelping, and Sandeman turned round and used atrocious language. Wherever the man learnt it I could never guess.

"That's one thing I do hate about the beggars, and one good reason why I won't have Joan down here. They're so damned cruel. It never seems to strike them that dumb beasts can feel," he told me as we shouldered through the press. Our goal was the marquee set up by the provincial government in honour of the Muslim saint who sleeps at Kefr Ammeh, who slept there as a Christian saint before the Muslim conquest, and as a god of ancient Egypt long before the birth of Christendom. One end of the marquee was open to the crowd; at the other, in the place of honour on a long divan, sat the representative of government, a black-bearded effendi, receiving the respectful compliments of divers notables. The atmosphere was reverent as in a church, till Sandeman with loud "Ha, ha!" strode in out of the sunlight, Snap at his heels, shook the official violently by the hand, nodded to all the company, which rose to greet him, and flopped down comfortably in the place of greatest honour, where Snap immediately jumped up beside him. The other visitors were mildly scandalised by the apparition of a dog on the divan above them; the representative of the provincial government betrayed alarm, until the omdeh of Kefr Ammeh, rising in his place, explained that Snap was not as other dogs which never wash but wander to and fro, eating all manner of abomination. This dog, he said, performed ablutions twice a day, lived in a house, slept in a bed, and fed on bread and milk and beans and onions. In all respects he was his master's soul.

The representative of the provincial government, thus reassured, and anxious to propitiate the soul of Sandeman, gave the dog a sweetmeat with his honourable hand, while all the notables showered praises on him. We drank a cup of coffee and some water, and ate sickly sweetstuff, while musicians squatting in the tent mouth made a merry din; then Sandeman sprang up abruptly, wrung the great man's hand once more, touched his hat to all the others and marched out with Snap behind him.

I had overtaken him before I realised that half the men who had been sitting in the tent were coming with us, anxious, no doubt, to pay their court to one so arrogant. Those who were not fortunate enough to gain a place beside him attached themselves to me as we proceeded on our homeward way. Among these was the omdeh of the place, a fine old man in splendid silken raiment, who at once began to pour into my ear the praise of Sandeman.

The town, nay all the country, were His Honour's servants. He was so strong and yet so generous, of such a brilliant and farseeing mind and yet benevolent. Of a verity he was the marvel of his time for might and justice. A perfect Englishman, and all was said! All Kefr Ammeh loved him as men love the water brooks. Would I be good enough to find out from His Excellency whether there was anything displeasing to him in the place, and afterwards let him (the omdeh) know, that he might have it altered. The population was, alas, uncivilised, however much devoted to His Grace, and might offend through ignorance of good behaviour. He (the omdeh) would far rather lose his right hand, he declared with vehemence, than that anything should happen to aggrieve that prince of Englishmen. There had been no disorder, praise to Allah, since his coming, but naturally there existed in the place a few bad characters who might by some unhappy outbreak smirch its fame. One of the outlying hamlets, Mît Gâmûs, was a veritable hornets' nest of fearless brigands. He therefore begged me, as a personal favour, to persuade His Highness not to come into the fair again like this incognito, but with outrunners and attendants as became his state. Thus he would be guarded from the rude touch of the crowd, and the sweetest, most delightful of all little dogs would be secured from hurt.

I called to Sandeman to stop and listen, and bade the omdeh make his own request. He did so, but with evident reluctance, and in broken phrases which contrasted strongly with the eloquence of his discourse to me. While he frequently declared his love for Sandeman, I saw that he was very much afraid of him. All the bystanders supported his petition, talking baby Arabic intelligible to the perfect Englishman.

"Does Your Honour think of visiting the fair tonight? Let him but order, and we will provide a score of men happy and proud to be his guard of honour."

"Who told you that I thought of visiting the fair to-night?" snapped Sandeman. He murmured: "Beastly cheek!" beneath his breath. "Why should I come out when I am comfortable in the house? They seem to think their beastly fair attractive," he remarked aside. I told him that I thought the omdeh had some fear of trouble with the crowd.

"Oh, that's another matter. Then we'll come, you bet! But don't you tell 'em that," said Sandeman with glee. I told the omdeh and the other notables that His Honour felt no great desire to see the fair again. They seemed relieved, and parted from us with a storm of blessings.

"Seems quiet enough," observed my friend some four hours later as we moved once more amid the multitude, under the flare of torches, deafened by a thousand discords. "Let's turn in somewhere, see a show or two. This place looks promising. Come on, old man!"

He paid down money at a wicket and we passed into a crowded circus tent. Our entrance was unheeded by the audience, all intent just then upon the antics of a clown who held the ring alone. I recognised the jester of my former visit, and tried desperately to get Sandeman out again under pretext of the foulness of the atmosphere. But in a trice he had become absorbed in the performance as completely as the fellâhîn around us.

"That's our omdeh to the life! Look, just below us in the third row, there's the man himself and all his family, enjoying it as much as anyone!" he whispered, and then forgot me and the world together for a while.

Having finished his performance of the omdeh, the clown put on a wig of tow, an old pith helmet, and a Frankish collar, hung something like a pipe between his teeth, took in his hand a whip and swaggered up and down with elbows raised, now exclaiming, "Wow! Wow!" now looking back and whistling for a dog.

"That's me! That's devilish good! The cunning beggars!" came from Sandeman, entranced, and presently his laugh rang out above the others. That betrayed us. I caught the

omdeh's gaze directed at us, and never have I seen such
mortal terror in an old man's face. He sprang up on his
seat and shrieked to the buffoon to stop, calling him evil
names and cursing his religion. Not content with that, he
scrambled down into the arena with remarkable agility
for one so old, and flung himself upon the jester with
intent to kill. Many of the audience followed his example,
while others called aloud on Allah and the local saint.
Sandeman wanted to go down into the *mêlée* and protect
the clown. I deterred him by main force and dragged him
from that pandemonium out into the street of tents, telling
two soldiers who were standing by the door to stop the
riot. We waited till the noise within had quite subsided,
when the omdeh came rushing out like a madman, flung
himself at Sandeman's feet and told him that the clown
was captured and awaited judgment. Sandeman swore
horribly and told him not to be a fool, which made the
old man look more scared than ever as we moved away.

"What silly fools the beggars are!" sighed Sandeman,
"spoiling the best part of the show like that! Whatever do
they think I am—an ogre? What? Of course it was cheek
of the feller, but I thought it damned amusin'. No need to
half kill the joker, anyhow! Surprisin' beggars! Absolutely
mad, of course. I sometimes feel as if I were bewitched,
changed somehow, not myself at all, the way the beggars
look at me! Can't grasp their point of view, you see. It's
pretty maddening. Makes one downright homesick. I've
had enough of this. Let's get indoors."

My friend was nearly crying with vexation. I told him
that in my opinion the beggars, as he called them, were
afraid of him, and suggested that the frightful language
he employed habitually might peradventure have something to do with it.

"Oh, that! They're used to that. They like it!" he made
light rejoinder, and went on to enlarge upon the subject
of the homesickness which seized him sometimes when
alone with them. He told me the whole history of his
love for Joan, which dated from his sixteenth year, described his home, his earliest recollections, his first ride
to hounds and other private matters in a sentimental tone.
There dwelt in truth a very honest, simple soul beneath
his self-assertive outward shell. After midnight, in his
study in the rest house, he described to me the height of
his ambition: "Two thousand a year. You can't ask a girl
to marry you on less, and a little country house—I know
the very place I want in Devon—among trees, you know—

I love the drip of trees after a shower—with decent shooting and a few good neighbours—and Joanie! I should be a
king, by Jove! And here I am in this damned furnace of a
country, acting nursery governess to a lot of bally monkeys.
But there, the beggars are all right. I'm feeling down."

At this point he had paused with one hand on his brow,
the other stroking Snap, who lay upon his knees as usual,
when a droning, nasal chant, uplifted suddenly, assailed
our ears. Coming from just outside the house, it startled
me.

"My old Ghafîr," said Sandeman. "He's at his prayers.
Whenever I wake up at night I hear that noise. It's damned
pathetic, the religion of these beggars. Fine, I call it!—He's
a rum old boy. God knows who pays him for his job.
He's never had a sou from me, I know. I've a jolly good
mind to give him something now."

He went to the window and called to the Ghafîr. The
man came running. "O Ghafîr! A sovereign for you!
Catch! Have you got it?"

"Praise be to God," replied a drowsy voice out of the
darkness. That old night watchman, who had kept the
rest house from its first foundation, was never seen again
in Kefr Ammeh.

The Ghafîr had all his life been saving money, little by
little, for the purpose of that pilgrimage to Mecca which,
being pious, he accounted life's true aim. I gathered this,
with other matters incidental to this story, afterwards from
an Egyptian friend in Kefr Ammeh, who had been my
host on more than one occasion of my visiting the place.
The sovereign he received from Sandeman that night made
up the sum he had put before him as the minimum required for his long journey. He had hoped to set forth in
another year or two. This godsend made it possible to
start at any time; and, as it wanted but a week of the
departure of the yearly pilgrimage, he resolved at once to
break the fetters of his worldly calling. By dawn he had
made made up a bundle of his few belongings, with which
upon his back and staff in hand, he set out for the railway
station at the peep of day. Wrapped in the praises of the
Lord, he stepped out gladly, never turning to look back at
the white house which he had guarded faithfully for fifteen
years. About a mile from his own place, passing the hamlet
known as Mît Gâmûs just as the sun was rising, he met
some young men going forth to work. One of them, who

was leading two white water buffaloes, hailed him by name, inquiring: "Whither away?"

He answered with a phrase which told them that he was a pilgrim. The young men asked him who would guard the rest house in his absence. He replied that Allah knew; the house was in His keeping; all was well. At that those young men exchanged lightning glances, and sped him on his way with hearty blessings.

Beside a sakieh they stood and watched him trudging on, a plume of dust uprising from his heels, then one of them remarked: "The praise to Allah. The gun which never misses is without a guardian. Meet in the palm grove at the fall of night. We must devise a stratagem."

Another cried: "The stratagem is found already. Lo, the watchmanship is vacant, and we alone have knowledge of the fact! Let one of us become the watchman till our end is gained."

"Dost thou consent to play the part, O Mustafa?"

"At thy pleasure," answered Mustafa, a swarthy youth, a kind of servant to the previous speaker, who was called the Sheykh Ridwân. "If thou desire it I will go tonight and be Ghafîr."

"Capital!" exclaimed Ridwân. "Thou wilt make friends with the two servants and learn from them the habits of the Englishman. We shall await thee here tomorrow at this hour, for thy report."

The Sheykh Ridwân, aged seventeen, was a romantic dreamer. He had battened upon tales of strange adventure till the sober facts of life appeared unreal to him. He saw that quiet countryside as wonderland, and planned, while he performed his daily tasks, such exploits as had earned renown for brave and wily ones of old. Those exploits, being always well rewarded in the chapbooks, he thought would lead perforce to high preferment and his recognition as the choicest spirit of the age. A mighty talker, of some eloquence upon his favourite subject, possessing, he alone of all his entourage, the power to read aloud from printed books; being, moreover, the son of a rich farmer, he had infected with his views a group of youths of his own age. They formed a band, united by most horrid vows. They pricked themselves with knives to get inured to pain; they prowled by night in order to get used to darkness. They thought of exploits which might make them famous, and if they heard of any treasure greatly guarded, would instantly devise some plan to get at it, with no idea of theft, but simply that mankind might

recognise their dauntless guile. On the few occasions of
their action hitherto they had succeeded; but when, as
happened naturally, they bragged of their success, the
men whom they had hoodwinked made complaint against
them to the father of the Sheykh Ridwân, whose anger
gave the youths a sense of failure through injustice.

"When Ali El Masri performed his clever rogueries at
the court of Er-Rashîd," said young Ridwân with bitterness, "those whom he tricked sought only to outwit him in
return and, when they failed, became his servants and
admirers. But these low dogs come fawning to my father.
They have neither heart nor liver. May they perish utterly!"

Therewith he swore to be revenged on them. Their names
were entered in the black book of the band, and never
mentioned without solemn execration. Any game at their
expense was counted fair. It was this admixture of re-
vengeful spite with their romance which made the band
the growing terror of the neighbourhood. The father of
Ridwân, although indulgent to his son, alluded sometimes
to the English as relentless rulers, without indulgence for
the sports of youth, who would not scruple to arrest the
band in its entirety and cast it into prison if they came to
know of it; and since the coming of the English ghoul to
Kefr Ammeh, the omdeh, through the fear of him, had
threatened action.

The band had seen the clown's performance in the
circus; they had seen the Englishman, the small white ball
and the small white dog at play upon the dust heaps many
times. Moreover, two of them had served the ghoul when he
went out to shoot, and so beheld the wondrous gun which
never missed. But while the other fellâhîn surveyed the
prodigy with awestruck eyes, as a mystery whose inner
meaning would never be revealed in this low world, Ridwân's small gang, intoxicated with romance, beheld him
as a potent lord and possible magician—in fact, the only
monster in the country. To overcome him by some stratagem would mean for them the moral lordship of the
district. Ridwân's most cherished daydream was to picture
the Englishman, outwitted by his skill, bestowing on him
rank and honours as did monarchs of old days; and his
disciples, taking fire from him as usual, saw in the English
ghoul their road to glory.

At first their mind had been to carry off the small
white dog, returning it after a while politely with a full
description of the stratagem they had employed to gain
it. But from the moment when they saw the gun which

never missed, cupidity usurped the place of sportiveness. With such a gun the band would be invincible. And now, in the departure of the old Ghafîr, they saw their opportunity to get possession of it. Mustafa, after his first night as watchman at the rest house, brought them hopeful news. He had been accepted as the new Ghafîr without a question. The Berberine cook, with whom alone he had held conversation, had asked him what had happened to the old Ghafîr, and, hearing he had gone upon the pilgrimage, had given praise to God. He had learnt from the said cook that the khawâgah was going to the capital to spend a night; Selîm the waiter would attend him thither, and the cook was thinking surreptitiously of going to Dumyâtt to see some friends. He had asked Mustafa to give food and water to the small white dog at sunset for fear lest it should die and he (the cook) be blamed; had asked him, too, to see that it was kept indoors lest it should stray, when equal blame would be his portion.

"Tomorrow, then, towards midnight!" cried Ridwân emotionally.

At the time appointed the band approached the rest house, armed with pistols, quarterstaves and rusty scimitars. First they crawled about the dust heaps on their bellies for an hour to make quite sure that no one of the village watchmen lurked in that direction. Then they stole up to the house.

Mustafa waited with the door key in his hand. He opened for them and they entered, shuddering, in supernatural awe of their own daring. They closed the house door, lit a candle they had brought with them, and set out to explore the house. The small white dog, aroused from sleep, flew at them, barking, till in their terror they struck hard and made it dumb. For long they could not find the gun, search as they would. At last a queer-shaped case, which they had passed repeatedly, was made to open. It contained the treasure. With that in hand they went away again, creeping till they were out of earshot of the house, when they careered with horrid yells across the plain, in terror of themselves, such awful malefactors!

The Berberine cook returned next morning from Dumyâtt to find the small white dog a lifeless corpse and the gun stolen. He praised the Lord, then gashed his forehead with a knife, likewise his arm, and bandaged up the wounds. He then ran weeping to the omdeh's house, where in the courtyard he fell down and rubbed his visage in the mire, exclaiming: "Woe! Oh, woe! The house is broken open. The soul of the khawâgah, the beautiful, the priceless little snow-white dog, is foully slain. I fought with twenty. I was wounded, overcome. I am but now awakened from the swoon. O Allah! What to do? O Lord, relieve me!"

At that cry, the omdeh, the watchmen, and all the elders came together. They hurried out across the dust heaps to the scene of the crime. The rest house soon became the centre of a wailing crowd. When the omdeh, in tears, appeared in the doorway holding reverently in his arms the body of the small white dog, there were cries of mourning as upon the death of true believers. "Woe! Woe! O cruel day!" the people moaned. "Behold us ruined, shamed and made a dunghill. The good khawâgah will no longer smile on us. His goodness will be changed to fury. This priceless little dog was his son, and innocent of all offences."

"Wallahi, I will have the lives of all concerned!" exclaimed the omdeh in a frenzy. "See that this corpse be buried with all honour, as one that was the soul of our good lord. I go to telegraph the dreadful tidings to the mudîrîyeh. What can I do? My face is blackened till the Day of Judgment. I feel that I shall not recover from this great calamity. Nothing worse than a murder has been committed in my jurisdiction hitherto, and now some devils have assailed our lords the English. I must hasten to the telegraph. O High Protector!" In tears he ran away across the dust heaps. In answer to the omdeh's telegram to the mudîr there came this message: "Inexpressibly horrified. Use all means to discover and arrest the miscreants. Am telegraphing to the noble victim of the wicked plot."

Immediately upon receipt of this command, the omdeh and the elders formed a court of law and summoned witnesses. The Berberine cook, under interrogation, mentioned the new night watchman and his likeness. The man described was recognised as Mustafa, a well-known member of the band of Sheykh Ridwân. Exalted by his wrath and fear above all ties of neighbourhood, the omdeh forthwith sent the village watchmen with orders to arrest not only the aforesaid Mustafa, but also Sheykh Ridwân and all his house. The gang which had intimidated a whole countryside was captured easily and brought to trial in an hour. The father of the Sheykh Ridwân strove hard to intercede for him, offering vast sums of money for his liberation, but the omdeh raised his arms to Heaven, crying: "Allah witness, I am helpless to befriend thee now. The crime is too excessive. All the land is moved with it. The Government will wipe out Kefr Ammeh and sow the ground thereof with salt as a memorial, if before sunset it is not avenged."

"But what proof have you that any of these lads are guilty?" roared the father of Ridwân.

"They shall confess their guilt before thee," said the omdeh grimly, and he ordered Mustafa to be brought forward.

Ridwân, that high-strung youth, was weeping bitterly, which made Mustafa, who loved him as his eyes, more resolute in keeping silence under question.

"What, O son of a dog?" thundered the omdeh. "Thou wilt not speak? Thou floutest me? Wait only! We will find a way to make thee speak. Here, watchmen, take those three dogs who are grinning there, and give them each ten stripes with the nailed whip."

"By Allah, we know nothing of the matter," howled the prisoners, all saving Mustafa, who in his obstinacy seemed of stone. On him the omdeh's wrath was concentrated. "Ha, I will make thee speak!" he cried once more.

"Put out his eyes!" bellowed the crowd. "Tear off his fingernails. Pull out his tongue to make him speak and save our lives!"

The omdeh, though he paid no heed to their advice, still thought it an occasion on which modern dilatory methods might be put aside. Mustafa was slightly tortured. His frame went rigid and his eyes turned over in his head, but not a word escaped him. Such fortitude destroyed the patience of the crowd. They spat upon him where he lay upon the ground.

"Where is the gun which never missed? Inform me!" shrieked the omdeh.

"Who slew with felon hand the small white dog? Inform me straightway!"

Mustafa compressed his lips and seemed to sneer.

"Then thou shalt forfeit thy right hand!" the omdeh cried. "My patience and my mercy are exhausted. The trial has already lasted for three hours. Here, make him kneel! Bring out the bucket of hot pitch. Now, O worst of malefactors, if thou confess not thou wilt lose thy hand of honour. Speak, I say!"

But Mustafa maintained a rigid silence.

The execution was just over when Sandeman thrust his way through the crowd, which had been too much absorbed in gazing at the horrid sight to notice anyone who came behind it.

The surprise at his sudden reappearance, the cries of

sorrow and condolence, the indescribable confusion which
arose when they discovered that the anger in his face was
for the justice done upon his foe prevented anyone from
thinking of the unfortunate Mustafa, who had swooned
away, till Sandeman himself commanded them to carry
the poor creature gently to the rest house, and to fetch a
doctor.

"He is a wretch unworthy of Your Honour's notice!"
wailed the crowd. "He murdered in cold blood Isnâb, our
chief delight!"

At ten o'clock that night, Sandeman came into my flat
at Cairo in a half-hysterical condition and told me the
amazing story: how his own omdeh had flogged three
men and cut off one man's hand, in presence of a crowd
and with the popular approval, all for pure love, as it
appeared, of him (George Sandeman) and horror at the
death of poor dear Snap! What in the world was he to do?

"Rummy beggars! Unaccountable beggars!" he kept
muttering. "I'm deadly sick about it, yet I want to laugh.
It hurts, I tell you. This business does for my career out
here. I lose the best part of my income and all hope of
Joanie. . . . If you'd seen what I saw! I can't make out
the beggars. God knows what kind of a beast they think
I am. When I was doing what I could for the poor devil,
a chap came up to me, as pleased as Punch because he'd
found a golf ball. Seemed to expect me to rejoice exceedingly! What does go on in their confounded heads?"

Late as it was, I called a cab and took him off to see
the chief of his department who, by good fortune, was at
home and able to receive us. I was the spokesman. Having
heard the story to an end, he ordered Sandeman a glass
of brandy, ere pronouncing: "I cannot see that you are in
any way to blame for this occurrence, Mr. Sandeman. The
only criticism of your conduct which I have to make is
that you ought to be at Kefr Ammeh at this minute and
not here. You ask me what you are to do? Use your own
judgment. You seem to have unbounded influence in Kefr
Ammeh. Strictly speaking, I suppose we ought to make
what is called an 'example' of your omdeh, but the case
is quite unusual, in no sense exemplary. . . . I should think
that you might let the matter rest, if rest it will. But I will
take advice upon the subject. Good night."

I had to support Sandeman to the cab in waiting. He
seemed dazed and did not speak till we had driven off.

"Well, thank the Lord!" he sighed at length. "I breathe
again. It's jolly decent of him not to go for me. . . . Poor

little Snap! I used to say I'd kill the man who teased him even, but when I saw that feller's hand chopped off. . . . Damned plucky feller! . . . He shall never want while I'm alive. . . . Don't tell Joanie anything about this business, mind. . . . I'll go down and frighten 'em a bit, and then proclaim a general amnesty. It was the thought of punishment for the affair that turned me sick. They're like dumb animals, at times; they aren't responsible. And, say what you like, old man, they are ingratiatin' beggars! What?"

HALIDE EDIB: A CHANGE OF FAITH

[from *Sıneklı Bakkal*, The Clown and His Daughter]

*Perhaps the only Turkish novelist well known in
English-speaking countries, Halide Edib began as a
prominent writer of that generation greatly influenced
by the nationalist ideology of Ziya Gökalp. Her pierc-
ing social satires made way for the more compassionate portrayals of her later works.*

*Her search for the truly humanitarian, perhaps the
mystical, brought her into abrupt conflict with the
strident secularism of Kemalist Turkey. The Clown
and His Daughter is one of her most finished works;
this portion of it treats one of the most sensitive
subjects in the Islamic world with the special insight reserved to women.*

The wheels of Fate were turning, as ruthlessly and as
blindly as ever. They had made a Moslem girl love a
Christian. They had crushed Rabia. Yet God in His mercy
had made the Christian's mother die, so that he might
disappear. Perhaps he would never return. The prospect
was painful. But it gave her a chance to overcome her
guilty passion in his absence. She was under trial. Fate
was testing the strength of her attachment to her faith.

It was natural for her to attribute the incalculable movements of life to the Unseen. The world she lived in was
that of the soul. All external signs of human achievement
and omnipotence were as shadows compared to the work-
ings of the unseen forces. That was the conviction of her
Eastern soul. The earliest stratum of human reason was
linked up with the Imam's grim and inhuman metaphysics.
An avenging God, a pitiless Fate, ruled human destiny.
Jealous of all human happiness, they snatched the cup of
joy from one's mouth before one could taste it. Yet in
Rabia's mind, stratum after stratum of rational thought,

which put a less gloomy complexion on the designs of the
Unseen, had been formed since her childhood. In these
regions of thought Vehbi Effendi ruled supreme. He had
interpreted human destiny in a gentler and kinder way.
However, no matter from what angle she faced the situation, it resolved itself into a single aspect. The death of
Peregrini's mother, which had called him away at the very
moment when she had realised her love for him, was a
warning. She must tear that sinful feeling out of her
heart.

For a week a mighty battle raged in her mind. Fortunately for her, every hour was full. Engagement followed
engagement. She was constantly trotting from one corner
of the city to another. She came home worn out, her
throat aching. Her silence in the evenings seemed only
natural. Yet both Pembeh and Rakim noticed a new, deep,
vertical line between her eyebrows. Her face was rigid, full
of the determination to solve some difficult problem.

Her nights had become intolerable. She took to reading
for hours before she went to bed. Pembeh grumbled, and
her body ached with fatigue. But sleep meant torturing
dreams. Was there anyone in the world who had such
endless dreams as Rabia? And now they were not comfortable dreams; they were mostly nightmarish. All the
formative forces of her life were up in arms. They appeared before her in the guise of terrible and distorted
human faces. Emineh's was the most unbearable. She always dreamed of her mother's mouth, that straight scar
across her face. It had been Emineh's most characteristic
feature. It was contorted with an ugly sneer, and an in-
credibly long tongue—the tongue of a reptile—protruded
from the ugly mouth and mocked Rabia. The Imam was
always present. He did nothing but chant awesome verses
out of the Koran, just as he used to in the old days,
terrifying Rabia with the horrors of Hell if she did not
purge her heart of this unholy passion. Sometimes she
dreamed of Vehbi Effendi. She appealed to him, begging
him to make Peregrini a Moslem, that she might have her
heart's desire. But he seemed sorrowful. She couldn't make
out whether he was on Emineh's side or on hers. The worst
of it was that after two long weeks her heart was as
rebellious, as painfully torn, as in the beginning. Nothing
would make it resign itself to losing Peregrini. She chuckled
to herself, saying: "No wonder the poets sing that hearts in
love are like minced and roasted liver sold in the bazaars!"

By the time she had touched the rock bottom of misery

she had also reached a decision. It was totally different from that to which all the forces of her bad dreams had been leading her. She didn't even know that she had found a solution to the dilemma. But in her heart she had come to the conclusion that life was infinitely more precious and important than any metaphysical consideration. She would wrest her happiness from the jaws of Fate. She would have Peregrini as her husband.

On a Thursday, before the end of that memorable month, Peregrini came to the shop. It was rather early in the morning.

Rakim's face lighted up. His presence, thought the dwarf, may pull Rabia out of her gloomy mood.

"When did you come back, Signor?"

"Last night."

"May Allah make you live long! I have heard of your loss," said the dwarf, repeating the traditional sentence of Moslem condolence.

Peregrini's response, or rather lack of response, puzzled him. The man hardly listened, neither did he speak of his journey or his mother's death. On such occasions the Italian might be expected to become expansive or to philosophise. He did neither. His face seemed almost haggard, but in his eyes burnt the fire of deliverance and the unmistakable look of one who has reached a momentous decision.

"Could I see Rabia Hanim at once?"

"Of course. You go upstairs and knock at the kitchen door. Auntie is busy washing; no need to announce you. It will do her good. She was in one of her unbearable tantrums. . . ."

Rakim heard the Italian go hurriedly up the stairs. He himself was soon busy serving a customer.

"Re, sol, la, si, la, sol," Rabia sang in the room. She was writing a simple air for her Palace pupils, sitting by the brazier, a sheet of music paper on her lifted knee. She wetted her pencil and drew her shawl round her shoulders.

"Re, sol, la, si, la, sol . . . oh come in, Uncle. . . ." She turned to scold Rakim for disturbing her, but she started to her feet, pulling her shawl over her head. Peregrini, standing at the door with a grave face, smiled at her childish gesture.

"But I've seen your hair so many times, you absurd little lady!"

"That was because I couldn't keep my veil on before the Prince."

Damn the Prince, he thought; but aloud he said, "I must talk to you, Rabia, on very serious business."

"Must you? Pray take a seat on the divan, there by the window."

It was when she herself had taken a seat at a considerable distance from him on the divan that she remembered his bereavement.

"May Allah make you live long!" She repeated the phrases as lugubriously as was proper, though her blood was racing with joy through her veins. This was the moment of the final solution of her life's problem.

"I am all alone in the world." He stopped for a long moment; perhaps he was paying his last filial homage to the memory of the dead.

"May Allah give you patience!" She again gave the conventional answer with the proper measure of gravity, but the golden eyes watched his face with a furtive glitter behind the long brown fringe of silky lashes.

"I've come to ask you to be my wife. I—I can't live without you."

She looked at him with eyes that had no trace of shame. Their honesty and sincerity confounded him. "I also cannot live without you, Signor. But how can we marry? We belong to two different Faiths."

"We could go away to a place where such things don't matter. You can stick to your faith. I have none."

She looked away from him. The colour was fading from her cheeks. She had the air of one who had thought out things carefully and had come to definite conclusions. Fate had struck her its last blow. She had been unconsciously expecting a different proposition. She knew that she could no more break the chains of custom than she could fly. Further, she could never leave her environment. She realised that it had even a stronger hold upon her than her faith. It was a complete knockout.

Meanwhile he was not altogether unaware of her possible reaction to such an offer as his. Probably a part of her bewitching personality was due to her being a well-rooted soul, one which could not be transplanted in alien soil. He himself was a wanderer. He must leap over the barriers and accept such a life as she lived if he wished to have her for his wife. No other way of having her was possible. How different from all his other infatuations, in which no element but that of desire had reigned supreme! He was as full of consideration for her as he had been for his mother. He realised the great earnestness of purpose,

the capacity for lasting attachment in the girl. Well,
against her simple background, values seemed more real
than in his own changeable world. Although they were
so totally different, yet there seemed an intangible resemblance between his mother and this girl. His eyes were
on her face. But her lashes were veiling her eyes. Very
slowly he saw two drops glistening on her lashes. They
fell on her cheeks, and she lifted her eyes to his. The
agony, the despair in their depths burnt him. "Baptism by
fire!" he murmured; then, in a determined voice, he addressed Rabia.

"I see that I must become a Moslem and marry you.
Will you be my wife then, Rabia?"

Her face had assumed a drawn look; it seemed as though
an invisible hand were pulling her features towards her
temples. In her this was a sign of supreme inner concentration.

"I will be your wife, always," she said with great
simplicity.

He was on his knees beside her, his hands clutching hers.

"Twice we are brought into the world," he said. "Once
by our mother, and once by the woman we love."

He rose immediately, and kissed her hand, carrying it to
his forehead in expression of his veneration for her. And
she felt that it was not at random that the people of her
land called the man a girl married "her Fate." The words
were the truest expression of her feelings for this man. He
was "her Fate."

"I will go and see Vehbi Effendi now, about the formalities of conversion. How soon will you marry me,
Rabia?"

"The sooner the better."

That evening, after the usual ritual of rising and kneeling
and bowing her forehead to the floor, Rabia lifted her
hands and talked with her God.

"Lord," she said: "He has said to me, 'I will take you,'
and I have said to him, 'I take you,' and that in our faith
constitutes marriage. He is going to accept the true Faith,
and be one of us. Bless us, O Lord!"

On Friday mornings the shop was fuller than on week-
days, for Rakim closed it at noon. That he did not attend
the Friday prayers was a known and generally accepted
fact. But he could not lack in respect for such a communal
affair as the Friday prayers; so he had to pull down the

shutters during the time of the service. He served the customers and cracked more jokes with them than ever. This Friday he was in a jolly mood. Rabia had been a little talkative the night before. She had even helped him to cut the coloured paper festoons hung across the ceiling of the shop. Rakim changed them every month. There were geese, ducks, and other creatures, and quaint boats, alternating with rows of green cypresses. At intervals some shadow-play puppets in coloured cardboard dangled from the line.

What a humorous twist Rabia's clever fingers had given to the noses of those cardboard rogues! He chuckled. He had made such a success of that shop! And Rabia had become so much more popular than she had ever been! Oh, they were earning a lot of money. The Sinekli-Bakkal was Rakim's world, and Rakim's grocery was the hub of it.

"Uncle Rakim, an oke of soap."

It was Muharrem, the young terror of the street, whom everyone called "the Sinekli-Bakkal Bastard." Rakim didn't like the boy. The fellow mimicked him in public; further, his mother, a washerwoman and a foul-mouthed virago, frightened him not a little.

"What a lot of soap you buy, Muharrem!"

"For mother's washing. The time is coming when she won't be washing the dirt of the rich," the boy said significantly.

"Have you by any chance inherited a fortune from your unknown father?"

"If I ever catch that swine of a father, I will defile his carcass!"

"Shuuuuuut, you filthy mouth! Tell me, on what are you going to feed yourself when your mother washes no more for the rich?"

"I am apprenticed to Fehmi Effendi, the cobbler."

"That is why you have a clean face. Let us celebrate it with a sugar cock. What colour shall it be?"

"A green one, Uncle," said the boy, licking his lips.

Though Rakim presented his well-behaved juvenile customers with sugar cocks on sticks, this was the first time Muharrem had been given one. The boy lingered, feeling that he was in favour, and becoming confidential.

"I wish you would tell Rabia Abla about my job. I will mend her shoes for nothing when I have a shop of my own. You see, I once filched a piece of sugar years and years ago, and there was a row in front of the shop. I am afraid she thinks of me as——"

Muharrem had no time to finish the sentence, for Vehbi Effendi's tall figure stooped and entered the shop.

"I want to see Rabia Hanim."

"Please go up to her room, sir. I will call her. She is at Granny Zehra's across the street."

As Rabia hurried across the street and the dwarf struggled to catch up with her, she leaned over him twice and asked the same question, "Does he look annoyed?" But she hardly listened to the answer he gave her: "How should I know? he never shows his feelings on his face." Surely there was something unusual on foot! Here was Vehbi Effendi coming on a Friday, when he had to direct such a solemn ceremony a few hours later! Rakim was eaten up with anxiety. He was very curious, too. He must go up and listen at the door. Oh, when would the customers stop coming!

Rabia found Vehbi Effendi sitting on the divan with his usual detached air. She thought his face rather pale, but his eyes had their habitual serenity and friendliness.

"Good morning, Effendim."

"Good morning, my child."

She squatted by the brazier, stirring the fire with the tongs. Framed in the coloured kerchief wound about her head, her face retained its composure. But he sensed her inner agitation from the almost imperceptible tremor of her fingers, and the way in which she kept her eyes fixed on the fire, as though she was almost afraid to meet his gaze.

"Shall I make you a cup of coffee, Effendim?"

"I don't take coffee today."

So he was fasting. The moment of silence which followed seemed interminable. "I will marry Peregrini even if Vehbi Effendi does not approve," she was saying to herself, but in some vague manner she knew that she would be miserable without his full consent. Without realising the strength of his hold on her mind, she felt that she would be inconsolable if he withdrew that unobtrusive but all-pervading protectiveness.

"Peregrini came to see me last night. He wants to become a Moslem and marry you."

Her eyes flew to his, their depths filled with a dumb prayer. He smiled.

"Are you sure your attachment is not a passing fancy, Rabia?"

She shook her head. The mixture of fervent conviction and humour in her gesture amused Vehbi Effendi.

"I have always wanted to marry that infidel since I was

that high. I would have remained single if he had not asked
me to be his wife."

How mysterious are the designs of the supreme Artist!
thought Vehbi Effendi. How queer and incongruous the
human material He mixes in His pictures! A little Koran-
chanter in the back street of a Moslem city, and an ex-
monk and musician, a Christian aristocrat! "No one may
dare to question Thy Wisdom, O Lord!" he said to himself.
But he had meant to speak of the incompatibility of their
characters, rooted in the difference of their worlds, their
cultures and the rest. Such things might have a greater
hold on Peregrini's mind than Rabia could imagine. She
might discover it when it was too late. The Past might stand
between them, might wreck their life. . . .

"You two belong to such different worlds, my child. He
belongs to a different class and circle; Sinekli-Bakkal may
lose its romance for him."

She smiled her crooked smile again. With a fatalistic
gesture she shrugged her shoulders, and her forefinger
passed over her forehead.

"I shall have to read whatever is written there."

"May it be a happy writing, Rabia."

"In the absence of your father," the Dervish continued,
"I will make all the arrangements. You understand that you
cannot see your future husband before you are made man
and wife. It will take a week to go through the formalities
of conversion in an official sense. He desires to be called
Osman. Do you approve?"

She nodded her head. There was profound relief in her
face. Vehbi Effendi was going to remain the friend and the
spiritual guide he had always been.

"How soon do you wish to be married, Rabia?"

"The sooner the better, Effendim."

Oh, the shameless hussy! She was calling herself every
hard name now. But nothing mattered. She heard him, as
in a dream, say: "I will write to Tewfik tonight. A brother
Dervish is going to Damascus. You, too, can write a long
letter to your father."

"Uncle, Uncle," she called out as she unfastened the
kerchief round her head.

"What is it you want, Rabia?"

"Were you at the door? You frightened me! Come in and
sit by me. I have a tale to tell."

"Let it be a short one and a gay one."

"Surely. . . . I have taken your advice, I am going to marry."

"What, what? Whom are you going to marry?"

"A man called Osman," she laughed.

"Is he one of the gentleman attendants of the Prince? You have been mighty queer since you started going to the Palace."

"This man is going to become a Moslem, to give up his own religion in order to marry me."

Her face was radiant. The fact that Peregrini had really no convictions of a religious nature to change didn't matter at all.

"So it is Peregrini after all! The fellow takes a religion as a child takes a ticket to enter a show," he growled.

"You are being nasty, spiteful!"

He grinned. He was not. He liked Peregrini well enough. The man understood him most wonderfully.

"I am glad, Rabia. Between ourselves, you were getting too old for anyone to ask you in marriage. What's more, I was afraid you would marry Vehbi Effendi. You were so upset when he called. He is not so cheery as the other one."

"For shame! Vehbi Effendi is a saint. I am not fit to wipe the very dirt under his shoes. You absurd Uncle! If I married everyone I loved I should marry you too."

"So you would, you faceless girl!" He spat at his collar, invoking the unseen powers to guard him from such a fate. "That poor innocent infidel knows not what is coming to him. I believe you would be marrying us all if custom allowed so many husbands. Why, you are like a whirlpool, you are like a haunted well; anyone who falls in can never be fished out!"

"Talking like a story book, are you?" The tears began to well out of her happy eyes, and she wiped them on her sleeve as she sobbed: "Oh, why isn't Tewfik here with us?"

"There, there, wipe your eyes on my hanky, you messy girl. He will celebrate the wedding in Damascus."

When Pembeh came in for lunch she found the dwarf in a boisterous and impish mood. He was turning somersaults sideways in Rabia's room—monkeyish somersaults—by way of rejoicing over Rabia's engagement, and Rabia sat on the divan laughing and beating time on her knees.

Sabiha Hanim gave the news to Selim Pasha. He shook his head.

"She is worth a change of faith. I hope he will stick to his new religion."

"He may stick to Rabia at all events," she laughed.

"Has she consulted you by any chance?"

She laughed again. This was by far the most exciting event of the year.

"Years ago she asked me what would happen if a Moslem girl married a Christian. She had got so far, the minx. Evidently she understood that the only way to marry a Christian was to make him turn Moslem."

"Curious. She didn't seem to care for such a comely lad as Bilal, and now marries that little man. Women are hard to understand. . . ."

Just then Rabia came in, followed by Bilal. They had evidently met outside and walked on together. She was very gracious to him. She was in such a turmoil of emotion that she could have embraced the very Devil in those days. The Pasha now saw her for the first time since the painful episode in his office during Tewfik's imprisonment. She came up to him smiling, behaving as though there had never been any such episode. No half measures for this wonderful creature!

"My congratulations, Rabia. I hear that you are bringing a new soul into the Moslem congregation of Sinekli-Bakkal!" he said in his old quizzical tone.

"Who could think that the cruel, horrible man who ordered us out of his office as though we were dogs could be this same old darling? I suppose he leaves his heart outside the door of his office," Rabia thought. But there was not the slightest trace of resentment in her heart.

"Peregrini has turned Moslem for the sake of Rabia," Sabiha Hanim was explaining to Bilal, who looked perplexed, as he had not yet heard the news. "Perhaps they will marry even before you do, my son!"

"Oh, that man!" came the scornful, almost involuntary comment from Bilal.

"What do you mean by 'oh, that man'?" Rabia snapped. "He is the greatest musician alive!"

"Quite so," Bilal hastened to assure her. "My congratulations. I suppose I better leave you; you may want to talk things over."

"You needn't. I have only come to read my father's letter to Hanim Effendi. I have to hurry back as fast as I can after that."

Bilal brought a chair for her, and she at once took the letter from her bosom and began to read it. She was obviously choosing the passages which would interest Sabiha Hanim, for she stopped now and then, scanning the sheets in her hand, and putting some of them back into her bosom without reading them.

Tewfik had given her a vivid description of Hilmi's life. It sounded as though Hilmi had experienced a complete revision of values since he had left Istanbul. Who could think of him as a man toiling to make both ends meet, actually working in the garden to grow vegetables for that purpose, and above all, who could imagine his pretty and elegant wife slaving in the house? "He has grown a beard, and wears the native costume. The governor allows him to move about and receive friends. The exiles here have the greatest respect for him. He is a great comfort and an example of courage to us all. There is nothing in the world I wouldn't do for him."

Rabia folded the sheets. Selim Pasha's cool, clear grey eyes were slightly dimmed. There was a vagueness and a warmth in their expression which seemed alien to the man. Sabiha Hanim gazed at the letter in Rabia's hands rather hungrily.

"Do read us some more, something about Tewfik himself," she begged.

Rabia began to read again. Tewfik was telling stories in the bazaars to earn a living until he received the leather set of shadow-play figures from Istanbul. Then he would hire a shop and start giving his proper show. As it was he had become quite a popular figure. His Arabic was not fluent enough, but he could always pretend to talk a language with its proper intonation, accent, and inner rhythm. That always kept his listeners guessing for a time. But his mimicry of animals and his dialogues in which he made them talk like human beings were a great success. So far his specialty had been the street dogs in Istanbul. Now he had taken up the camels. He had invented a scene in which a group of caravan camels discussed the numbers of strange pilgrims whom they carried to Mecca on pilgrimage. "I am happy enough living with Hilmi Bey. The evenings give me the illusion of being still in my native city. But during the day there are moments when I cry like a child. I am generally surrounded by a number of exiles, of course by the derelict and destitute ones. They loaf on the benches or beg in the street. They have lost all account of the years. Most of them do not know why they have been exiled. Their homesickness, their dire poverty, are heart-breaking. I try to cheer them up, and feed them with tripe soup on Fridays when I earn a few extra coppers. . . ."

Rabia stopped and hastily folded the letter. The rest of it must be kept from Selim Pasha. She looked at him furtively. His colour had heightened. He was wondering about the numbers of the men whom he had dispersed to the four corners of the Empire during the last twenty years. Thousands probably. And most of them to much more uninhabitable places than Damascus. He had never thought of them as individuals. Rabia's tact in skipping over the rest of the sufferings of those poor devils whetted his imagination. Well, he had been nothing but the handle of a huge soulless machine. He had to turn and turn. . . . He had had no qualms of conscience over the rights or wrongs of his official actions. But now, thinking as an individual, he was finding it all a little painful.

"Listen, Rabia, in August it is the thirty-second anniversary of the Sultan's accession to the throne. There will be an amnesty of a sort. I'll try to get as many of the Damascus exiles as I can on the list."

He followed Rabia into the corridor.

"Sorry I couldn't get your father back before your marriage, my child. When is it really going to be?"

"In April, Pasha. Thank you all the same."

Rabia's coming marriage had become the event of the year in the Sinekli-Bakkal. The place hummed and buzzed with gossip. The cobbler's wife, a woman who rarely indulged in idle talk, had become quite talkative, discussing Rabia's marriage while her man drank the customary hollyhock tisane before going to bed. The women at the fountain and the men in the coffee house fell on the news and enlarged upon it. But it was a bit of a shock to the youthful element round Mr. Big Brother. They had the feeling of having missed something. Who could think of Rabia as an ordinary girl, falling in love and marrying! And marrying such a middle-aged man, in such romantic circumstances! When Mr. Big Brother spat backwards, wiped his moustache on his sleeve, and eyed them, saying: "We will call her husband Uncle Osman," his word became law. They would fetch and carry for the husband as they had done for Rabia Abla. They discussed at some length the wedding present which they would offer. It was to be a toy pump, the model of the one which the local squadron owned. They would have their local yell engraved on a metal placard to be fastened on the pump: "The raiser of dust, the burner of hearts!"

The preparations for the wedding were in the hands of the Princess Nejat. As Sabiha Hanim believed that she had a prior right to meddle in Rabia's life, the younger woman came often to the Konak to discuss matters with her old mistress. The house, including the shop, was being white-washed and repaired. Because of Osman's mode of life the Princess wanted to have the rooms furnished in European style. Sabiha Hanim was all for preserving the native aspect of the place. Rabia backed the older woman, so a compromise was arrived at. In Rabia's room over the kitchen Osman's piano was to be placed. He played at all sorts of hours. It wouldn't be suitable to have music at any hour in a room over the street. Rabia accepted a table and armchairs, but she grumbled at a bedstead. It would make her dizzy to sleep at such a height.

"He is giving up habits of forty years' standing, Rabia. Aren't you ashamed to be so selfish?" scolded the Princess. But Rabia remained adamant in the matter of pictures. She wouldn't have images in a room where she prayed. Let Osman hang as many pictures as he wished on the walls of the room over the shop. The attic was turned into a room for the dwarf, and the room which he had oc-cupied previously would be Pembeh's. The dining room would still be the kitchen. It was spacious and pleasant. A table and chairs—instead of stools and a tray on a low stand—were accepted by popular vote.

The next difficult problem was Rabia's bridal dress. The Princess was for white. She wanted to make a modern bride of Rabia. Sabiha Hanim insisted on purple velvet with silver lotuses embroidered all over it. "We could hire it," Rabia proposed rather timidly. But it was no con-cern of hers. Sabiha Hanim, Selim Pasha, and the Princess were paying all expenses. Unable to restrict their lavishness, Rabia left them to their own devices. She would have no feasting, no wedding ceremony in her house, beyond the religious ritual which would make her a wife in the eyes of the world.

The preparations lasted two months, and during that time Rabia was as busy as ever. Her calmness and matter-of-fact bearing surprised Pembeh. But that was only during the day. At night she lay awake, thinking of the life she would live with Osman. And he, on his side, continued his daily round of lessons, but at night he paced up and down in his lodgings, dreaming of Rabia, devising extraordinary schemes of life in the Sinekli-Bakkal.

"Strange that I should accept a new creed? But am I

accepting it really? Islam to me is not a religion, it is a way of living, a mere label and a code of human relationship. I can't enter the Sinekli-Bakkal as an inhabitant without that label pinned on my coat. I shall still have my back garden, the preserve of my private life and thoughts. I shall pass under the purple wistaria every day, joking with the women at the fountain. We will let Rakim carry on with the shop. Damn it, why can't I see my future wife and talk things over with her before the marriage ceremony? Well, it is going to be a happy life, good days following good nights, when we will sleep together and wake up together to begin it all over again. She may bear me sons, sons to play with, to teach, to scold. In the month of Ramazan we may give shadow plays for the street children when our bambini are big enough.[1] One of the boys must be like his grandfather—a great clown! Oh, it is going to be as fascinating as a circus!"

---

[1] One of these shadow plays was included in *Anthology of Islamic Literature*, pp. 371–377.

TAHA HUSSEIN: STUDENT DAYS

[from *Al-Ayyām*, Days]

*Taha Hussein has been considered the foremost
modern Arab man of letters. Certainly he is one of
the comparatively few of them to achieve a wide international reputation. He became a professor, Minister
of Education, and—what is more significant—acknowledged arbiter of literary style. That eminence
was not quickly or easily won. His early thesis on
Al-Maarri, his theories about pre-Islamic Arabic
poetry, and his outspoken criticism of the Egyptian
educational system all aroused storms of outraged
protest. Nor did his passage from enfant terrible to
respected man of letters occur at the expense of his
ideals or his art. He remained as incisive a critic and
independent a thinker as he became soon after he
left his small village as a poor blind boy to come
to study at Al-Azhar in Cairo.*

*There are scores of other works to choose from,
but his autobiography of childhood and youth is still
one of his most compelling books, and, according to
one authority, "has a good claim to be regarded as
the finest work of art yet produced in modern Egyptian literature." It is, of course, critical of Al-Azhar
and of many aspects of modern Egyptian life. But
more than that, it is a sensitive personal document, a
deep introspection of a type hitherto rare in Islamic
letters.*[1]

The boy sat down on this carpet in the corner of the
room, resting his hand or arm on the window at his left.
He had no time now to dream, but only to pass over in
his mind the things that were uppermost in it: incidents on
the road or in the court of the Azhar, points from lectures

[1]See Pierre Cachia, *Tāhā Husayn* (London, 1956), one of the very
finest studies of a modern Islamic writer.

on tradition or on law. But these reminiscences were short-lived; for when his brother deposited him in his corner it was not with the intention of leaving him to dream or to go over his lessons, but simply of giving himself time to get the food ready for lunch.

This meal varied from day to day, not so much in its menu, which consisted always of beans cooked in butter or oil, as by the atmosphere in which it was eaten. For one day it was silent and another day clamorously noisy. When the boy was alone with his brother they lunched in oppressive gloom, almost without exchanging a word; they spoke in short sentences and the boy replied to his brother in monosyllables. But what a hullabaloo when the young sheikh's friends were invited! There were sometimes three and sometimes four, even occasionally five; but the fifth was important for a different reason, and it is better not to mention him now.

These young students came to spend a pleasant hour together; they completely neglected the boy, and addressed never a word to him, so that he had no need to make any reply.

He preferred it so, for he loved listening. And what a host of things there were to listen to and wonder at! Nothing could be more varied than the conversations which took place over that low circular table. The guests sat all round it on the floor; in the centre of it was placed a huge dish full of beans cooked in butter or oil, and beside it a great bowl full of mixed pickles soaked in water. The young men took a drink from this bowl before beginning to eat; one of them drank first and then passed the bowl on to his neighbour, but it was never offered to the boy. When they had each taken their share of this tart apéritif, they started eating. The table was piled high with loaves, some of which were bought and paid for, others drawn as an allowance from the Azhar. The meal was nothing less than a competition to see which of them could eat the most, who could consume the largest quantity of loaves, gulp down the greatest number of mouthfuls, swallow the most considerable amount of beans in sauce, or devour the largest share of the turnips, peppers and cucumbers which were intended to help all this down. The din of eager laughing voices flooded through the room, burst out through the window on the left and dropped echoing into the street below; it overflowed through the door on the right and cascaded into the well of the building, where it interrupted the bickerings or whispered undertones of the workers' wives on the first floor. The women stopped to listen to the hubbub of talk and laughter wafted to them by the wind, as if they found a pleasure in it paralleled only by the delight which the young men took in swallowing their food.

The boy sat silently amongst them with his back bent like a bow. His hand travelled in a hesitant, apologetic way between the loaf laid on the table in front of him and the bowl which stood some distance away in the middle of the table. It kept colliding with a crisscross of other hands, which moved so rapidly up and down that in a short time they had completely scoured the bowl. This aroused in the boy an astonishment mingled with disgust. He could not admit the compatibility of this passion for beans and pickles with the noble thirst for knowledge, the vivacity and penetration of mind which he recognised in these young men.

They did not let their lunch occupy any great length of time. Not a quarter of an hour passed before the bowl was empty and the table clean, apart from an odd crumb or two and half of the loaf which had been put in front of the boy. He had been unable, or unwilling, to eat more than half of it. In another moment the table had been lifted up by one of them, taken outside the room and cleared of the remains, to be brought back to its place clean and smooth except for the spots of butter and sauce which had been dropped on it. Another went to fetch some wood-charcoal and prepare the samovar—that species of tea-kettle which the Persians and Russians use. He filled it up with water, then after lighting the fire and arranging the coals round it he put it back in the place where the bowl had been, with the tea glasses on the edge of the table in front. Then he sat down again and waited for the water to boil. Whereupon the young men resumed their conversation, but this time in a quiet, languorous tone. For their energies were occupied at the moment in digesting the mixture of hot and cold, solid and liquid, which they had just put inside them. Then suddenly the voices dropped again and were quiet. The room was possessed by a solemn stillness, broken only by a thin, feeble vibration, inter-mittent at first, but soon becoming continuous.

The young men were enthralled. They broke the silence all together with a single word pronounced quietly, but in a firm, sustained tone: "Allaah!" Their voices lingered over the word as if they had been stirred to ecstasy by soft music heard a long way off. There was nothing strange in this;

for what they were listening to was the wheeze of the water beginning to shift uneasily above the place where, without either noise or smoke, the charcoal was burning away. The student responsible for the tea watched intently over the samovar, concentrating eye and ear and mind upon it, until when the wheezing of the water changed to a bubbling he took a china teapot and, putting it close to the samovar, turned the tap carefully so that a little of the boiling water ran out into the teapot. Then he closed the tap again and cut off the flow of water. After this he replaced the lid of the teapot and shook it gently to and fro so that the little hot water that was in it could warm every part of the pot. As soon as it was warm he got up and poured this water away. For the tea must never come into contact either with cold glass or cold metal, which spoil its taste. After waiting for a few seconds he poured the water gently into the pot, without filling it to the brim. Then he picked up the tin of Indian tea, took a pinch of it and dropped it into the pot, which he then filled up to the brim before picking it up very carefully and putting it on the embers for a few seconds. Finally he raised it in triumph and invited his friends to hold out their glasses.

Throughout this process the others waited in silence, watching jealously every movement their friend made, in case he should infringe any of the regulations. When the glasses were full, the teaspoons began to circle in them with a gay tinkle of metal against glass that fell like music upon the ear. Then the company raised their glasses to their mouths and began to suck the tea in with their lips in long sips, making an unpleasant sound which drowned the noise of the spoons playing in the glasses. They continued drinking with scarcely a word, except for this invariable remark, which had to be made by one of them and assented to by the rest: "So much to quench the fire in the beans!" When they had finished the first round the glasses were filled a second time, after fresh water had been poured into the pot to replace what had been drawn off. But this time the company was taking more interest in the tea than in the unhappy water which, as it absorbed the heat of the fire, first moaned, then sang plaintively, then burst into weeping as it boiled. But the young men paid no attention to it, unmoved either by its music or its tears. They were intent on the tea, and on this second round especially. The first round was intended to quench "the fire in the beans." But as for the second, that was destined simply for their own delight and the satisfaction of their bodies as a whole. It gave refreshment not only to their mouths and throats but to their heads too; at all events when they had finished this round they recovered their wits and became intelligent again. Their tongues were loosened, their lips began to smile, their voices were once more raised in conversation. But now it was not food and drink they were discussing. They were no longer preoccupied with physical needs and could turn their attention to things of the mind. They remembered what one sheikh had said in the first lecture, or another in the second, and found something to laugh at in each. They recalled an objection one of them had made to the sheikh, and discussed it amongst themselves. One would consider it so strong as to be conclusive, while another thought it unconvincing and even nonsensical. One of them would take the place of the sheikh in question, and another that of the student who had made the objection, while a third set up as judge of the debate. The judge would interfere from time to time to bring one of the speakers back to the point or to support one of them with a forgotten argument or a proof left out. The student responsible for the tea was not debarred from the discussion, but on no account must he let his mind wander too far. He had added more tea and water to what was left in the pot, and the glasses had been drained and refilled. The tea ran at least to a third round; there were normally three glasses, but while the number might not be decreased, there was no objection to raising it.

The boy was still crouching in his corner, back bent and eyes lowered. His tea was passed to him in silence, and in silence he drank it. He paid attention to what went on and listened to what was said around him, understanding some of it, though missing more. But everything he heard, whether understood or not, enthralled him; and he asked himself yearningly how soon he would be able to talk and argue as these young men did.

Nearly an hour had gone by. Everyone had drunk his tea, but the table remained as it was, with the samovar in the middle and the glasses dotted round the edges. Noon was approaching, and the company would have to break up so that each of them might quickly look over the midday lesson before going in to hear it. They had prepared it together the night before, but there was no harm in a rapid revision to reconsider any word which was at all obscure or ambiguous. No doubt the text was clear and the com-

mentary lucid. But El-Bannân[2] complicates the simple and
ties knots where all seems plain. El-Sayyid Jurjâny's[3]
penetrating mind draws dark secrets out of clarity itself;
while ʿAbdul-Hakîm[4] is often clear enough, but even he
creates unnecessary difficulties. As for the commentator,
he's an imbecile who has no idea what he means. Now
there are only a few minutes left before noon, so we must
hurry to the Azhar, where the muezzins will be giving the
call to prayer. The service will have begun while we are
still on the way there. When we reach the Azhar it will
already be over, and the students will have started forming
circles round their sheikhs. No matter. We have missed
the common prayer, so we will say it together after the
lecture and still be praying in company. It is better not to
say prayers before the lesson, when one's mind is distracted
by the difficulties and problems in it requiring to be solved.
When the lesson is over, when we have listened to it and
discussed it, and delivered ourselves of its intricacies and
puzzles, we shall be able to devote our whole hearts and
minds to prayer.

The boy's brother was calling him, in a phrase which,
throughout those years, he never ceased to use: "Now, sir,
up with you!" So up the boy got, still rather dazed, and
stumbled along at his brother's side till they reached the
Azhar. His guide put him in his place for the grammar class
and went off to Sheikh Sâlihy's lecture in the Chapel of
the Blind.

The boy listened to the grammar lesson and understood
it without effort. He found the sheikh's explanations and
repetitions tedious in the extreme. When the lesson was over
and the students had dispersed the boy remained in his
place. Sooner or later his brother would come to drag him
away all urgently without a word, out of the Azhar and
along the road they had taken at dawn and in the middle
of the morning, then deposit him in his place in the corner
of the room, where the old carpet was stretched out on a
rotten worn-out mat. From that moment the boy set himself
to face the hours of agony.

What tortured the boy was solitude: blank, unending
solitude. He stayed still in his corner from before the mid-

[2] A modern writer on rhetoric.
[3] A fourteenth-century Arabic philosopher of Persia. To be distinguished from his more famous namesake, the rhetorician ʿAbdul-
Qâhir Jurjâny.
[4] Author of treatises on theology who lived at the court of the Mon-
gol rulers of India in the first half of the seventeenth century.

dle of the afternoon, at which time his brother left him
and went off to one of his friend's rooms elsewhere in the
building. The meeting place was never fixed; it might be one
room in the morning, another in the afternoon and a third
in the evening.

After the midday lecture, then, his brother went off and
left him alone for a period which varied from day to day.
The group spent the time in a leisurely fashion, joking and
telling stories about their teachers or other students. Their
voices rose, and their laughter echoed through the building
until it reached the boy frozen in his corner; a smile might
flitter across his lips, but in his heart there was only pain,
because he could not hear what they were saying. In the
morning he had at least been able to listen to their
anecdotes and sallies of wit, and to add his ghost of a
smile to their boisterous outbursts of laughter.

The boy knew very well what followed. Soon they would
have had enough of this relaxation and be tired of telling
stories at the expense of their teachers and fellow students;
then they would gather round afternoon tea in quiet,
orderly conversation, before going over any points that had
cropped up in the midday lecture; then they would prepare for the evening lecture, which was to be given by the
Imam, Sheikh Muhammad ʿAbdu, sometimes on the
Dalâ'il el-Iʿgâz,[5] and on other days on the Koran. During
their preparation for this lecture they would talk about the
Iman himself, discussing his extraordinary qualities, recalling his judgments on the sheikhs, or theirs on him, and
repeating the crushing replies with which he used to silence
questioners or objectors and make them a laughingstock to
their fellows. The boy yearned with all his heart to be with
them and to listen to what they said. It may be, too, that
deep inside himself he felt a longing for one of the cups
of tea that were being passed round there; he was not
different from them in desiring, at the proper times, morning and evening, his share of tea. But all was denied him.
The others went on joking and arguing and studying and
drinking tea only a few paces away. But he could take no
part in this, nor could he ask his brother for permission to
join the company and share these pleasures of body and
of mind.

He could not bring himself to make such a request;
for the last thing he could bear to do was to ask anyone

---

[5] Lit. Proofs of the Miracle, i.e., book of the proofs that the Koran
is a miracle, by ʿAbdul-Qâhir Jurjâny, prince of Arabic rhetoricians
(eleventh century).

for anything. If he had spoken to his brother about it, no matter whether the reply had been harsh or gentle, it would have tortured him just the same. So the best thing was to control himself, to say nothing of his passion for learning, his need for conversation or his craving for tea. He must withdraw altogether and go on crouching there silently in his corner, absorbed in his own thoughts. But how could he do this when his brother had left the door wide open, so that he heard first of all the sound of their voices and laughter, then later on a minute or two of silence, which told him that the master of ceremonies was breaking the charcoal to light the fire for tea. All these sounds stirred in him desire and dread, hope and despair—enough to unnerve him and reduce him to utter misery. It was all the worse in that he could not even budge from his place, or take the few short steps which would bring him to the door of the room, so as to be nearer to the voices and have more chance of catching a few words here and there. This would have been a great consolation to him. But alas, he could not move from his place; not because he did not know the way to the door—he had learnt that long ago, and a few short, careful paces would have brought him there—but because he was ashamed to be surprised by some passer-by as he stole along with cautious, furtive steps. He was especially anxious not to be caught by his brother, who used to visit the room now and again to fetch a book, perhaps, or some food or other to eat with tea at odd times of the day. Anything in the world was better than to be met by his brother as he fumbled nervously along, and to be asked: "What do you want? Where are you going?" So he saw that by far the best thing was to stay where he was, and to stamp down these yearnings that welled up inside him, together with others no less bitter and insistent for that house far away in the country village which was his home.

There, when he returned from school, worn out with play, he would make a meal off a crust of dry bread while he joked with his sisters or described to his mother some amusing incident that had occurred that day at school. When he was tired of this he could go out of the house, bolting the door behind him, and walk on till he reached the wall of the house opposite; he turned southwards alongside this until he reached a spot where he bore right, and arrived after a time at a shop belonging to Sheikh Muhammad ʿAbdul-Wâhid and his younger brother El-Hagg Mahmûd. Here he sat talking and telling stories and listening to the sheikh's customers, both male and female, whose simple country conversation delighted him, not only by its variety and strangeness, but by its very simplicity.

Sometimes there were not many customers. Then one of the owners of the shop, having nothing to do, would start a discussion with the boy, or read to him from a book. Sometimes, instead of visiting the shop, the boy would go outside the house and sit cross-kneed on the bench against the wall, listening in silence to the conversations his father used to hold there with his friends from the time of after-noon prayer until the muezzin called them away to even-song and to their suppers.

Sometimes, instead of going out, the boy would stay indoors with a school friend who had come to see him, bringing a book of exhortation or some tale of the con-quests of Islam. Then his friend would read to him until sunset called him home to supper. So the boy never felt lonely, never knew the torture of inactivity, hunger or ex-clusion, never yearned in vain for a cup of tea.

All these memories kept crowding in on the boy's brain as he lay there in utter immobility. His dreams were cut short for a moment by the call of the muezzin to afternoon prayer from the Mosque of Baibars.[6] The man's voice was utterly hateful to the boy; it contrasted so harshly with the voice of the muezzin in his village at home, which was more melodious than any he had ever heard. How many times had this man amused and entertained the boy, and in what a variety of ways! How often had he taken him up the minaret and let him give the call to prayer in his place, or accompany him in the invocation which followed it! But here in this room the boy loathed hearing the call to prayer, for he could not join in it and did not even know where it came from. He had never once been in the Mosque of Baibars and did not know the way to the minaret. He had never set foot on its steps, and had no idea whether the staircase was straight and broad or as narrow and twisty as the steps in the minaret at home.

Of all this he knew nothing, and there was no way of learning it, only this waiting, this eternal immobility. Ah, what agonies one can be condemned to by a passion for learning!

[6]Baibars II El-Gâshenkir (1247–1325) was a Mameluke slave who won his freedom and was for two years Sultan of Egypt. His *khanqa*, or convent mosque, in Sharia El-Gamaliya is one of the finest in Cairo.

This interminable blankness was nothing if not exhausting. Drowsiness would come upon him as he crouched on his mat, and often he would be forced to lie down and surrender himself to sleep. His mother used to tell him that to sleep in the afternoon was extremely harmful both to body and mind. But what could he do? How could he shake off this pernicious slumber?

He woke with a start, hearing a voice call him in words that rang in his ears year after year: "Sir, are you asleep?" It was his brother come to see how he was getting on and to bring him his supper. This was a pleasant meal consisting of a loaf of bread and a piece of Greek cheese or a slice of sesame cake. Every weekday, after putting this meal in front of him, his brother would say good night and go off to attend the Imam's lecture at the Azhar.

The boy attacked his food with more or less appetite, but in either case he left nothing uneaten. He used often to eat very little when he was with his brother, who made no comment or remark on the subject. But when he ate alone he used to finish everything, even if he had to force his appetite. He was afraid that his brother, when he came back, would see that he had left some of his food and imagine he was ill or unhappy. And the last thing he could bear was to give his brother pain or anxiety.

So he set to and ate everything. When it was finished he went back again to his own corner and surrendered himself to listless inactivity. As the day began to decline and the sun descended towards the west, a slow, haggard melancholy came down upon the boy. The muezzin sang out his call to evening prayer and told him that the day was done. He felt the shadows closing in upon him and knew that if anyone else had been with him in the room he would have lit the lamp and driven them away. But he was alone, and as far as folk with eyes could tell he had no need of any lamp. The boy knew only too well that they were mistaken. For in those days he drew a sharp distinction between darkness and light. If the lamp was lit he found it friendly and companionable, whereas darkness was sheer desolation. Perhaps it was only the fruit of youthful imagination and a nervous temperament, but the strange thing was that he sensed the darkness with his ears as a constant tingling sound like the hum of a mosquito, only louder and coarser. Its impact stung his ears and put terror into his heart. He felt compelled to change his posture; rising to a sitting position he supported his elbows on his knees, hid his head in his hands and abandoned himself to that inescapable buzz. If in the afternoon, solitude forced him asleep, in the evening it stirred him into a wakefulness worse than a nightmare.

He might in the end have become accustomed to the sound of darkness and even found it reassuring, but there were various other sounds in the room which combined to madden him. The house belonged to the Wakfs,[7] which is as much as to say that its origin was lost in the vast backwardness of time; its walls were rotten with age and full of cracks containing hordes of insects and other small animals. These creatures seemed to have made it their business, after nightfall, to keep watch and ward over the boy as he lay crouching in his corner. There were inconsiderable scratchings, light movements this way and that, now furtive, now hasty—enough to make the boy shiver with fear. When his brother came in, whether alone or with friends, and the lamp was lit, all these sounds and shiftings ceased as though they had never been. This was the main reason why the boy never dared to mention them to anyone. The least of his fears was that, if he said anything about the matter, people might call him an idiot or cast doubts upon his courage or intelligence. So he preferred to keep quiet and master his apprehensions as best he could.

There was the muezzin calling to the last prayer of the day. A gleam of hope stirred in him for a moment, then betrayed him to blank despair. The Imam's lecture was over and the boy's brother would soon be coming in to light the lamp, put away his portfolio and take anything he needed in the way of books, food and so on, diffusing through the room as he did so a little comfort and peace, and ridding it for a time of that intolerable solitude. But then he would throw the boy his bedclothes, stay long enough to see him roll himself up in the rug and lay his head on the pillow, then put out the lamp and go off, shutting the door behind him and turning the key in the lock. He must have imagined, as he walked away, that he had left the boy sound asleep, when in fact he had abandoned him to a long-drawn-out nightmare of insomnia.

In three or four hours' time he would come back, after he had eaten his dinner and drunk his tea, talked of this and that with his friends and worked with them on the next day's lessons. He would turn the key in the lock and light up the lamp, imagining all the time that the boy was sunk in a sweet, peaceful slumber, when in fact he had

[7]Religious endowments administered by the Ministry of Wakfs.

never tasted sleep and had only been waiting in frightened impatience for his brother to return.

The young man put out the light and lay down on his bed. Soon the sound of his breathing, now disturbed and now more regular, showed that he had fallen asleep. Then at last there flooded through the boy a blissful sense of release; his spirit was filled with confidence and his mind wrapped up in the serenest quiet.

And then, without any perceptible transition, he slid out of consciousness into a downy sleep.

TRANSLATED BY HILARY WAYMENT

ARABIC AND PERSIAN POETRY

In modern times Arabic and Persian poetry are linked far less by common forms, as they were in the past, than by common problems and patterns of solution. It would be wrong to imply that Arabic and Persian poetry immediately before the nineteenth century had nothing good to offer; but no one—least of all the Arabs and Persians—would care to defend the proposition that it was very good either. In fact, the condition of Islamic poetry was quite poor until the revivals of the nineteenth century.

The Arabs felt the revival first and in a way more triumphantly than the Persians did, since the Arabs were under Turkish rule. For both literatures, revival of poetry involved prose as well; for both it concentrated on a search for new forms and some degree of imitation of European forms. Both used literature a little too freely, to its detriment, in the service of politics; and both were burdened with some very mediocre talents.

Their experiences and productions have not all been similar, either. Arabic poetry has in general been the more inventive and word-conscious; Persian poetry has been the more clever in adapting popular traditional forms to please the ears of the times. Both have undergone, and are still undergoing, vast changes; but there are many signs (for instance in the poetry journals of Beirut and Teheran) that poetry may be on the verge of reassuming its traditional primacy within the two greatest Islamic literatures.

Rather than to attempt to present biographical material on the poets, which is often difficult to obtain, or even analyses of the individual poems, which would have to be prohibitively lengthy, the poems will stand here on their own, a challenge alike to them, their poets, and their translators.

Arabic Poetry

Ahmad Shawqi

To a Late Composer

Every day another reception and garlands of rhetoric
   over a tomb.
This man taught the nation nothing, planted no deserts
   with pylons.
We remnants are enriched, but his friends and family
   were impoverished.
Slander arrested him in kennels of aphrodisiac and
   hashish.

But beams make tears of what they play on. He filled
   ears and throat
With the turmoil of his presence first, then with his stiff
   quiet.
Unthought stresses of voice and instrument replaneted his
   firmament
Beyond the mason on the site he built for duration
Set for perpetuity more than the seedsman, explored
   properties
Rare in the luckiest tendril or the talented stone.

The sands were dry and ready for the fall.
An Alexandrian nightingale with a sky-nest
Lighted on the shore from a dark flowering hill
He chose where only the kites circled in a cleft
An hour when the food-gatherers were away busy
He chose to struggle with the two horizons
And alert as a parrot he intercepted
The surprise of the world's shouts and whispers.

A frenzy in the sands was fretting
For his harangues and elegiac speech
For soliloquies on the reed
And sighs which through gaping notches
Achieve the slopes and parapets
In continents of the pure dead.

The house of earth was opened, down its corridors of art
Consolation was blown from the cool belts. And do not
   lament
For art. There is always nourishment streaming in the
   crevices of air,
The calendar's quickening restores the corpses, and the
   meteors
In the shafts of Karnak make bonfires among the pillars
And what washes through Egypt is tired and brilliant as
   wax.

The master, relaxed: the end of his blaze was disaster.
He quitted his disquiet, even the random and epilectic
Revelations, by which he committed more monuments
   to us
Than legions have left banners in this sand.

> Still in the lay kingdom chants a boy,
> Frail as bamboo, pink with tossing
> The ball of twine that cradles space

He clings to the suburbs, restless, locking his hands
—And the premise of art is an alabaster blush.

TRANSLATED BY HERBERT HOWARTH AND IBRAHIM
SHUKRALLAH

Maruf Al-Rusafi

Sleepers, Wake!

Begone, begone, Baghdad! Depart from me;
   No wise am I of thee, not mine art thou;
Yet, though I suffered oft and much of thee,
   Baghdad, it pains me to behold thee now
Upon the brink of great catastrophe.

Misfortune past misfortune fell upon
   Thy life so sweet, and turned it all to rue;
Canst thou no more produce a noble son?
   Nay, thou art barren of the free, the true,
Whose sons of old were heroes, every one.

The witnesses of Ignorance, behold!
   Humble thee to her shrine in worship mean;
Wilt thou not spurn her in rebellion bold

Remembering the glory that has been,
The empire of Rashid, the Age of Gold?

The sway supreme no foreman dared defy
    Thy clouds of fortune rained abundantly,
The palace of thy splendour soared on high,
    True learning had its resting-place in thee,
The crescent of thy greatness filled the sky.

Ahmad Zaki Abu Shadi

The Maiden of Bekhten

Ramses sits on his high throne, and on either hand
Slaves attending; richly-jewelled his courtiers stand.
Liquid floweth the music; the lute's low, vibrant notes
Softly answer the silver singing of silver throats;
Still and lovely as chiselled marble, the maidens sing
Fair as ever an artist dreamed, to delight a king.
Row on row the mighty chiefs with offerings rare
Lifted up in the pride of power superbly stare;
Costly-broidered the great fans upraised on high
Swing sweeping the rathe breeze and refreshingly;
Brightly flash in the vast chamber the carvings gay
Outgleaming the spring's mantle of rich array.
Precious offerings these, precious and proud they are,
Hither brought for the king's pleasure from near and far;
But the king, the most might, with high disdain
Stares askance, and the gifts speak him fair in vain,
Naught accounts he of all their worth and their
    eloquence,
Nay, though wondrous fine they be reckoned long ages
    hence:
Though his loyal lieges strove to the uttermost,
Yea, and more, for the royal favour, 'twas labour lost.

Now the Maiden of Bekhten cometh, apparelled all
Softly in fine linen, the nymph of the festival,
Gift of her father chosen, the most delectable,
Far exceeding whatever magic of words can tell.

Then from his high throne, flashing in golden pride,
Ramses in majesty descends, and to his side
Draweth her, and she in the wonder of loveliness
Draweth the king's heart to love resistanceless.

Great is the pomp of beauty; the glory of mortal power
Swift fadeth; beauty's pomp is deathless flower;
Many symbols of lesser gods in the world we view;
Beauty mirrors the One, the Everliving, the True.

TRANSLATED BY A. J. ARBERRY

Abbas Mahmud Al-Aqqad

Satan felt superior to his own wiles,
Superior to those who followed him like sheep.
The debauched and the saintly
Seemed far too much alike to him.
Why bother to corrupt
Those who had lost all trace of good?
And if they had not lost it,
Why rob them of what they had?
Was it worth coveting?
Poor Satan! He had lost his faith in evil.
It had lost its power. Poor Satan!
What a spectacle: a devil
Losing faith in evil!

TRANSLATED BY JAMAL AHMED

Love's Compound

Love is not mere friendship, son,
Neither enmity alone;
Love an equal compound is
Mingled of both qualities.
Purest enmity's to share
With the sweetest friendship there,
Free for all, to yield and rape—
And but few on earth escape!

Competition

I gave her respite from deceiving,
And duped myself into believing
Her love was true and tender;
But though I strove with utmost daring

To try my patience past all bearing,
She wins—and I surrender!

Cheat Me!

Cheat me once, or cheat me twice;
With a thousand thousand lies
Wondrous in variety
Fraudulently cozen me!
Never, O my heart's delight,
Shalt thou bridge the infinite
Firmament of difference
'Twixt thy folly and my sense!

Lie to me, and lie anew,
As thy fancy bids thee do;
What is worth my wealth of wit
If thou be not cheating it?
Plunder me, as takes thy will,
I have wit in plenty still:
Where's the harm, to steal a grain,
Or a couple, from my brain?

TRANSLATED BY A. J. ARBERRY

Abu Al-Qasim Al-Shabi

Fate must respond
If a people will to live.
Night must go
And chains must break.
Grasp life with tenderness, embrace it,
Or die where you stand.
So nature tells us,
So the hidden spirit speaks.

Blood roared in my veins;
There was a blizzard in my heart.
O Mother Earth, I cried,
Do you hate all humanity?
Blessed, she answered, are the unyielding,
Blessed those who brave the tides.
Cursed are they who lag behind.

Life is alive and buoyant;
It loves its image,
It hates the dead.

TRANSLATED BY JAMAL AHMED

Khayr Al-Din Al-Zirikli

Lament

I weep for a land fashioned to beauty fair
  Beyond compare;
I weep for a heritage of glory and fame
  A hard, far aim.

I weep for spirits too indolent to urge men
  To battle again;
I weep for the splendour of empire and the boast
  Turned all to a ghost.

Abd Al-Majid Ibn Jallun

Who Art Thou?

I had forgotten the bright stars and moon,
The beauty of the sunset, and of morn,
And through the radiance of the stars and moon
By memory's soft whisper I was borne
Back to a youth, that passed away so soon.

And lo, the shadows lifted; and a light
Glowed in the blossoms of a garden green
Wherein all living things were fresh and bright,
And dancing magic phantasms were seen
Bathed in a lustre that dispersed the night.

Then 'mid the perfume of those shining flowers
A light appearing led my footsteps on
Toward a wondrous palace, tall with towers,
Until I stood within its courts, alone,
My heart enraptured by its silent bowers.

And now I heard a voice that called to me;
As in a dream I raised mine eyes, and lo!
I gazed upon a lofty balcony.

"Ha! Who art thou? I would that I might know;
But scarce I think I ever looked on thee."

"I—I am but an unremembered ghost
Whose world was once conterminous with thine,
But now our age of happiness is lost;
No memory lingers of our love divine;
Out of thy heart its wizardry is tossed—

Tossed out my love, that life may all possess
With other charms; and so my passion spurned,
My flowering mead of roses, comfortless,
By the cold winds of casual scorn is turned,
My garden fair, into a wilderness.

Who am I? Hast thou then forgotten quite
Our days together, and my cup of wine
Wherewith I moved thy spirit to delight,
And quenched thy thirst with joy, and rapture fine,
And made thee tread life's furthest, holiest height?

Who am I? Thou hast drunken from my bowl
Honey, my love, the molten fire thereof,
The frankincense and attar of my soul;
I was the chattel of thy poet's love;
I did not think passion could perish whole."

Wakened my dreaming heart her prick of woe;
Her brooding phantom vanished into space,
And I was standing on this soil I know
And gazing rapturously at the moon's face
Out of the shadows of our earth below.

Time has entranced my heart, so full of care
I have betrayed my friends of long ago:
Sweet ghost, forgive me! For the griefs I bear
Have drugged my spirit, and I no more know
If I wax sane, or mad, of my despair.

TRANSLATED BY A. J. ARBERRY

Persian Poems

Qaani

To a Benefactor

What cheek!
He believes
God the cause
of all my poverty
and misery
and only
His servants rich.

TRANSLATED BY OMAR POUND

Bahar

The Miracle of Spring

Recall how with frozen fingers December's clouds out-
spread
Over the fields and uplands a mantle of ice and snow;
Over the buried roses, over a world of dead
Vengeful as any hangman stalked the exultant crow.

But lo, the abiding wonder! Spirit, that never dies,
Surges anew and vital through the upstanding trees.
See, those spear-armed horsemen, the spreading tulips,
rise
Over the plains triumphant, hills, yea, and mountains
seize.

Behold, the eager lily leaps to delight the eye,
Spurning the bent narcissus crouched in his self-regard.
Deep in the springing corn-shoots the gleaming violets
lie;
Bright with a myriad jewels the wheat-swept fields are
starred.
Under the nodding willow the poppy lies in blood—
Sudden the blow that smote her, drenched her in crimson
flood.
And now, mid the green profusion of wheat, in mingled
hue

Note how the lily argent with lily azure glows;
So, when the sky is stippled with scattered rain-clouds
   through
Here and there betwixt them the vault of heaven shows.

Random Thoughts

Above the surface of this low, mean sphere,
Below the heavens' high, enamelled bowl,
None, small or great, lives in contentment here:
Shall I be meanly satisfied in soul?
Deep have I plunged in every subtlety,
Far to the frontier of life's secrets fared:
Being? 'Tis but a dim horizon, we
A point of doubt that on its rim appeared.
Save for that one small, glittering point of doubt
No lustres on that dark horizon rise.
I loved all truths, and yearned to find each out,
But, truly, all was fantasy and lies.
Joy, sorrow, foul and lovely, worst and best,
Are naught but fantasies to my survey:
Dawn's glad effulgence gleams not in my breast,
Nor the last lustre of departing day.
All rebel thought, uprooted from my mind,
Drowns in the whirlpool of a mighty ease,
As when a ship unmasted to the wind
Of fortune yields, and tosses on its seas.

Creation from the start was shaped to be
By nature subject to two monstrous laws:
First, to the influence of heredity,
Next, faculty acquired, a second cause.
If from my ancestors derives my soul,
What in God's name am I, the unfortunate?
If mind and spirit are of my control,
Why shall heredity my doom dictate?
One forebear was a saint and mystic high,
And one an officer and governor:
My father was a poet; therefore I
Should be a poet, saint, and warrior.
My grandfather a merchant was, and so
My father urged me to engage in trade;
Yet all his upbringing was doomed to go
To waste; more loss upon my soul was laid.

No auditor am I, ascetic none,
Merchant nor courtier, officer nor wit;
Curious of all things, but not skilled in one,
Learned in each trade, yet ignorant of it.
Hard as a rock, and heaven's jealous zone
Each instant looses arrows at my heart,
As if I were a red mark on a stone
Set up, fair target for some archer's art.

TRANSLATED BY A. J. ARBERRY

A Critical Tribute to Sir Edward Grey[1]

To London speed, O breeze of dawning day
Bear this my message to Sir Edward Grey.
To thee in skill, wise Councillor of State,
Ne'er did the world produce a peer or mate!
Great Peter's schemes to thine were shifting sand,
And weak by thine the plans that Bismarck planned.
Ne'er from Toulon Napoleon's hosts had gone
If on the Pyramids thy name had shone.
Had Paris been in league with thee, in vain
The German hosts had swamped Alsace-Lorraine.
Had England 'gainst the States sought help from thee
No Washington had won them victory.
Had thy prestige companioned England's arms
Ne'er had the Boers caused England such alarms.
Would Kuropatkin's hosts before Japan
Have fled had he been guided by thy plan?
Had the Manchus been aided by thy thought
The rebels ne'er against their king had fought.
And had thy schemes included Persia's life
Not fruitless had remained this storm and strife.

You nurse the wolf-cub in your arms: a deed
Which folly prompts, and which to grief will lead.
To this o'erbearing partner you submit,
And bow your head, bereft of sense and wit.
Your pacts with Russia made in time gone by
Brought loss unseen by your short-sighted eye.

---

[1]An architect of the Anglo-Russian agreement of 1907, which was designed to end the rivalry of the two powers in Iran by establishing spheres of influence, an agreement widely resented, of course, within Iran. [Ed.]

In Afghanistan, Persia and Tibet
Before your foe a three-doored wall you've set.

Not I but human nature tells you plain
That pacts weigh naught compared with present gain;
The more since Russia longs for India still
As longs the hawk for partridge on the hill;
Else why did she o'er Persian lands let loose
Her Cossack hordes to crown her long abuse?

O cursed obstinacy, which did raise
This veil, and set the feet in such a maze!
Headstrong and rash you wrought a deed of shame
Which stolid Turk and vagrant Arab blame.
Woe to that judgement cool, that reason bright,
Which now have put you in so dire a plight!
All hail that judgement, hail that insight rare,
Of which, men say, you hold so large a share!

TRANSLATED BY E. G. BROWNE

Qulzum

The tyranny of silence shall be broken—
New shining words by us, the poets, spoken;
Whereas a diver threads dull pearls upon a string
We choose the words which soar—and give them wing.

TRANSLATED BY J. C. E. BOWEN

Iraj

Epitaph

Know ye, fair folk who dwell on earth
Or shall hereafter come to birth,
That here, with dust upon his eyes,
Iraj, the sweet-tongued minstrel, lies.
In this true lover's tomb interred
A world of love is sepulchred.
Each ringlet fair, each lovely face,
In death, as living, I embrace:
I am the selfsame man ye knew,
That passed his every hour with you.

What if I quit the world's abode?
I wait to join you on the road;
And though this soil my refuge be,
I watch for you unceasingly.
Then sit a moment here, I pray,
And let your footsteps on me stray:
My heart, attentive to your voice,
Within this earth's heart will rejoice.

Nosratullah Kasemi

Sting and Antidote

Said wasp to bee:
they loathe me
stone my nest
smoke me out
and even pay
for cyanide
to move me,

but you,
with your hexagons
and pollen dances,
they house in luxury.

Said bee: to sting
and still be loved
you must give honey.

TRANSLATED BY OMAR POUND

Khanlari

Night the Plunderer

Night came to plunder, and with open fist
Seized all that stirred within the hollow vale:
Long since the river was his captive—list,
And you might hear the river's plaintive wail.

The garden's treasure, purple, crimson, white,
All vanished into night's far-plundering hand;
The walnut bough lifted its foot in fright
High o'er the apple branch, and upwards spanned.

Like a black smoke its swirling skirt night drew,
Hastening from the lowland to the hill;
The forest's hands and feet were lost to view,
The concourse of the trees was hushed and still.

"Night! night!" the screech owl's warning echo leapt,
And a leaf shivered on a willow limb;
Along the earth a wandering straggler crept
Until the thick mintbushes swallowed him.

Night drew a long, warm sigh, to sleep at last
Reposeful after strife and stress, content:
A poplar and some ancient willows fast
Fled o'er the hillock's brow, incontinent.

Faridun Tavalluli

Evening Shadows

The owl calls, and the nightmare in its wildness
Fixes its eyes on the flame of a lightless candle;
The wind roars, coming softly to the ear,
The howl of a hungry beast from a distant forest.
The sky, dull, heavy, like a bit of lead,
Crushes the dread-casting, fright-compounding night.
Dark night touches the wall of the world,
In the hope of opening the casement of "morrow."
Anon a dried branch touches another,
And in that darkness of night the bond of silence severs.
Death, mayhap, is breaking the bones of life,
Or a dead body trembles in the coffin.
Suddenly, from the sun's torch a scarlet spark
Flies in undulation to the black-blue mountain's top;
A partridge calls, and night, disturbed, goes on its way;
Morning lauchs and a group goes slowly to the river.

TRANSLATED BY G. M. WICKENS

Sad Love

Below the ancient plane
That since so long ago,
   Head lifted so,
   Solitary

Stands in the plain
    A lonely tree,
Love, too worn out to weep
    For Fate,
Too sad, too desolate,
    Love lies asleep.

And now the ravens come
Swooping on the crowded wing,
    Come clamouring
    To their lost tree
    That is their home
    Where they would be
At eventide; they sweep
    In flight
Calling, that through the night
    Still they may sleep.

As coming from afar
Heavy and slow of breath
    Night entereth;
    Winking on high
    Each flickering star
Looks down, to spy
What haps on earth. A peace
    Profound
And awful reigns; no sound;
    Eve's whispers cease.

Anon out of the heart
Of some black, lowering cloud
    That caps a proud
    Far mountain-head
    Quick lightnings dart,
    Sudden and red.
From a dark corner bathed
    In gloom
A spirit from the tomb
    Stirs, shadow-swathed.

Beside the ruined tower
Where once a fortress rose
    A flame now glows.
    The nymph of night
    Kindled this hour;
    There, by the bright

Fire she is sleeping. Lo,
   Around
The gleam a ghost aswound
   Sweeps, and shrills woe.

Down from the mountain's brows
A wind, drawn suddenly,
   Upon the tree
   Rushes unpent
   And thrust its boughs
   To the earth, bent.
So, with a twisted limb
   The plane
Seizes sad love again
   And wakens him.

TRANSLATED BY A. J. ARBERRY

Radi Adharkhushi

House of Love

Every pomp has its instability,
Every possession holds the source of beggary;
From pomp and possession flee, into Love,
For that house has a door to Light.

Freethinkers

Shackled to our past and our own age,
To thought-in-pawn and earlier utterance,
More worthy than any of prisoner's title:
Let us assume the name of "freethinkers"!

Abu Al-Qasim Halat

The Pickpocket's Repentance

In a street, one night, I saw two pickpockets;
   At mere sight of them, the hair stood up on my body.
One, en route, was complaining to the other:
   "I vow a thousand times never again to touch a person's pocket.
Because one evening a smart young fellow

'Induced' me to pick his pocket, and
When I got his wallet out and opened it up,
   Nothing was to be found in it but my wife's picture."

Muayyad Thabiti

Snow

Snow has come and capped every woman and every
   mountain,
   This year its coming is very precious.
The world in whiteness has become like a royal falcon's
   breast,
   The welkin in blackness like the wing of a swallow.
People have all fled from lane and market,
   Hiding in their houses like bees in the hive.

Mascud Farzad

The Moon and the Chain

The chain of loneliness weighs heavy on the foot of my
   soul,
   Alas! With such a foot walking is not possible.
Since, at the world's board, king and beggar have their
   portion,
   Why is there nothing for us, save the portion of the
     onlooking?
Why will one atom of joy not fit in my narrow heart,
   When in every corner of it there is room for a hundred
     mountains of grief?
How long can one see wisdom trampled by folly?
   Come, blindness, and release me from the evil of sight!
The night of hope is void: a barrier has come between
   the road and me;
   Rise, O moon of new hope, maybe you will show the
     road.
The mind was distraught, and distraught poetry was born
   of it:
   A distraught-bearing mind is more to my liking than
     barrenness.

TRANSLATED BY G. M. WICKENS

Furugh Farukhzad

Lagoon

Oh, if I had a way to the sea,
I would have no fear of going down.

In the lagoon, water falls short of its course,
Diminishes to nothing from its rest;

Its soul will be the region of destructions,
Its depth the grave of fishes.

Gazelle, O deer of wildest land,
When in your passage through a flower field
You come upon a singing stream
Facing the blue color of the sea, flowing.

Remember the dream of the dreamless one,
Remember the death in the lagoon.

The Earthly Signs

Then no one thought of love
Then no one thought of victory
And no one
then thought of no-thing.

What bitter and black days
Bread has defeated
the astonishing power of prophecy
The hungry and unfortunate prophets
ran away from the holy promise lands
And the lost lambs of Christ
Then did not hear
The "Hay, Hay" sound of shepherding
in the consternation of fields.

The lagoons of alcohol
With those acrid and poisoned steams
pulled down the static multitude of the enlightened
into their depth
And crafty mice
chewed up the golden pages of books
in old cupboards.

And the sun was dead
And no one knew
the name of that sad dove
that flew away from hearts is faith.

Oh, the sound of a prisoner
Would your helpless complaint ever
from any side of this detested night
burrow toward the light?
Oh, the sound of a prisoner
Oh, the lost sound of sounds . . .

A Cold Season

And this is I
A lonely woman
On the threshold of a cold season
At the beginning of the understanding of the contami-
    nated existence of earth.
And the simple despair and sadness of sky
And the weakness of these cemented hands.

On the threshold of a cold season
In the circles of the mourning of mirrors
And the mournful society of these pale experiences
And the sunset being pregnant with the knowledge of
    silence
How is it possible to command someone who goes so
    patient,
    heavy,
    wondering,
to stop.
How is it possible to say to man that he is not alive,
    has never been alive.

Dear stars
Dear cardboard stars
When lies billow in the sky
Then how is it possible to rely on the surahs of disgraced
    prophets?
We, like corpses dead a thousand years, will gather to-
    gether; and then
The Sun shall judge the rottenness of our dead bodies.

Salaam, O innocent night
Salaam, O innocent night, you who change the eyes of
    the desert wolves

into the bony pit of faith and trust
And on the side of your brook the spirit of willows
smell the kind spirits of apes
I came from the indifferent world of thoughts, words
      and sounds,
And this world is like the nest of snakes,
And this world is full of the sound of the movement of
      people's feet
that, just as they kiss you,
In their imagination weave your noose.

Look here
How the soul of the one who spoke with the word
and played with the glance
and found comfort with fondling; away from running
on the imaginary scaffold,
has been crucified.

Fortunate corpses
Dejected corpses
Quiet and reflective corpses
Well-countenanced, well-dressed, well-fed corpses
In the stations of certain times
And in the doubtful field of temporary lights
And the lust of buying the rotten fruits of vanity
Oh,
What people at the crossroad are looking for accidents
And the sound of the stop whistle
In the moment that a man must, must, must
be smashed under the wheel of time
A man who is passing by the wet trees.

TRANSLATED BY BAHRAM JAMALPUR

MOHAMMED IQBAL: IS RELIGION POSSIBLE?

[from *The Reconstruction of Religious Thought in Islam*]

*By 1934, when the following was published, Moham-
med Iqbal had emerged not only as a major world
poet, some of whose poems we have already sampled
in this book, but as one of Islam's most important
and influential thinkers in modern times. The Reconstruction of Religious Thought in Islam, his most
comprehensive statement along these lines, rein-
vigorated the earlier and more direct appeal to rationalism of the Arab Modernists.*

*In his appeal to the predominantly civilizing func-
tion of Islam in human development, he provided that
philosophical erudition and profundity which modern
Islam had hitherto lacked. In his concern, manner,
finesse, and force in doing so, however, he achieved
something far grander, something closer to the ideals
of his favorite German philosophers: he became one
of the greatest Moslem philosophers since Averroës.*

Broadly speaking, religious life may be divided into
three periods. These may be described as the periods of
"Faith," "Thought," and "Discovery." In the first period
religious life appears as a form of discipline which the
individual or a whole people must accept as an uncondi-
tional command without any rational understanding of the
ultimate meaning and purpose of that command. This attitude may be of great consequence in the social and
political history of a people, but is not of much consequence in so far as the individual's inner growth and
expansion are concerned. Perfect submission to discipline
is followed by a rational understanding of the discipline
and the ultimate source of its authority. In this period,
religious life seeks its foundation in a kind of metaphysics
—a logically consistent view of the world, with God as a
part of that view. In the third period, metaphysics is

displaced by psychology, and religious life develops the ambition to come into direct contact with the ultimate Reality. It is here that religion becomes a matter of personal assimilation of life and power, and the individual achieves a free personality, not by releasing himself from the fetters of the law, but by discovering the ultimate source of the law within the depths of his own consciousness. As in the words of a Muslim Sufi—"No understanding of the Holy Book is possible until it is actually revealed to the believer just as it was revealed to the Prophet." It is, then, in the sense of this last phase in the development of religious life that I use the word religion in the question that I now propose to raise. Religion in this sense is known by the unfortunate name of Mysticism, which is supposed to be a life-denying, fact-avoiding attitude of mind directly opposed to the radically empirical outlook of our times. Yet higher religion, which is only a search for a larger life, is essentially experience and recognized the necessity of experience as its foundation long before science learnt to do so. It is a genuine effort to clarify human consciousness, and is, as such, as critical of its level of experience as Naturalism is of its own level.

As we all know, it was Kant who first raised the question: "Is metaphysics possible?" He answered this question in the negative; and his argument applies with equal force to the realities in which religion is especially interested. The manifold of sense, according to him, must fulfil certain formal conditions in order to constitute knowledge. The thing in itself is only a limiting idea. Its function is merely regulative. If there *is* some actuality corresponding to the idea it falls outside the boundaries of experience, and consequently its existence cannot be rationally demonstrated. This verdict of Kant cannot be easily accepted. It may fairly be argued that in view of the more recent developments of science, such as the nature of matter as "bottled-up light waves," the idea of the universe as an act of thought, finiteness of space and time and Heisenberg's principle of indeterminacy in nature, the case for a system of rational theology is not so bad as Kant was led to think. But for our present purposes it is unnecessary to consider this point in detail. As to the thing in itself, which is inaccessible to pure reason because of its falling beyond the boundaries of experience, Kant's verdict can be accepted only if we start with the assumption that all experience other than the normal level of experience is impossible. The only question, therefore, is whether the normal level is the only level of knowledge-yielding experience. Kant's view of the thing in itself and the thing as it appears to us very much determined the character of his question regarding the possibility of metaphysics. But what if the position, as understood by him, is reversed? The great Muslim Sufi philosopher, Muhyuddin Ibnul Arabi of Spain, has made the acute observation that God is a percept; the world is a concept. Another Muslim Sufi thinker and poet, Iraqi, insists on the plurality of space-orders and time-orders and speaks of a Divine Time and a Divine Space. It may be that what we call the external world is only an intellectual construction, and that there are other levels of human experience capable of being systematized by other orders of space and time—levels in which concept and analysis do not play the same role as they do in the case of our normal experience. It may, however, be said that the level of experience to which concepts are inapplicable cannot yield any knowledge of a universal character; for concepts alone are capable of being socialized. The standpoint of the man who relies on religious experience for capturing Reality must always remain individual and incommunicable. This objection has some force if it is meant to insinuate that the mystic is wholly ruled by his traditional ways, attitudes, and expectations. Conservatism is as bad in religion as in any other department of human activity. It destroys the ego's creative freedom and closes up the paths of fresh spiritual enterprise. This is the main reason why our medieval mystic techniques can no longer produce original discoverers of ancient Truth. The fact, however, that religious experience is incommunicable does not mean that the religious man's pursuit is futile. Indeed, the incommunicability of religious experience gives us a clue to the ultimate nature of the ego. In our daily social intercourse we live and move in seclusion, as it were. We do not care to reach the inmost individuality of men. We treat them as mere functions, and approach them from those aspects of their identity which are capable of conceptual treatment. The climax of religious life, however, is the discovery of the ego as an individual deeper than his conceptually describable habitual selfhood. It is in contact with the Most Real that the ego discovers its uniqueness, its metaphysical status, and the possibility of improvement in that status. Strictly speaking, the experience which leads to this discovery is not a conceptually manageable intellectual fact; it is a vital fact, an attitude consequent on an inner biological transformation which cannot be captured in the net of logical categories. It can embody itself only in a world-making or world-shaking act; and in this form alone the content of this timeless experience can diffuse itself in the time-movement, and make itself effectively visible to the eye of history. It seems that the method of dealing with Reality by means of concepts is not at all a serious way of dealing with it. Science does not care whether its electron is a real entity or not. It may be a mere symbol, a mere convention. Religion, which is essentially a mode of actual living, is the only serious way of handling Reality. As a form of higher experience it is corrective of our concepts of philosophical theology or at least makes us suspicious of the purely rational process which forms these concepts. Science can afford to ignore metaphysics altogether, and may even believe it to be "a justified form of poetry," as Lange defined it, or "a legitimate play of grownups," as Nietzsche described it. But the religious expert who seeks to discover his personal status in the constitution of things cannot, in view of the final aim of his struggle, be satisfied with what science may regard as a vital lie, a mere "as-if" to regulate thought and conduct. In so far as the ultimate nature of Reality is concerned, nothing is at stake in the venture of science; in the religious venture the whole career of the ego as an assimilative personal centre of life and experience is at stake. Conduct, which involves a decision of the ultimate fate of the agent, cannot be based on illusions. A wrong concept misleads the understanding; a wrong deed degrades the whole man and may eventually demolish the structure of the human ego. The mere concept affects life only partially; the deed is dynamically related to reality and issues from a generally constant attitude of the whole man towards reality. No doubt the deed, i.e., the control of psychological and physiological processes with a view to tuning up the ego for an immediate contact with the ultimate Reality is, and cannot but be, individual in form and content; yet the deed, too, is liable to be socialized when others begin to live through it with a view to discovering for themselves its effectiveness as a method of approaching the Real. The evidence of religious experts in all ages and countries is that there are potential types of consciousness lying close to our normal consciousness. If these types of consciousness open up possibilities of life-giving and knowledge-yielding experience, the question of the possibility of religion as a form of higher experience is a perfectly legitimate one and demands our serious attention.

But, apart from the legitimacy of the question, there are important reasons why it should be raised at the present moment in the history of modern culture. In the first place, the scientific interest of the question. It seems that every culture has a form of Naturalism peculiar to its own world-feeling; and it further appears that every form of Naturalism ends in some sort of Atomism. We have Indian Atomism, Greek Atomism, Muslim Atomism, and Modern Atomism. Modern Atomism is, however, unique. Its amazing mathematics which sees the universe as an elaborate differential equation; and its physics which, following its own methods, has been led to smash some of the old gods of its own temple, have already brought us to the point of asking the question whether the causality-bound aspect of nature is the whole truth about it. Is not the ultimate Reality invading our consciousness from some other direction as well? Is the purely intellectual method of overcoming nature the only method? "We have acknowledged," says Professor Eddington, "that the entities of physics can from their very nature form only a partial aspect of the reality. How are we to deal with the other part? It cannot be said that that other part concerns us less than the physical entities. Feelings, purpose, values, make up our consciousness as much as sense-impressions. We follow up the sense-impressions and find that they lead into an external world discussed by science; we follow up the other elements of our being and find that they lead—not into a world of space and time, but surely somewhere."

In the second place we have to look to the great practical importance of the question. The modern man with his philosophies of criticism and scientific specialism finds himself in a strange predicament. His Naturalism has given him an unprecedented control over the forces of nature, but has robbed him of faith in his own future. It is strange how the same idea affects different cultures differently. The formulation of the theory of evolution in the world of Islam brought into being Rumi's tremendous enthusiasm for the biological future of man. No cultured Muslim can read such passages as the following without a thrill of joy:

> Low in the earth
> I lived in realms of ore and stone;
> And then I smiled in many-tinted flowers;

Then roving with the wild and wandering hours,
O'er earth and air and ocean's zone,
      In a new birth,
        I dived and flew,
          And crept and ran,
And all the secret of my essence drew
Within a form that brought them all to view—
        And lo, a Man!
        And then my goal,
Beyond the clouds, beyond the sky,
In realms where none may change or die—
In angel form; and then away
Beyond the bounds of night and day,
And Life and Death, unseen or seen,
Where all that is hath ever been,
          As One and Whole.
          (*Rumi:* Thadani's Translation.)

On the other hand, the formulation of the same view of evolution with far greater precision in Europe has led to the belief that "there now appears to be no scientific basis for the idea that the present rich complexity of human endowment will ever be materially exceeded." That is how the modern man's secret despair hides itself behind the screen of scientific terminology. Nietzsche, although he thought that the idea of evolution did not justify the belief that man was unsurpassable, cannot be regarded as an exception in this respect. His enthusiasm for the future of man ended in the doctrine of eternal recurrence—perhaps the most hopeless idea of immortality ever formed by man. This eternal repetition is not eternal "becoming"; it is the same old idea of "being" masquerading as "becoming."

Thus, wholly overshadowed by the results of his intellectual activity, the modern man has ceased to live soulfully, i.e., from within. In the domain of thought he is living in open conflict with himself; and in the domain of economic and political life he is living in open conflict with others. He finds himself unable to control his ruthless egoism and his infinite gold-hunger, which is gradually killing all higher striving in him and bringing him nothing but life-weariness. Absorbed in the "fact," that is to say, the optically present source of sensation, he is entirely cut off from the unplumbed depths of his own being. In the wake of his systematic materialism has at last come that paralysis of energy which Huxley apprehended and deplored. The condition of things in the East is no better. The technique of medieval mysticism by which religious life, in its higher manifestations, developed itself both in the East and in the West has now practically failed. And in the Muslim East it has, perhaps, done far greater havoc than anywhere else. Far from reintegrating the forces of the average man's inner life and thus preparing him for participation in the march of history, it has taught him a false renunciation and made him feel perfectly contented with his ignorance and spiritual thraldom. No wonder then that the modern Muslim in Turkey, Egypt, and Persia is led to seek fresh sources of energy in the creation of new loyalties, such as patriotism and nationalism which Nietzsche described as "sickness and unreason," and "the strongest force against culture." Disappointed of a purely religious method of spiritual renewal which alone brings us into touch with the everlasting fountain of life and power by expanding our thought and emotion, the modern Muslim fondly hopes to unlock fresh sources of energy by narrowing down his thought and emotion. Modern atheistic socialism, which possesses all the fervour of a new religion, has a broader outlook; but having received its philosophical basis from the Hegelians of the left wing, it rises in revolt against the very source which could have given it strength and purpose. Both nationalism and atheistic socialism, at least in the present state of human adjustments, must draw upon the psychological force of hate, suspicion, and resentment which tend to impoverish the soul of man and close up his hidden sources of spiritual energy. Neither the technique of medieval mysticism nor nationalism nor atheistic socialism can cure the ills of a despairing humanity. Surely the present moment is one of great crisis in the history of modern culture. The modern world stands in need of biological renewal. And religion, which in its higher manifestations is neither dogma, nor priesthood, nor ritual, can alone ethically prepare the modern man for the burden of the great responsibility which the advancement of modern science necessarily involves, and restore to him that attitude of faith which makes him capable of winning a personality here and retaining it hereafter. It is only by rising to a fresh vision of his origin and future, his whence and whither, that man will eventually triumph over a society motivated by an inhuman competition and a civilization which has lost its spiritual unity by its inner conflict of religious and political values.

As I have indicated before, religion as a deliberate enterprise to seize the ultimate principle of value and thereby to reintegrate the forces of one's own personality is a fact which cannot be denied. The whole religious literature of the world, including the records of specialists' personal experiences, though perhaps expressed in the thought-forms of an out-of-date psychology, is a standing testimony to it. These experiences are perfectly natural, like our normal experiences. The evidence is that they possess a cognitive value for the recipient, and, what is much more important, a capacity to centralize the forces of the ego and thereby to endow him with a new personality. The view that such experiences are neurotic or mystical will not finally settle the question of their meaning or value. If an outlook beyond physics is possible, we must courageously face the possibility, even though it may disturb or tend to modify our normal ways of life and thought. The interests of truth require that we must abandon our present attitude. It does not matter in the least if the religious attitude is originally determined by some kind of physiological disorder. George Fox may have been a neurotic, but who can deny his purifying power in England's religious life of his day? Mohammed, we are told, was a psychopath. Well, if a psychopath has the power to give a fresh direction to the course of human history, it is a point of the highest psychological interest to search his original experience which has turned slaves into leaders of men and has inspired the conduct and shaped the career of whole races of mankind. Judging from the various types of activity that emanated from the movement initiated by the Prophet of Islam, his spiritual tension and the kind of behaviour which issued from it cannot be regarded as a response to a mere fantasy inside his brain. It is impossible to understand it except as a response to an objective situation generative of new enthusiasms, new organizations, new starting points. If we look at the matter from the standpoint of anthropology it appears that a psychopath is an important factor in the economy of humanity's social organization. His way is not to classify facts and discover causes; he thinks in terms of life and movement with a view to creating new patterns of behaviour for mankind. No doubt he has his pitfalls and illusions just as the scientist who relies on sense-experience has his pitfalls and illusions. A careful study of his method, however, shows that he is not less alert than the scientist in the matter of eliminating the alloy of illusion from his experience.

The question for us outsiders is to find an effective method of inquiry into the nature and significance of this extraordinary experience. The Arab historian Ibn Khaldun, who laid the foundations of modern scientific history, was the first to seriously approach this side of human psychology, and reached what we now call the idea of the subliminal self. Later, Sir William Hamilton in England and Leibnitz in Germany interested themselves in some of the more unknown phenomena of the mind. Jung, however, is probably right in thinking that the essential nature of religion is beyond the province of analytic psychology. In his discussion of the relation of analytic psychology to poetic art he tells us that the process of artistic *form* alone can be the object of psychology. The essential nature of art, according to him, cannot be the object of a psychological method of approach. "A similar distinction," says Jung, "must also be made in the realm of religion; there, also, a psychological consideration is permissible only in respect of the emotional and symbolical phenomena of a religion, wherein the essential nature of religion is in no way involved, as indeed it cannot be. For were this possible, not religion alone but art also could be treated as a mere subdivision of psychology." Yet Jung has violated his own principle more than once in his writings. The result of this procedure is that instead of giving us a real insight into the essential nature of religion and its meaning for human personality, our modern psychology has given us quite a plethora of new theories which proceed on a complete misunderstanding of the nature of religion as revealed in its higher manifestations, and carry us in an entirely hopeless direction. The implication of these theories, on the whole, is that religion does not relate the human ego to any objective reality beyond himself; it is merely a kind of well-meaning biological device calculated to build barriers of an ethical nature round human society in order to protect the social fabric against the otherwise unrestrainable instincts of the ego. That is why, according to this newer psychology, Christianity has already fulfilled its biological mission, and it is impossible for the modern man to understand its original significance. Jung concludes:

Most certainly we should still understand it, had our customs even a breath of ancient brutality, for we can hardly realize in this day the whirlwinds of the un-

Is Religion Possible? 199

chained libido which roared through the ancient Rome
of the Caesars. The civilized man of the present day
seems very far removed from that. He has become
merely neurotic. So for us the necessities which brought
forth Christianity have actually been lost, since we no
longer understand their meaning. We do not know
against what it had to protect us. For enlightened people
the so-called religiousness has already approached very
close to a neurosis. In the past two thousand years
Christianity has done its work and has erected barriers
of repression which protect us from the sight of our own
sinfulness.

This is missing the whole point of higher religious life.
Sexual self-restraint is only a preliminary stage in the ego's
evolution. The ultimate purpose of religious life is to make
this evolution move in a direction far more important to
the destiny of the ego than the moral health of the social
fabric which forms his present environment. The basic
perception from which religious life moves forward is the
present slender unity of the ego, his liability to dissolution,
his amenability to re-formation and his capacity for an
ampler freedom to create new situations in known and unknown environments. In view of this fundamental perception, higher religious life fixes its gaze on experiences
symbolic of those subtle movements of reality which
seriously affect the destiny of the ego as a possibly
permanent element in the constitution of reality. If we
look at the matter from this point of view, modern psychology has not yet touched even the outer fringe of
religious life, and is still far from the richness and variety
of what is called religious experience. In order to give you
an idea of its richness and variety I quote here the substance of a passage from a great religious genius of the
seventeenth century—Sheikh Ahmad of Sarhand—whose
fearless analytical criticism of contemporary Sufiism re-
sulted in the development of a new technique. All the
various systems of Sufi technique in India came from
Central Asia and Arabia; his is the only technique which
crossed the Indian border and is still a living force in the
Punjab, Afghanistan, and Asiatic Russia. I am afraid it is
not possible for me to expound the real meaning of this
passage in the language of modern psychology, for such
language does not yet exist. Since, however, my object is
simply to give you an idea of the infinite wealth of experience which the ego in his Divine quest has to sift and

pass through, I do hope you will excuse me for the apparently outlandish terminology which possesses a real substance of meaning, but which was formed under the inspiration of a religious psychology developed in the atmosphere of a different culture. Coming now to the passage. The experience of one Abdul Momin was described to the Sheikh as follows:

> Heavens and Earth and God's throne and Hell and Paradise have all ceased to exist for me. When I look round I find them nowhere. When I stand in the presence of somebody I see nobody before me: nay even my own being is lost to me. God is infinite. Nobody can encompass Him; and this is the extreme limit of spiritual experience. No saint has been able to go beyond this.

On this the Sheikh replied:

> The experience which is described has its origin in the ever varying life of the *qalb*; and it appears to me that the recipient of it has not yet passed even one-fourth of the innumerable "Stations" of the "Qalb." The remaining three-fourths must be passed through in order to finish the experiences of this first "Station" of spiritual life. Beyond this "Station" there are other "Stations" known as *Ruh*, *Sirr-i-Khafi*, and *Sirr-i-Akhfa*; each of these "Stations," which together constitute what is technically called *Alam-i-Amr*, has its own characteristic states and experiences. After having passed through these "Stations" the seeker of truth gradually receives the illuminations of "Divine Names" and "Divine Attributes" and finally the illuminations of the Divine Essence.

Whatever may be the psychological ground of the distinctions made in this passage it gives us at least some idea of a whole universe of inner experience as seen by a great reformer of Islamic Sufiism. According to him this *Alam-i-Amr*, i.e., "the world of directive energy," must be passed through before one reaches that unique experience which symbolizes the purely objective. This is the reason why I say that modern psychology has not yet touched even the outer fringe of the subject. Personally, I do not at all feel hopeful of the present state of things in either biology or psychology. Mere analytical criticism with some under-standing of the organic conditions of the imagery in which religious life has sometimes manifested itself is not likely to carry us to the living roots of human personality. Assuming that sex-imagery has played a role in the history of religion, or that religion has furnished imaginative means of escape from, or adjustment to, an unpleasant reality, these ways of looking at the matter cannot, in the least, affect the ultimate aim of religious life, that is to say, the reconstruction of the finite ego by bringing him into contact with an eternal life-process, and thus giving him a metaphysical status of which we can have only a partial understanding in the half-choking atmosphere of our present environment. If, therefore, the science of psychology is ever likely to possess a real significance for the life of mankind it must develop an independent method calculated to discover a new technique better suited to the temper of our times. Perhaps a psychopath endowed with a great intellect—the combination is not an impossibility—may give us a clue to such a technique. In modern Europe Nietzsche, whose life and activity form, at least to us Easterns, an exceedingly interesting problem in religious psychology, was endowed with some sort of a constitutional equipment for such an undertaking. His mental history is not without a parallel in the history of Eastern Sufiism. That a really "imperative" vision of the Divine in man did come to him cannot be denied. I call his vision "imperative" because it appears to have given him a kind of prophetic mentality which, by some kind of technique, aims at turning its visions into permanent life-forces. Yet Nietzsche was a failure; and his failure was mainly due to his intellectual progenitors such as Schopenhauer, Darwin, and Lange whose influence completely blinded him to the real significance of his vision. Instead of looking for a spiritual rule which would develop the Divine even in a plebeian and thus open up before him an infinite future, Nietzsche was driven to seek the realization of his vision in such schemes as aristocratic radicalism. As I have said of him elsewhere:

The "I am" which he seeketh,
Lieth beyond philosophy, beyond knowledge.
The plant that groweth only from the invisible soil of
the heart of man,
Groweth not from a mere heap of clay!

Thus failed a genius whose vision was solely determined by his internal forces, and remained unproductive for want of expert external guidance in his spiritual life. And the irony of fate is that this man, who appeared to his friends "as if he had come from a country where no man lived," was fully conscious of his great spiritual need. "I confront alone," he says, "an immense problem: it is as if I am lost in a forest, a primeval one. I need help. I need disciples: I need a *master*. It would be so sweet to obey." And again: "Why do I not find among the living men who see higher than I do and have to look down on me? Is it only that I have made a poor search? And I have so great a longing for such."

The truth is that the religious and the scientific processes, though involving different methods, are identical in their final aim. Both aim at reaching the most real. In fact, religion, for reasons which I have mentioned before, is far more anxious to reach the ultimately real than science. And to both the way to pure objectivity lies through what may be called the purification of experience. In order to understand this we must make a distinction between experience as a natural fact, significant of the normally observable behaviour of reality, and experience as significant of the inner nature of reality. As a natural fact it is explained in the light of its antecedents, psychological and physiological; as significant of the inner nature of reality we shall have to apply criteria of a different kind to clarify its meaning. In the domain of science we try to understand its meaning in reference to the external *behaviour* of reality; in the domain of religion we take it as representative of some kind of reality and try to discover its meanings in reference mainly to the inner *nature* of that reality. The scientific and the religious processes are in a sense parallel to each other. Both are really descriptions of the same world, with this difference only that in the scientific process the ego's standpoint is necessarily exclusive, whereas in the religious process the ego integrates its competing tendencies and develops a single inclusive attitude resulting in a kind of synthetic transfiguration of his experiences. A careful study of the nature and purpose of these really complementary processes shows that both of them are directed to the purification of experience in their respective spheres. An illustration will make my meaning clear. Hume's criticism of our notion of cause must be considered as a chapter in the history of science rather than that of philosophy. True to the spirit of scientific empiricism we are not entitled to work with any concepts of a subjective nature. The point of Hume's criticism is to emancipate empirical science from the concept of force which, as he urges, has no foundation in sense-experience. This was the first attempt of the modern mind to purify the scientific process.

Einstein's mathematical view of the universe completes the process of purification started by Hume, and, true to the spirit of Hume's criticism, dispenses with the concept of force altogether. The passage I have quoted from the great Indian saint shows that the practical student of religious psychology has a similar purification in view. His sense of objectivity is as keen as that of the scientist in his own sphere of objectivity. He passes from experience to experience, not as a mere spectator but as a critical sifter of experience who by the rules of a peculiar technique, suited to his sphere of inquiry, endeavours to eliminate all subjective elements, psychological or physiological, in the content of his experience, with a view finally to reach what is absolutely objective. This final experience is the revelation of a new life-process—original, essential, spontaneous. The eternal secret of the ego is that the moment he reaches this final revelation he recognizes it as the ultimate root of his being without the slightest hesitation. Yet in the experience itself there is no mystery. Nor is there anything emotional in it. Indeed with a view to securing a wholly nonemotional experience the technique of Islamic Sufiism at least takes good care to forbid the use of music in worship and to emphasize the necessity of daily congregational prayers in order to counteract the possible antisocial effects of solitary contemplation. Thus the experience reached is a perfectly natural experience and possesses a biological significance of the highest importance to the ego. It is the human ego rising higher than mere reflection, and mending its transiency by appropriating the eternal. The only danger to which the ego is exposed in this Divine quest is the possible relaxation of his activity caused by his enjoyment of and absorption in the experiences that precede the final experience. The history of Eastern Sufiism shows that this is a real danger. This was the whole point of the reform movement initiated by the great Indian saint from whose writings I have already quoted a passage. And the reason is obvious. The ultimate aim of the ego is not to *see* something, but to *be* something. It is in the ego's effort to *be* something that he discovers his final opportunity to sharpen his objectivity and acquire a more fundamental "I am" which finds evidence of its reality not in the Cartesian "I think" but in the Kantian "I can." The end of the ego's quest is not emancipation from the limitations of individuality; it is, on the other hand, a more precise definition of it. The final act is not an intellectual act but a vital act which deepens the whole being of the ego and sharpens his will with the creative assurance that the world is not something to be merely seen or known through concepts, but something to be made and remade by continuous action. It is a moment of supreme bliss and also a moment of the greatest trial for the ego:

Art thou in the stage of "life," "death," or "death-in-life"?
Invoke the aid of three witnesses to verify thy "Station."
The first witness is thine own consciousness—
See thyself, then, with thine own light.
The second witness is the consciousness of another ego—
See thyself, then, with the light of an ego other than thee.
The third witness is God's consciousness—
See thyself, then, with God's light.
If thou standest unshaken in front of this light,
Consider thyself as living and eternal as He!
That man alone is real who dares—
Dares to see God face to face!
What is "Ascension"? Only a search for a witness
Who may finally confirm thy reality—
A witness whose confirmation alone makes thee eternal.
No one can stand unshaken in His Presence;
And he who can, verily, he is pure gold.
Art thou a mere particle of dust?
Tighten the knot of thy ego;
And hold fast to thy tiny being!
How glorious to burnish one's ego
And to test its lustre in the presence of the Sun!
Rechisel, then, thine ancient frame;
And build up a new being.
Such being is real being;
Or else thy ego is a mere ring of smoke!

Jawīd Nāma[1]

---

[1] A long poem by Iqbal himself, recently translated in its entirety by A. J. Arberry (London, 1966). [Ed.]

KING ABDULLAH: LAWRENCE AND CHURCHILL

[from *Mudhakkirātī*, My Memoirs]

By all accounts the first king of Jordan was an extremely canny and sensitive man. He was also very knowledgeable about Arabic poetry, and on several occasions bested some of Al-Mutannabi's finest lines, not an easy accomplishment. Perhaps he was not the favorite of his father's friends, and the kingdom he was asked to rule was difficult to define, but he proved himself every inch a king, and also a major moderate theorist of Arab nationalism. Ostensibly for that moderation and his friendship with the British, highlighted somewhat in the following selections from his well-written memoirs, he was assassinated as he left his prayers in the Aksa Mosque in Jerusalem on July 20, 1951.

We had been established at Wadi-Ais a week when twenty-seven camelmen under the command of Captain Lawrence arrived,[1] from my brother Faisal, to supervise the wrecking of the railway. I did not like his intervention as I was suspicious of his influence among the tribes. I explained, however, that he had come to damage the railway, that he was an engineer and that he represented our ally, Great Britain, but although these words made some impression, the general dislike of Lawrence's presence was quite clear. He tried to make contact with the tribes but could not do so because of the guard which was placed over him to prevent the Turks from killing him, and thus causing ill-feeling between us and the British. In Faisal's army, however, he had a free hand and through the money he spent and the words he talked became the uncrowned

[1]The date of Lawrence's arrival is given in *The Seven Pillars of Wisdom*, his autobiographical account which has been published in countless editions, as March 15, 1917.

king of the Arabs and was regarded as the moving spirit in the revolt.

He was certainly a strange character. His intrigues went as far as an attempt to influence me against my own father on the pretext that my father was obstinate.[2] I sent his messenger back with this reply: "Tell your friend that my father is my lord and king. I shall be content with this relationship to the end of my days." In fact Lawrence rendered the Arabs the greatest service by reiterating that my father was determined in his aims. Lawrence appeared only to require people who had no views of their own, that he might impress his personal ideas upon them.

The British attempt to support Ibn Saʾud was extremely well arranged. It should be remembered that Britain had undertaken to prevent any Amir who had connections with the Government of India from opposing the Arab revolt. On the other hand, the Arab leaders of the revolt were not to draw such Amirs into the Arab movement, for fear of complications with India. When Ibn Saʾud and his Wahabis violated the frontiers of the Hejaz, Britain declared her neutrality, and obliged Iraq and Transjordan to remain neutral too. Transjordan did all it could to assist Mecca, but Iraq withheld its support. This is an instance of Lawrence's activities against the Hashimites.[3]

We once sent a force to damage the railway, with Lawrence as explosives' expert. He returned dissatisfied with the result, and blamed the officer in command for not being willing to wait long enough. Even so a locomotive was blown up, a whole train damaged and eleven kilometres of the line put out of action. However, we were soon relieved of his presence, as he became ill and returned. I acknowledged his valuable services, but still did not like his interference.

At dinner we all assembled in the large hall, where I made the acquaintance of Mr. Winston Churchill. During

[2]On the subject of the relations between King Husain and his sons on the one hand and Lawrence on the other, Sir Ronald Storrs has written: "I myself incline to doubt whether King Husain ever loved Lawrence. There were moments when he and his sons suspected him of working against them, and more than once let fall hints . . . that he should not be allowed to mingle too much with Arab tribesmen. Faisal spoke of him to me with a good-humoured tolerance which I should have resented more if I had ever imagined that Kings would like King-makers."

[3]The Wahabi invasion of the Hejaz took place in 1924. Lawrence had left the Colonial Office and had ceased to have any hand in the shaping of British Near Eastern policy in 1922.

the conversation Mr. Churchill asked about what happened at Shajarah[4] (a small village in northern Transjordan).

"I hear there was an attack by a band of brigands and murder was committed. My Government attributes this to your influence, but luckily I have two broad shoulders to carry the Government's protest for you."

I said with a smile, "I thank Your Excellency, but this is the first I have heard of such an incident. I cannot, ever, of course, prevent people from defending their own country."

I looked at Ghalib Bey al-Shaalan and asked him about the incident. He rose from his seat, stood at attention and saluting me said, "This may have been an act of robbers, but as for people of our country, they are awaiting your orders."

Dinner was over, and cigarettes and cigars were offered. I took some snuff from a golden box enamelled green, with the rays of the setting sun in red. Mr. Churchill asked for the box, which then contained a French snuff called "Randah," and took some, sneezed and laughed. We fixed nine-thirty next morning for a meeting with Mr. Churchill.

The meeting took place as arranged. On the English side there were Mr. Winston Churchill, Sir Herbert Samuel, Mr. Deedes the Chief Secretary for Palestine, and Colonel Lawrence, while on the Arab side, there were Auni Abd al-Hadi and myself. The Colonial Secretary opened the conversation by mentioning the noble aims which had led Britain and the Arabs to join hands in the war, and the hopes placed in that spirit of co-operation during the war. He then mentioned how Britain had endeavoured to prevent the events that took place between France and the Arabs and went on to communicate his Government's advice to me.

Amir Faisal ibn Husain should leave Syria and put himself up as a candidate for the Kingship of Iraq, as France would never work with him. There were many candidates for the throne of Iraq, including Ibn Sa๖ud and Khaz๖al Khan. I should therefore influence my father to accept the nomination of Faisal and the people of Iraq to accept him. I myself should remain in Transjordan in full agreement with Great Britain and carry on a policy of appeasing the French. Mr. Churchill hoped that thus France would reconsider the position and he hoped that in six months

[4] Where there had been a collision with French police who seem to have crossed the ill-defined border.

he would be able to congratulate us on the return of Syria to our hands.

With regard to Palestine, he mentioned the Balfour Declaration and said that he could not discuss this matter, which would be left to the High Commissioner.

I said, "If you wish to nominate Amir Faisal to the throne of Iraq, I shall be pleased to use my influence to persuade both him and my father to take this course. But with regard to the people of Iraq, I cannot write to them as I have had no contacts with them."

He answered, "If you do not do so, you may lose everything, as it is possible that Ibn Saʾud may reach Mecca in three days, and England has done what she can."

I then said, "With regard to that, if the Arabs want to exchange one dynasty for another, that is their affair. But what is the position of Ibn Saʾud in the eyes of Britain today? Is he a King, a Sultan, a Sheikh of a tribe or what?"

He rose from his chair and walked over to the window, and with his left hand on his side, turned to Lawrence and said, "Tell the Amir that I cannot reply to his question before asking the Cabinet."

Then I said, "With regard to your advice, I quite agree, but I must submit it to the leaders of my country. They are with me here and I shall give you a reply tomorrow morning at the same hour. As for the people of Palestine, they refuse the Balfour Declaration and insist on the retention of the Arab character of Palestine. We shall not agree to the annihilation of the Arabs for the sake of the Jews. The Arabs are not like trees, which, when cut, grow again."

He said: "I am afraid I have tired you. I shall look forward to your reply tomorrow morning."

I feel I must say something now about the man who played so great and important a part during the two world wars, especially as concerns his attitude to the Arab cause while he was Colonial Secretary in the Government of Lloyd George.

Winston Churchill is unique among the men Great Britain has produced in recent times, and it fell to his lot to preserve the United Kingdom and the Empire by what seems like a miracle. He carried the burden of responsibility with complete awareness of Germany's strength and gigantic preparations, and of the hatred which every German had for Great Britain. He also knew that the

United Kingdom was unprepared as a result of the ill-judged policy of its Government from the fall of Lloyd George's Cabinet to the time of Chamberlain when the war began.

How many times did he warn his people about Germany! How prophetically he spoke without getting a proper hearing, till eventually he had to bear the burden of the very disasters of which he had given the nation so clear a warning. The British people had to endure enormous sacrifices and hardships during this terrible war, and without their loyalty and supreme efforts even a Churchill would have failed. England is a country which can bear every kind of misfortune and catastrophe, and in Churchill she found an effective leader of her quiet, hard-working, gentle and courageous people. She gave the whole world an example of true nationalism, of patient endurance, of defence in a righteous cause, of sacrifice of life and property in the interests of the country, of national pride and honour. Britain fully deserved the laurels of victory, and Churchill's leadership was an inspiration.

The retreat at Dunkirk was an example of courage and patience. The attack on the French fleet at Oran; the destruction of the Italian battleships at Taranto; General Wavell's campaign and the rout of Graziani; the annihilation of the Italian armies in Ethiopia and Eritrea; the preparations in Britain against a German invasion; the courage and sacrifice of the R.A.F.; the counterattacks on the enemy everywhere—all these are actions to be admired and marvelled at, the more so as these glorious deeds were not performed in one theatre of war only, but took place in theatres scattered all over the earth and the seven seas.

The heroic stand of Great Britain, fighting the Axis alone, before America entered the war, and before Hitler attacked Russia, vindicates the truth about England and her Prime Minister. Nothing but the determined defence of Britain made the Germans invade Russia, thinking that a decision could be obtained there.

Let me add that it was Mr. Churchill who urged me to arrange for my brother Faisal to become King of Iraq, while I remained in Transjordan and endeavoured by peaceful negotiations to recover the unity of Syria, and it was he who tried to bring about a reconciliation between my father and Ibn Saʾud.

In conclusion I wish the Arabs to realize that friendship with Britain involves alertness of spirit. Britain does not care for inefficiency, nor does she bestow her confidence on people who are untrustworthy or lacking in courage and resource. She does not believe in sentiment, but in realism and determination. Therefore be strong, loyal and alert and Britain will be with you and will put her trust in you.

TRANSLATED BY G. KHURI

SADEGH HEDAYAT: SOLITUDE

[from *Būf-i Kūr*, The Blind Owl]

Like some of his fellows, but hardly together with them, Sadegh Hedayat went to Belgium in 1926 to study engineering, and the following year moved to France to study architecture. There he began to write in a variety of forms, and returned to Iran to pursue a career in literature. Depressed by the literary censorship, he traveled in India in 1935–36. The Blind Owl, his most famous book, was first published in a limited edition in Bombay in 1936. Hedayat's reputation was increasingly enhanced within Iran and abroad by his prolific output thereafter.

Hedayat sought his themes in the lives of the common people of his own country. Stylistically he was heavily in debt to many European writers, although his pessimism and penchant for psychological analysis were not entirely derivative. He was much preoccupied with dreams and visions, and wrote essays on magic and primitive religion. In his hauntingly beautiful stories, somewhat reminiscent of Kafka (whom he admired) and others, he developed a strange and supple new form of prose in Persian.

There are sores which slowly erode the mind in solitude like a kind of canker.

It is impossible to convey a just idea of the agony which this disease can inflict. In general, people are apt to relegate such inconceivable sufferings to the category of the incredible. Any mention of them in conversation or in writing is considered in the light of current beliefs, the individual's personal beliefs in particular, and tends to provoke a smile of incredulity and derision. The reason for this incomprehension is that mankind has not yet discovered a cure for this disease. Relief from it is to be found only in the oblivion brought about by wine and in the artificial

211

sleep induced by opium and similar narcotics. Alas, the effects of such medicines are only temporary. After a certain point, instead of alleviating the pain, they only intensify it.

Will anyone ever penetrate the secret of this disease that transcends ordinary experience, this reverberation of the shadow of the mind, which manifests itself in a state of coma like that between death and resurrection, when one is neither asleep nor awake?

I retired as deep as I could into the depths of my own being like an animal that hides itself in a cave in the wintertime. I heard other people's voices with my ears; my own I heard in my throat. The solitude that surrounded me was like the deep, dense night of eternity, that night of dense, clinging, contagious darkness which awaits the moment when it will descend upon silent cities full of dreams of lust and rancour. From the viewpoint of this throat with which I had identified myself I was nothing more than an insane abstract mathematical demonstration. The pressure which, in the act of procreation, holds together two people who are striving to escape from their solitude is the result of this same streak of madness that exists in every person, mingled with regret at the thought that he is slowly sliding towards the abyss of death. . . .

Only death does not lie.

The presence of death annihilates all superstitions. We are the children of death and it is death that rescues us from the deceptions of life. In the midst of life he calls us and summons us to him. At an age when we have not yet learnt the language of men, if at times in our play it is that we may listen to the voice of death. . . . Throughout our life death is beckoning to us. Has it not happened to everyone suddenly, without reason, to be plunged into thought and to remain immersed so deeply in it as to lose consciousness of time and place and the working of his own mind? At such times one has to make an effort in order to perceive and recognise again the phenomenal world in which men live. One has been listening to the voice of death.

Lying in this damp, sweaty bed, as my eyelids grew heavy and I longed to surrender myself to non-being and everlasting night, I felt that my lost memories and forgotten fears were all coming to life again: fear lest the feathers in my pillow should turn into dagger blades or the buttons on my coat expand to the size of millstones; fear lest the breadcrumbs that fell to the floor should shatter into fragments like pieces of glass; apprehension lest the oil in the lamp should spill during my sleep and set fire to the whole city; anxiety lest the paws of the dog outside the butcher's shop should ring like horses' hoofs as they struck the ground; dread lest the old odds-and-ends man sitting behind his wares should burst into laughter and be unable to stop; fear lest the worms in the foot bath by the tank in our courtyard should turn into Indian serpents; fear lest my bedclothes should turn into a hinged gravestone above me and the marble teeth should lock, preventing me from ever escaping; panic fear lest I should suddenly lose the faculty of speech and, however much I might try to call out, nobody should ever come to my aid. . . .

I used to try to recall the days of my childhood, but when I succeeded in doing so and experienced that time again, it was as grim and painful as the present.

Other things which brought their contribution of anxiety and fear were my coughing, which sounded like that of the gaunt, black horses in front of the butcher's shop; my spitting, and the fear lest the phlegm should some day reveal a streak of blood, the tepid, salty liquid which rises from the depths of the body, the juice of life, which we must vomit up in the end; and the continuous menace of death, which smashes forever the fabric of the mind and passes on.

Life as it proceeds reveals, coolly and dispassionately, what lies behind the mask that each man wears. It would seem that everyone possesses several faces. Some people use only one all the time, and it then, naturally, becomes soiled and wrinkled. These are the thrifty sort. Others look after their masks in the hope of passing them on to their descendants. Others again are constantly changing their faces. But all of them, when they reach old age, realise one day that the mask they are wearing is their last and that it will soon be worn out, and then, from behind the last mask, the real face appears.

The walls of my room must have contained some virus that poisoned all my thoughts. I felt sure that before me some murderer, some diseased madman, had lived in it. Not only the walls of the room itself, but the view from the window, the butcher, the old odds-and-ends man, my nurse, the bitch and everyone whom I used to see, even the bowl from which I ate my barley broth and the clothes that I wore—all these had conspired together to engender such thoughts in my brain.

A few nights ago when I took off my clothes in a cubicle
at the bathhouse my thoughts took a new direction. As the
attendant poured water over my head I felt as though my
black thoughts were being washed away. I observed my
shadow on the steamy wall of the bathhouse. I saw that I
was as frail and thin as I had been ten years earlier, when
I was a child. I remembered distinctly that my shadow had
fallen then in just the same way on the wet wall of the
bathhouse. I looked down at my body. There was something lascivious and yet hopeless in the look of my thighs,
calves and loins. Their shadow, too, had not changed
since ten years before, when I was only a child. I felt that
my whole life had passed without purpose or meaning like
the flickering shadows on the bathhouse wall. Other people
were massive, solid, thick-necked. Doubtless the shadows
they cast on the steamy wall of the bathhouse were bigger
and denser and left their imprint for some moments after
they had gone, whereas mine was effaced instantaneously.
When I had finished dressing after the bath my gestures and
thoughts seemed to change again. It was as though I had
entered a different world, as though I had been born again
in the old world that I detested. At all events I could say
that I had acquired a new life, for it seemed a miracle to
me that I had not dissolved in the bath like a lump of
salt.

My life appeared to me just as strange, as unnatural, as
inexplicable, as the picture on the pen case that I am using
this moment as I write. I feel that the design on the lid of
this pen case must have been drawn by an artist in the
grip of some mad obsession. Often when my eye lights on
this picture it strikes me as somehow familiar. Perhaps this
picture is the reason why. . . . Perhaps it is this picture that
impels me to write. It represents a cypress tree at the foot
of which is squatting a bent old man like an Indian fakir.
He has a long cloak wrapped about him and he is wearing
a turban on his head. The index finger of his left hand is
pressed to his lips in a gesture of surprise. Before him
a girl in a long black dress is dancing. Her movements are
not those of ordinary people—she could be Bugam Dasi.
She is holding a flower of morning glory in her hand. Between them runs a little stream.

I was sitting beside my opium brazier. All my dark
thoughts had dissolved and vanished in the subtle heavenly
smoke. My body was meditating, my body was dreaming

and gliding through space. It seemed to have been released from the burden and contamination of the lower air and to be soaring in an unknown world of strange colours and shapes. The opium had breathed its vegetable soul, its sluggish, vegetable soul, into my frame, and I lived and moved in a world of vegetable existence. But as, with my cloak over my shoulders, I drowsed beside the leather ground sheet on which my brazier stood, the thought of the old odds-and-ends man for some reason came to my mind. He used to sit huddled up beside his wares in the same posture as I was then in. The thought struck me with horror. I rose, threw off the cloak and stood in front of the mirror. My cheeks were inflamed to the colour of the meat that hangs in front of butchers' shops. My beard was dishevelled. And yet there was something immaterial, something fascinating, in the reflection that I saw. The eyes wore an expression of weariness and suffering like those of a sick child. It was as though everything that was heavy, earthy and human in me had melted away. I was pleased with my face. I inspired in myself a certain voluptuous satisfaction. As I looked into the mirror I said to myself, "Your pain is so profound that it has settled in the depths of your eyes . . . and, if you weep, the tears will come from the very depths of your eyes or they will not come at all." Then I said, "You are a fool. Why don't you put an end to yourself here and now? What are you waiting for? What have you to hope for now? Have you forgotten the bottle of wine in the closet? One gulp, and there's an end of everything. . . . Fool! . . . You are a fool! . . . Here I am, talking to the air!"

The thoughts that came into my mind were unrelated to one another. I could hear my voice in my throat, but I could not grasp the meaning of the words. The sounds were mingled in my brain with other sounds. My fingers seemed bigger than normal, as always when the fever was on me. My eyelids felt heavy, my lips had grown thick. I turned round and saw my nurse standing in the doorway. I burst out laughing. My nurse's face was motionless. Her lustreless eyes were fixed on me, but they were empty of surprise, irritation or sadness. Generally speaking, it is ordinary stupid conduct that makes one laugh, but this laughter of mine arose from a deeper cause. The vast stupidity that I saw before me was part of the general inability of mankind to unravel the central problems of existence and that thing, which for her was shrouded in impenetrable darkness, was a gesture of death itself.

She took the brazier and walked with deliberation out of the room. I wiped the sweat from my forehead. My hands were covered with white flecks. I leaned against the wall, pressing my head to the bricks, and began to feel better. After a little I murmured the words of a song which I had heard somewhere or other:

"Come, let us go and drink wine;
Let us drink wine of the Kingdom of Rey,
If we do not drink now, when should we
    drink?"

When the crisis was coming upon me I could always feel its approach in advance and was filled with an extraordinary uneasiness and depression as though a cord had been tied tightly around my heart. My mood was like the weather before the storm breaks. At such times the real world receded from me and I lived in a radiant world incalculably remote from that of earth.

Then I was afraid of myself and of everyone else. I suppose this condition of mine was due to my illness, which had sapped my mental strength. The sight of the old odds-and-ends man and the butcher through the window filled me with fear. There was something frightening in their gestures and in their faces.

TRANSLATED BY D. P. COSTELLO

TALES FROM THE TRIBES

[from *Tales from the Arab Tribes, From Town and Tribe,* and *Told in the Market Place*]

> It would be a serious omission, indeed a misrepresentation, if this anthology did not include a generous helping of the folk literature, seldom written down, which has continued as a staple of life throughout almost all the Islamic world and has nourished many of its more sophisticated writers in modern times and long before.
>
> C. G. Campbell, who assembled the three volumes from which the following tales were selected, was an inveterate story hunter, and one of the most successful to ply his avocation in the central Islamic world since the compilers of the **Arabian Nights.** Unlike them, however, Campbell was not concerned about fitting the stories into any Chinese box pattern or cementing them together with any unifying numerological tale. They are given just as the translator recorded them, and are the basic raw material of past and present literary works.
>
> It is particularly fitting that these tales come from Iraq, Muscat, and Libya, which could not otherwise be well represented in this anthology.

The Story of the Two Dancers

Let it be written that the story was related by Hamed while we were awaiting the coming of the wild duck.

Once in Basra there was a dancing boy and a dancing girl and they were brother and sister. They were Circassians of great beauty, and they were slaves of a Turk who kept a dancing hall. So beautiful was their dancing that the great and noble Pashas and even the Wali of Basra himself would pay bags of gold to watch their dancing. And the

217

boy, whose name was Nasirulla, and the girl, whose name was Salma, were displeased at their situation, for whatever gold they earned, the Turk took it, and it appeared to them that they would remain forever slaves.

One day the boy Nasirulla said to his sister: Know you that a time will come when our beauty will fade, and then these mighty Pashas will no longer want to gaze at our dancing. Then will our Turkish master sell us to do manual work on the roads and fields, and they will work us so hard that we shall die in a few years in agony and misery. But as for our master, he will be rich from all this gold which he takes from us, and he will buy a house and live in it with his mistresses while we are starving, and this state of affairs is neither right nor is it just. The girl Salma replied: Indeed, you speak the truth, but how are we to escape from this Turk? For in the daytime he is watchful, and at night does he not chain us by the neck with an iron chain? And Nasirulla replied: We must kill this man. Salma turned pale and she said: Do you not know the penalties for slaves who kill their masters? And how will this benefit us, since they will find him dead and then they will commence to flog us? Anyway, how can you kill him, since you are only a weak boy?

Then Nasirulla said to her: Know you that I shall kill him, and when he is dead who will know of it? For the boys who serve the wines do not sleep in this house, and to them we can say, Our master is sick, and they will suspect nothing. And as for the visitors who come for entertainment, they never see our master. For do not we have to go to them and sit on their knees and kiss them and coax them until they give us gold. And indeed they little know that our master takes the gold off us when we get behind the screen. Salma agreed with the words of her brother and she said: Verily we should risk all and slay him.

The next day, when the dancing hall was closed for the night, Nasirulla took a mouse he had caught and he threw it in the great jar of wine, which had a neck as large as a wheel, and the mouse swam around in the wine, nor did it want to drown. Then Nasirulla called out to his master: Come and help me, for there is a mouse in the wine. And the Turk grew angry, for he thought: This is some trick of the boy to dip a bowl in the wine and steal some of it. So the Turk came over and he peered into the jar of wine. And as he was looking for the mouse in the jar, Nasirulla caught him a blow on the back of the head with an iron bar, and he fell forward stunned, with his head in the jar. Then

Nasirulla called his sister and together they lifted the legs of the Turk and they thrust him completely into the jar of wine. And upside down in the jar of wine the Turk met the Angel of Death. And Nasirulla and Salma took what gold they could find in the house and put it in their pockets. Yet it was not sufficient for them, for they did not know where the Turk kept his main hoard of gold.

The next night the boys who served the wine came to the dancing hall, and Nasirulla said to them: Know you that our master is sick, but you are to take the wine from the tap at the bottom of the jar as is your custom, and you will bring the money to me, for I am acting for our master, until, please God, it may be soon, he is recovered in health.

The boys drew the wine from the tap at the bottom of the jar, and they took it and gave it to the guests who were coming into the dancing hall. Then Nasirulla and Salma went out and they danced in a manner in which they had never danced before. And the Pashas and the Beys were amazed, for never had they seen such dancing, and they said one to the other: Never has the entertainment been so good as it is tonight, and even the wine tastes better and has more body to it.

And after their dance was finished Nasirulla and Salma went out and they sat on the knees of the Pashas and on the knees of the Beys and they kissed them and tickled their ears until they pulled out their bags of gold and they gave them money such as they had never given before. And that night when they closed the dancing hall Nasirulla and his sister counted their money and they said: If we can keep this up for one more week, then we shall have enough money to return to the Caucasus.

The next night the hall was even more crowded than it had been on the first night, for the Pashas and the Beys had told their friends of the excellence of the dancing and the quality of the wine. And again Nasirulla and Salma danced in the most exquisite manner and again they kissed and tickled the ears of the Ottomans and they received even more gold than before. And the noble Pashas and Beys said to each other: The wine at this hall gets better every night, and as for the dancing, there is none like it in the world.

And again on the third night and on the fourth night the dancing was perfect and the wine was getting richer and richer and Nasirulla and Salma collected much gold. But on the fifth night so many Turkish officers came to the hall that they could not all enter, and they quarrelled one

with the other and fought to get in and a noble Bey was
killed. And the Wali of Basra was informed of the affair.

On the morning of the sixth day soldiers came to the
cabaret and they asked Nasirulla: Where is Jamal Effendi,
the owner of this hall? Nasirulla's heart was full of fear and
he replied: Verily he has gone out to the market, nor do I
know when he will return. Then the Shawish in charge of
the soldiers said: We have been commanded by the Wali
to confiscate the wine of this hall, because it is said to be
of such quality that the officers of the garrison are fighting
with each other to get at it. And we have also been ordered
to take the dancing boy and the dancing girl who perform
here, for they have been inflaming the passions of the
garrison. But in future they will perform only before the
Wali himself.

Nasirulla's face went as pale as death, and he thought:
Now our secret is no longer a secret. But he said to the
Shawish: Know you that this wine is the finest wine in the
world, but it will spoil unless you have a large number of
men to move the jar. The jar must be kept vertical and
not shaken, for it is most delicate wine, and you must keep
the mouth of the jar tightly sealed, lest the cold air strike
the wine and spoil it. Then the Shawish went off to fetch
porters to take the jar of wine, and Nasirulla said to his
sister: Come, for we cannot delay further. Then Nasirulla
and Salma left the hall and they went out into the street,
and they took with them their gold.

When Nasirulla and Salma came out into the street the
time was day, and they thought: Wherever we go now we
will be seen by the people. It is better that we hide until
nightfall. So they slipped into a large warehouse which was
full of chests of Kuweit of enormous size. And Nasirulla
opened one of the largest chests and he found it full of
silk, so he emptied out the silk and hid it behind another
chest. Then he and Salma got in the chest and he closed the
lid, and with his knife he made a small hole that they might
breathe air within that chest.

And when they had been some time hidden in the chest,
Nasirulla and Salma heard footsteps approaching, and men
walked into the vault. And one man said to the other: Have
you packed the silks? The other man replied: Master, I
have packed them with my own hand in this chest. And
he tapped with his hand on the chest in which Nasirulla
and Salma were hiding. Then the master of the vault ordered: Rope the chest, and I will return in one hour with
the camels. But the servant said: Master, I must fetch

the porters to lift this chest before the rope can be passed around it, for alone I cannot lift it. And both the master and the servant left the store.

Salma was trembling with fear, and she said to Nasirulla: Let us escape before they return. But Nasirulla replied: Do not fear, for wherever this chest is going, we will go inside it. For it must be going a long way or they would not rope it, and any place is better for us than Basra. When the Wali finds the body of our master in his wine his brain will boil over even as the milk boils when it is left too long on the fire. But wait you here, and in two minutes I will return with bread and water, for this may be a long journey. And Nasirulla opened the box and he ran out into the street and he ran to a shop and he said: Give me bread and dates and cheese and take this gold. And Nasirulla bought a large bag and filled it with bread and dates and cheese, and he bought the largest bottle he could see and he filled it with water and ran back to his sister, and on the way back he bought two watermelons also. And Nasirulla got into the chest and he closed the lid, saying to his sister: Know you that these supplies may have to last us even for weeks, for perchance they are loading this chest onto a ship and sending it to India.

After a time the servant returned with porters, and they lifted the chest and roped it securely. Then they brought a camel, and loaded the chest and they set out. And Nasirulla and Salma heard the bells of many more camels and they said: This is no ship. Rather it is a caravan on the road to Baghdad. And for days and days the caravan marched, and at night it halted, and each day Nasirulla and Salma took only a sip of water, and a slice of watermelon and a few dates.

And when the days had joined to become a week the watermelons were finished, and when the weeks had joined to become a month, the water was finished, and only a few dates and a little cheese remained. And Nasirulla said to his sister: Know you that we were not on the road to Baghdad. Perchance we are on the road to Mecca through Busaiyir, or on the road to Syria by way of the desert. And Salma said: If we do not arrive within three days then I must call out to the camelmen that they release us, if only to kill us, for I am dying of thirst.

But the next day they heard around them the sounds of a large city and Nasirulla listened to the swearing and shouting of the people of the streets and he said: The tongue is Turkish. How have we arrived in Turkey without passing through a great city? This must be a special caravan carrying goods for the Sultan himself, that it has been able to halt away from the cities, and supplies of water and food have been sent out to be ready for it in the desert that it be not delayed.

The camels came to a halt and porters came and the great chest in which were Nasirulla and Salma was unloaded and carried by the porters for a long way, and finally it was set down on a stone floor. And Nasirulla and Salma knew not where they were. They heard a man come, and he cut the rope around the box, and he said in Turkish: I will go to summon the ladies that they may see the silks. And his voice was the voice of a eunuch. When the footsteps of the eunuch died away, Nasirulla opened the box and peered out, but there was nobody in sight.

So he and his sister staggered out of the chest, for they could scarcely walk from weakness, and they found themselves in a great hall, the walls of which were covered with marble and rare stones and with mirrors set in silver, and in the centre of the hall a fountain was playing. Nasirulla and Salma went to the fountain and they drank until their stomachs were filled. Then Nasirulla took his sister and said: Let us hide until we can find out what this place is, and how we can get out of it, for I do not suppose that it is closely guarded. And Nasirulla and Salma entered a small chamber which led off the main hall, and they found it crowded with the most beautiful dresses, made of rare cloths, and they were all for women, and there was not a single coat or cloak for a man in that room. Amongst the gowns and the dresses Nasirulla and Salma hid.

Then the eunuch returned to the large hall, and Nasirulla was amazed, for behind the eunuch followed hundreds and hundreds of the most beautiful girls, and the eunuch went up to the great chest and threw it open, and he cried: Ladies, see the latest chest of silks and fine cloths. But in the chest was only the skin of two watermelons, hundreds of date stones, an empty bottle and a smell of dirt, for verily Nasirulla and his sister had not left that box for over a month. And the ladies and the eunuch looked into the box and they were amazed what they saw. And the eunuch said: I will go to order the guards of the Palace to seize the camelmen that they may feel the bastinado until they die, for verily they have stolen the cloth which our Lord the Sultan had ordered for the ladies of his imperial harem.

Nasirulla heard the words of the eunuch and his heart

stopped through very fear, and he said to his sister: Do you know where we are? We are in the Harem of the Sultan himself, the most closely guarded place in the whole empire of the Ottomans, of which it is said that no man can enter it and no man can depart from it alive, and in this place there are only girls and eunuchs.

Nasirulla turned to the dresses in which they were hiding, and he took a dress which fitted him and he put it on, and his own clothes he hid. Salma also selected a new dress and put it on, for her dress was dirty, and after they had put on the dresses Nasirulla and Salma looked like sisters, nor could anyone who saw him tell that Nasirulla was a boy, for he wore his hair long after the fashion of the dancing boys, and his moustache was not grown.

Then they heard the eunuchs call out: Ladies, come to your food. Nasirulla turned to his sister and he said: Let us go and eat, for we are hungry. And Salma replied: What, shall we go amongst them? Nasirulla said: We will go and eat. There are many hundreds of girls here and two new faces will never be noticed amongst them.

So Nasirulla and Salma went out into the hall, and they went into another hall, which was even larger than the first, and in it was laid out a great feast. And they saw before them a hundred roast sheep, and a hundred roast peacocks, and many hundreds of chickens and ducks and pigeon and doves and partridges and quail, and from every direction hundreds of the most beautiful girls in the world were coming and sitting down to the meal and wine was brought for them by Negro slave girls.

Nasirulla and Salma sat down and ate of the feast until their stomachs were bursting, nor did anyone question who they were. And when all hands were withdrawn from eating, the Chief of the Eunuchs came round and he talked to some of the girls, and he came to Nasirulla and Salma and he said to them: Your faces are new. Were you part of the last present to our Lord? And Salma replied: Verily we are new here, and our desire is to be of service to our Lord and Master. But the eunuch sighed and he said: How can this be? It was different in the days when our master was a young man, though even then he rarely needed more than three hundred girls a year. But now he is old and his beard is white and his eyes are dim and even one girl would be too much for him. Yet we have three thousand in this place, and every month another hundred arrive as presents from the great rulers and governors, and these poor girls are condemned to live unloved and unseen in this vast harem, until they kiss and make love to each other from very sadness of heart.

And Nasirulla was amazed at the words of the eunuch, and he thought: While I am here and until I find a way out of this closely guarded place I will at least comfort some of these poor girls.

On the next day and on the following days Nasirulla examined all the doors and windows of the harem, but they were all guarded by eunuchs armed with swords, nor could anyone pass in or out. And the days lengthened into months, but Nasirulla could find no place unguarded save one, and this was a window which was covered by a grid of iron bars as thick as a man's wrist, and beneath the window was a lake, nor could anyone leave the window without swimming through the lake. And Nasirulla commenced to cut away at the bars, using diamonds and precious stones for the work, of which there was an abundance in the harem. But the cutting of each bar in such a manner that it could not be detected took weeks, and it was long before the work was nearing completion.

One day, just before Nasirulla had finished the cutting of the bars, Salma came to Nasirulla and her face was as pale as death, and she said to him: There is a rumour among the girls, and I believe this rumour to be true, that some eighty of them are become pregnant, and indeed they have children in their stomachs, and it is known that these cannot be the children of our Lord the Sultan. And after a short time these children will become known and they will become apparent even to the Chief Eunuch himself, and when that happens there will be such investigations and such floggings and tortures and executions that the fountain in this harem will spray only blood. And when Nasirulla heard the words of his sister he turned faint with fear, and he thought: Can such great consequences come from such little cause?

Then Nasirulla took his sister and they went to the window and they finished the cutting of the remaining bar. And in the lake beneath the window Nasirulla saw two naked boys, who were in the sixteenth year of their life, and they were swimming and amusing themselves in the water. Nasirulla said to his sister: We must get these boys out of the way and we must steal their clothes, for if we dive now into the water they may raise the alarm, and if we land from the lake in wet clothes, then we shall attract attention. And verily we cannot walk through the city in the silken dresses of the harem.

Salma realised the truth of her brother's words, and she saw the clothes of the boys, which were lying safe and dry on the far bank of the lake. So Salma called out to the boys, and they saw the faces of two beautiful girls at the window, for they knew not that Nasirulla was a boy, and they swam over to beneath the window, and Salma said to them: We are two and you are two, come up here and play.

And the boys replied: How can we do this when that window is covered by bars as thick as a man's arm? And is not that the Imperial Harem, the penalty for entering which is death by torture? Salma said: Do not fear. Just swarm up the wall and we will loosen the bars, nor will anyone see you, for the eunuchs never come to this window, as it is considered secure. And when you are inside we will hide you in a small chamber where none can see you, then let us amuse ourselves for an hour, and then you can return to the lake and to your clothes. And the boys thought: Verily there is no danger, and what a jest it will be to go into the Sultan's harem itself.

So they clambered out of the water and up the wall, and they were in a naked condition. Nasirulla and Salma loosened the bars and let the boys in and led them to a small chamber which had only one door and no windows, and they said: Here we can amuse ourselves unseen. And Nasirulla and Salma said to the boys: Wait here while we look around the corners and see that the eunuchs are sleeping peacefully. But when Nasirulla and Salma were outside the door, they shut it and drove home a great bolt which secured that door from the outside, and the two boys were left prisoners in that room.

Then Nasirulla and Salma stripped off their clothes and they dived into the water and swam over the lake to the clothes of the boys, and Nasirulla had tied around his waist a rope to which was tied much gold and rare jewels. And Nasirulla and Salma reached the clothes of the boys and they put them on and they became as two boys, for their long hair they wrapped in the turbans of the boys.

And as for the boys they sat in the small chamber and they said: How sportive are these girls, for they have locked the door on us. This is indeed a fine joke. But the minutes passed and passed and the boys became cold, for they were wet and naked, and they began to fear, for they thought: This is the Sultan's harem, and it is no place to be caught in through some foolish girlish trick. But the girls did not return and the boys sat naked and shivering with fear and an hour passed.

And out in the main courtyard of the harem the Chief Eunuch sat with his assistants who were not guarding the doors and he was watching some of the girls washing at a fountain. And he said to his comrades: Are not some of the figures of the girls changing, or do my eyes play me tricks? And the eunuchs answered: Verily your thoughts are our thoughts, and we have also seen many girls lately who are red-eyed from weeping. There is truly some matter here which requires investigation.

Then the Chief Eunuch sent for a wise woman and she came and examined the girls, and she said to the Eunuch: Verily these girls are blessed with children. The Chief Eunuch was horrified at the words of the wise woman, and he thought: Who can be the father of these children? It cannot be the Sultan our master, nor can he be from us the eunuchs, and apart from us there are only girls here, nor can a man enter this place. So he ordered two of the eunuchs to take one of the girls and they tied her up by her thumbs to the beam of the ceiling, and the Chief Eunuch said: There shall you remain until your thumbs pull out from your hands or until you tell us the truth of this matter. And the girl stayed for twenty minutes until she screamed out in agony, and she said: Know you that by magic, in the night, one of the girls in this harem becomes a boy, and she is one of the two Circassian sisters who are so much alike, and though in the daytime she is as a girl, yet at night she is a boy, and there is no doubt about this whatever.

The Chief Eunuch ordered the eunuchs: Go and fetch me the two Circassian sisters who are so alike. And they went off and they searched, but they returned and said: We cannot find them. The Chief Eunuch ordered them to go again and to search every room and every chamber in the great building of the harem. And they went and they searched and searched and they came to the chamber in which were the two naked boys, and they opened the door of that chamber and they found them within it, and they took them and chained them and brought them in front of the Chief Eunuch.

And the two boys wept and implored mercy from the Chief Eunuch, but he showed them no mercy. He commanded that they be tied by their thumbs to the beam of the ceiling, and that thing was done to them. He then ordered the eunuchs to flog them with whips until their lives were ended, for he thought: How can I show mercy when my own life is now in the most terrible danger?

And when the two boys were dead, the wise woman came to the Chief Eunuch and said: Verily, eighty of the girls in this harem are in a condition of pregnancy. The heart of the Chief Eunuch stopped beating from very horror, and he thought: Now my royal master will end my life. And he thought and thought and a way appeared open to him, and he said to himself: I will announce this to the Sultan in open court, then through very shame he cannot confess that he is not able to have fathered these children.

So the next morning the Chief Eunuch went to the Royal Diwan, and there in the presence of the great ministers and generals and the distinguished people of the country he announced in a high voice: Majesty, eighty of the ladies of your harem are blessed with children. And those sitting in the court were amazed, for the beard of the Sultan was white and his eyes were dim and he dribbled down his beard. And the Sultan said nothing to the Chief Eunuch. However, when the court was over the Sultan retired to a private chamber and he sent for his secretary, whom he trusted, and he said: Kill the Chief of my Eunuchs and take his body and bury it and let it be known in the court that he has died of sickness. And the secretary obeyed the orders of his master the Sultan.

And as for Nasirulla and Salma, when they had put on the clothes of the boys, they went into the city, and Nasirulla purchased weapons and two horses of the finest stock and six baggage ponies and they loaded them with supplies and they set out that very night for their own country, nor did they desire to linger in the lands of the Turks, and after many weeks of travel they arrived in safety. And Nasirulla married a wife and he gave his sister Salma in marriage, and when in the winter evenings he used to go to the wineshop and drink with his friends, he would say to them: Know you that I have eighty children. But they did not believe his words.

The Story of the Ass Which Became a Judge

Once a Shawi came to the town, and he had with him his ass loaded with grass for sale in the bazaar. And as he was passing the school he heard the teacher hitting and belabouring the boys and cursing them, even as he was hitting and cursing his ass, so he stopped to listen and he heard the teacher say: O you who think you are humans, there is no brain in your heads, there is only an empty space with a wind whistling through it. O that they had sent me donkeys to teach instead of boys, for I am such a good teacher that I could teach a donkey to read and write in a single day, and I would teach him to be more human than you; but you I cannot teach, for you have not the brains of a donkey.

And the Shawi was amazed at the words of the teacher, and he thought: The Muallim must be a magician if he can teach a donkey to read and write, and make him human, and it is true that there are many magicians in this town. Why should he not make my donkey into a clerk, so that I can receive his pay and become rich, instead of earning but a dollar a month carrying grass. So the Shawi went in to the teacher, and he led him aside and offered him money, saying: Teach my donkey to read and write, and make him human.

And the Muallim said to the Shawi: Give me fifteen dollars and I will teach your donkey to read and write and I will make him human. But do you beat your donkey? And the Shawi said: I beat him if he loiters by the way. But why do you ask this? And the teacher replied: Since you beat him he will hate you, and when he is human you will not be able to recognise him, and he will deny that he is your donkey and become angry and kick you. Is there any mark on your donkey by which you can recognise him? So the Shawi looked at his donkey and said: See this circle and line branded on his flank; by this shall I recognise him. And the Shawi left the donkey with the teacher, who said: Come tomorrow and take your human being.

And when the Shawi was gone the teacher, for he was not numbered amongst those who are honest, took the donkey and sold him in the bazaar, but the pack saddle and harness he kept. And the Shawi spent the night dreaming, thinking: My days of toil are over, for tomorrow I shall get my donkey a job as a clerk, and he will bring me his salary, and I shall live handsomely on it.

And when the morning came the Shawi went to the Muallim and asked him: Is the donkey human? And the teacher said: Indeed he is human, and possessed of the keenest brain and the finest intellect, for, know you, when I had transformed him into human shape and completed his education I heard that the king had summoned the wisest men in the country for a test, for he wished to appoint a judge to the court in this town, and I sent your donkey along with those that desired to take the test. And such was my teaching that your donkey came out first in the test, therefore he is now Qadhi and administers the law in this town. Therefore take his saddle and bridle, for now he does not require them, but give me twenty dollars more, for I had to buy him clothes suitable for a judge. And the Shawi asked: What is the salary of a judge? And the Muallim replied: A hundred dollars a day, and not less. Also, he can charge the petitioners in his court such fees as he may deem suitable, therefore you are now a wealthy man. But first you must make him realise he is your donkey, for he is but an ass and now believes himself human, therefore he may deny his state. And the Shawi said: In this there is no difficulty. How often have I not compelled that donkey to obey me when he refused to carry a load or when he loitered by the way. So the Shawi went off to the court of the Qadhi and his heart was full of joy.

As the Shawi came near to the door of the great court he heard a great noise and commotion, and the door of the court was flung open and two men were flung from it into the dust, and Negroes followed them, beating them with sticks. And the Shawi walked up to the men and helped them to their feet, shaking the dust from their clothes, and he asked and sympathised with them touching their situation. And the men replied to the Shawi and said: It was only that we called the Qadhi in that court an ass, for verily his ruling was that of a donkey. But he became inflamed with rage and his eyes grew red, and he summoned his guards and they beat us and flung us from the court. The Shawi answered them, saying: You did right in calling him a donkey, for a donkey he is, and I am his master, and I will soon make him repent and reverse his decision in your favour. And the men were amazed at the words of the Shawi, so they questioned him until they had learnt all that had happened between him and the Muallim; yet they did not laugh, for they were of those that are called Ayar, foxes who live by their brains off other men.

And one of the Ayar said to the Shawi: It is as you say, yet I think that if you tell him he is your donkey he will hit you, for he is mad with rage. How can you prove he is your donkey? The Shawi replied: Did you not see the mark of a circle and a line on his flank. This is my mark and by it I prove him mine. And the trickster answered: I saw no mark, for he was clothed in his robes and his cloak, but leave the affair in my hands and say only that which

230 MODERN ISLAMIC LITERATURE

I whisper to you, then shall you have your proof. Then one Ayar whispered with the other Ayar and they discussed the affair in confidence. And one of the tricksters went off to the palace of the king of the country, and the other Ayar muffled his face in his headcloth, and entered the court with the Shawi, saying: That which I whisper, that shall you say.

And the Ayar and the Shawi entered the court and took their place with the petitioners, and it came about that the Qadhi asked of the Shawi: What is your complaint in this high court? And the Shawi listened to the whispers of the Ayar and answered: Learned Qadhi, my donkey is strayed and some felon has covered him with cloth, and I require only from Your Excellency an Order that the cloth be removed and his flank examined for the mark, that I may prove him mine. And I request that the examination may take place in this very court before the witnesses and people of the court, and I request that the Order be written in the king's name. And the Qadhi said: In this there is no difficulty, for the removal of the cloth will facilitate justice and it will identify the donkey. So the Qadhi wrote: Bismillah, By the High Authority of His Majesty the King I do hereby command that the cloth be removed from the flanks of whatsoever the Shawi claims to be his donkey, and that in this very court in the presence of witnesses and the people of the court. And the Qadhi signed the paper and sealed it with his great seal and handed it to the Shawi.

Then the Qadhi asked the Shawi: What is the mark on the flanks?

And the Ayar whispered to the Shawi: Do not say a line and a circle, for perchance the mark is changed by magic. Say merely "Two." That is, one line and one circle, and one and one makes two. So the Shawi said: My mark is Two.

Meanwhile, the other Ayar went into the presence of the king of that country, for he knew the king loved a wager, and he saluted him and said: O king, is there a law in the country that the Qadhi must remove his pants in the presence of the people of the court or break the law? And the king said: This is impossible. It can never happen thus. And the Ayar said: O king, I wager you one thousand dollars that it is indeed so. And the king was astonished, but he agreed to the wager of the Ayar, and they left together for the court of the Qadhi.

When the king entered the court of the Qadhi the people arose and saluted him, but he bade them be seated, and he ordered the Qadhi to continue the work of the court. And the Qadhi said to the Shawi: Bring that which you suspect to be your donkey, that it may be uncovered and the truth revealed. And the Shawi said: O Qadhi. You are my donkey. Remove your clothes that I may see my mark of two. And the Qadhi was amazed with the words of the Shawi and he grew white with anger. But the Ayar took the Order from the Shawi and showed it to the king, who was astonished when he read the Order, but he said: The Order is clear. The Qadhi must remove his pants. And the Qadhi, though he went red from shame and anger, was compelled by the king to lift his robe and take down his pants in the presence of witnesses and in open court, in accordance with the Order. And the king demanded of the Shawi: Do you recognize your donkey?

And the Ayar whispered to the Shawi, and he spoke out and said: It is indeed he, for this donkey has a near flank and an off flank and one and one make two and my mark is two.

Then said the king: Take your donkey and put him in a stall and feed him with grass, for verily only a donkey would have written that Order which this Qadhi wrote. Thus it came about that the Qadhi was tethered in a stall and fed only with barely and grass, but as for the Shawi, he wept, saying: Before, my donkey was good and useful, but now he is become but a poor thing; for he cannot carry twenty maunds of firewood, and whenever I try to get him employment as a clerk men shake their heads and say: Take him away for we do not want him, since this donkey is as stupid as a judge.

The Story of the Fisherman and of the Daughter of the Sea

Once, in ancient times, there was a fisherman named Mohammed Ali el Berki, who used to live in a town which stood on the shore beside the sea, as if, as you might say, in Benghazi. And every day Mohammed Ali used to take a boat and row far out into the sea, and throw his net and take in fish. And every day he would take his catch of fish and sell it in the market, and with the money he would buy eleven flaps of bread, and some meat, and a few vegetables, such as carrots and tomatoes and parsley and cucumbers, and he would return with his provisions to his house, and his wife would cook a stew and they would eat, each one flap of bread and a little of the stew, for they were eleven in that house. There was Mohammed Ali, and his wife and they had nine children, and every child was a boy.

It came about that the wife of Mohammed Ali again became heavy with child, and, as the moon ripened to fulness, she brought forth a child, a girl. And Mohammed Ali was amazed that he had a girl, a daughter, since all his children were boys, but he went down to the sea, and he took his net, and he took his boat and he went out to fish, saying: I will see what luck this daughter has brought with her. And when he reached a place far from the shore he cast his net into the sea and he pulled it again from the sea. But in the net was something so heavy that he could not draw it out from the sea, and he pulled and pulled for many an hour, and he rowed towards the shore towing the net behind him, since he could not lift it out of the water. And when he reached shallow water he got out of the boat and inspected his net and he found in it a dead donkey, and he said: Verily this is the luck of a girl.

And Mohammed Ali returned to the town with his heart heavy with grief, and as he passed the oven he smelt the smell of the baking bread, and he halted, that the smell might enter his lungs, for he was hungry and he had no money with him.

And the baker came to open the oven, and he saw that Mohammed Ali was savouring the smell of the baking bread, and he took eleven flaps of bread to give to the fisherman, for, he said: Are you not eleven in your house, since every day you take eleven flaps?

And Mohammed Ali's mouth watered for the bread, but he said: Alas! Alas! Now we are twelve, though the twelfth is but a drinker of mother's milk, for there is born to me a daughter, and today I threw my net in her name that I might see what luck she brought me, and her luck was a dead donkey, so I have no money to buy bread and to-night my children will cry out in hunger.

But the baker was numbered amongst the generous, for he said: Take eleven flaps of bread even as you always take them, and take also twelve silver dollars, one for each of you, that you may buy provisions and stores for your house, and tomorrow, if, please God, your luck is good, you may give me the money, and a gift of a fish besides. And Mohammed Ali thanked the baker exceedingly, and he took the bread and the money, and he went to the Market of Greenstuffs and to the Market of Meat and he bought provisions for his house, then he set out for his home. And the house of Mohammed Ali was not far and not near to the town, as if, as you might say, as far as Berqa is from Benghazi. So after walking for a time he came to his home and he greeted his wife, and his children cried out to him, saying: What is the luck of our new sister, O our father? And he replied, saying: Verily her luck is a dead donkey!

Mohammed Ali gave the provisions to his wife, and he said: Verily we eat through the generosity of the baker, for the luck of my daughter is a dead donkey. And Mohammed Ali and his children ate of the food, and they thanked God and they praised the baker, and they said: If it please God, our luck will change on the morrow, for the luck of this baby must be more than a dead donkey!

On the next day Mohammed Ali went again to the sea, and again he threw his net in the name of his new daughter and on her luck, and again something was caught in the net, and Mohammed Ali found that he had caught a dead dog. So he grieved with exceeding grief, thinking: The luck of my daughter is but dead donkeys and dead dogs. And he returned to the shore and he went to the baker and he said: Today I cannot repay you, for the luck of my daughter was but a dead dog. Yet the baker was a charitable man, and generous, for he said: It matters not. Take eleven flaps of bread and twelve silver dollars more, and repay me when your luck changes! And the fisherman thanked the baker exceedingly, and he bought provisions from the market and he returned to his home, and he said to his wife and to his children: The luck of the girl was but a dead dog, and we eat through the generosity of the baker.

And the next day and the next day it happened in a like manner, and Mohammed Ali the Fisherman caught dead donkeys and dead dogs and dead cats and dead goats and dead hyenas, and he dumped them on the shore.

And on the seventh day he went again to the sea and he cast his net for the last time on the luck of his daughter, and he felt something heavy catch in the net and he drew it forth. Then verily he was amazed with the greatest of amazements, for in the net was a woman of exceeding beauty, yet she had no legs, but the tail of a fish, and with her a girl like the moon, whose skin was as the golden sand, whose hair was as the night, whose lips were ruby-red, yet she also was legless, and her tail was that of a fish. Then Mohammed Ali fell back in his boat from amazement and surprise. But the woman, the elder of the two, spoke to him and said: O Mohammed Ali el Berki! O Mohammed Ali el Berki! Do you not fear! And Mohammed

Ali, though he was shaking with astonishment and surprise, said: Who are you? Who are you? And whose daughter are you? And the woman replied: Do not ask of my father, for no human can say his name, but, know you, I am the Bride of the Sea and this girl is Marjan, and she is daughter to the King of the Sea! And Mohammed Ali was overcome with awe when he knew he had caught the Bride of the Sea, with her power to sink ships and drown sailors, and he said: Forgive me and pardon me, for I threw the net without intent, desiring only fish, and by some mishap I have caught you in my net! Then Mohammed Ali released the Bride of the Sea and the Daughter of the King of the Sea from the net. And Mohammed Ali saw that the fish-girl was as a moon, and he could not withdraw his eyes from gazing at her beauty, and she also looked at him, seeing him handsome.

Then the Bride of the Sea spoke and said: Our ransom shall be a boatload of pearls, and diamonds and turquoise and other jewels of the sea. Mohammed Ali said: I want nothing but your pardon, that I caught you in error. But the Bride of the Sea said: Our ransom shall be paid! And the Bride of the Sea was of a mind to swim away and to leave the fisherman, but the girl Marjan lingered, and she said: Will you not bring me some fruits of the land at this very place tomorrow. For I have never tasted the fruits of the land, and I hear that they are sweet.

The heart of Mohammed Ali grew glad when he knew that he would see the fish-girl Marjan again, and he promised her the fruits of the land on the morrow. Then Mohammed Ali rowed towards the shore, but when he was halfway to the shore fish-boys came, swimming like fish in the sea, and they had a great store of pearls and diamonds and turquoise, and they called out: O Mohammed Ali el Berki! Take these jewels, a gift from our mistress, the Bride of the Sea. And Mohammed Ali took pearls and diamonds from the hands of the fish-boys until his boat was heavily laden and near to sinking, and he said to the Pages of the Sea: Stop! For I can take no more! And he thanked the fish-boys with exceeding thanks and he went onwards to the shore.

And when he reached the shore he pulled up his boat on the beach, as if, as you might say, on the beach at Benghazi, and he called for a donkey and he loaded the jewels in sacks on the donkey and he carried them to the richest of the jewellers of that town, and he sold the jewels for a great price in gold. Then he went to the

baker, to that generous man, and he gave him a hundred
pieces of gold, and the baker was astonished at his wealth
and munificence.

Then he went to his home and he showed his wife and
his sons the gold, saying: The luck of today is not a dead
donkey! And he gave his eldest son a sack of gold, saying:
Buy me a new house, and hire servants and cooks, and
buy twenty sheep and kill them and bid the cooks to prepare them for our supper!

And the next day Mohammed Ali el Berki took donkeys
and he went to the fruit market, and he bought sack upon
sack of apples and peaches and pomegranates and grapes,
and he loaded them in a boat and carried them out into
the sea, to that place which the Bride of the Sea had appointed, and yet he took no man or sailor to help him,
that his meeting might be a secret.

And when he reached that secret place in the sea he
drew his oars into the boat and he waited. And after, perhaps, as you might say, an hour, perhaps longer, he saw
two handsome boys of the sea come riding on the waves.
And behind them, couched between two waves came
the Bride of the Sea and the Daughter of the King of the
Sea, with a host of servants and retainers. And Mohammed
Ali el Berki greeted them with the best of salutations, and
they replied: Mohammed Ali el Berki! Mohammed Ali el
Berki! Give us of the fruits of the land!

Mohammed Ali el Berki gave peaches to the Bride of
the Sea and to the Princess Marjan of the Sea, and they
ate of the fruit, and they said: Never have we tasted the
like of this before! And the Princess Marjan implored
Mohammed Ali to take the rest of the fruit to her father,
the King of the Sea, and she looked at him with eyes full
of pleading and desire, and she said: Never has the King
my father tasted such fruit and never have I seen a man
with two legs before! And Mohammed Ali el Berki gazed
at the girl Marjan and at the yearning in her eyes, and he
forgot his wife and he forgot his sons and even his
daughter he forgot!

So Mohammed Ali el Berki allowed the fish-boys and the
youths of the sea to harness ropes to his boat and he
travelled with the Bride of the Sea and with the girl
Marjan at a great speed over the surface of the sea, for the
fish-boys who towed his boat travelled faster than fishes,
having the tails of fish and the arms of boys. And when
they had gone, as you might say, for an hour, they came to
a place in the middle of the sea, and the Bride of the Sea

commanded them to halt. Then the boys of the sea took
hold of Mohammed Ali and began to remove his clothes,
but Mohammed Ali cried out to them in fear and alarm.
And the Bride of the Sea said: Your clothes must be taken
from you, for they will spoil in the salt water, since now
we go down to the Palace of the King of the Sea! But
Mohammed Ali was a man of the land, and he feared
greatly to go naked even as the Bride of the Sea and the
Princess Marjan of the Sea and her Pages and fish-boys
went naked, so he clutched with one hand at his garments
and he stuck a finger in his mouth and he said: This cannot
be! This cannot be! For how can I come with you without
pantaloons? And the Bride of the Sea saw that he was a
man of the land and not as were the people of the sea,
so she had compassion on him, and she struck Mohammed
Ali's boat with her staff, saying a magic spell, and she said:
Let everything in this boat be in the sea and under the
sea even as it was on the land and over the land, and let
nothing be harmed by the sea and let nothing be drowned
by the sea! Then the Pages of the Sea took the fruits and
provisions from the ship and dived into the sea, knowing
that the fruit would not lose its sweetness in the saltness of
the sea. And the fish-boys took Mohammed Ali el Berki
and they dived with him beneath the waves, and he was
amazed, for the water did not fill his lungs and did not
wet his clothes, and he breathed as easily as if he were on
land and over the land.

And Mohammed Ali el Berki was carried by the fish-
boys down and down into the sea, until he saw before
him a great palace made of green crystal and of mother-of-
pearl, and he entered the palace and he saw the King of
the Sea sitting in majesty and in state, and he saw fishes
and sea creatures and Jinn and spirits of the sea bring pearls
and diamonds and rare stones to pay as tribute. And the
King of the Sea returned the greeting of Mohammed Ali el
Berki and bade him to be seated. And the Bride of the
Sea entered and she gave of the fruits of the land to the
King of the Sea, and she said: This sailor has brought us
sweet fruits, and he released me and he released your
daughter when we were tangled in his net and within his
power, therefore should you reward him with the greatest
of rewards. And the King of the Sea ate of the fruit and
he saw that it was sweet, and he gave of the fruits to the
Queen of the Sea, and she also became pleased with the
sweetness of the fruit, and the King of the Sea spoke and
said: Let Mohammed Ali el Berki be given my daughter's

hand in marriage, that he may be rewarded for the graciousness of his conduct and for the nobleness of his character, and this is the greatest reward that we can give him!

Now who can refuse a command from the lips of the King of the Sea. And more, Mohammed Ali el Berki had forgotten his wife, and his nine sons, and he had even forgotten his daughter, for he had never seen such beauty as was the beauty of the girl Marjan before, not even, as you might say, in all Benghazi and in all of Tripoli. So the fisherman Mohammed Ali consented to the words of the King of the Sea, and he thanked him with exceeding thanks for his generosity and his munificence.

Then the King of the Sea commanded that a palace be built for Mohammed Ali el Berki, and the slaves and attendants of the King of the Sea built for him a palace of marble and emerald and crystal and garnet, and Mohammed Ali the Fisherman took the fish-girl Marjan to wife and he took her to bed.

And Mohammed Ali el Berki lived with his mermaid wife in happiness and in love, and he had no thought for the land. And as for food, they ate of the foods of the sea, which were many in variety and delicious in taste, but they were always cold, since who could light a fire under the sea, and sometimes, as they ate of the food, Mohammed Ali el Berki remembered the taste of roasting lamb and of hot rice, but again, when he took the girl Marjan in his embrace he forgot the taste of meat. And yet, one day as they were eating, Mohammed Ali el Berki exclaimed and said: Roast sheep's meat is hot on the fingers and it crackles on the tongue. And the girl Marjan exclaimed: I want roast sheep. Bring some for me!

And, though Mohammed Ali el Berki did not wish to leave his palace or to leave his wife of the sea, the girl Marjan drove him out, saying: Bring me roast sheep! Mohammed Ali, since he had perforce to go to the land, was of a mind to take presents to his wife and to his nine sons, and even to his only daughter, for their memory returned to him when he thought of the land. So he said to his wife of the sea: Bring me, then, twelve sacks of diamonds and of emeralds, for I must take them as presents to my brothers and to my mother who are living on the land. The girl Marjan commanded the fish-boys to load twelve sacks with jewels from her father's treasury, and they put their hands to that labour.

Now when Mohammed Ali had brought the fruits of the

land from the shore, there was, in one of the sacks, a single he-rat, yet Mohammed Ali knew it not. And there was, on that he-rat, a single he-flea, and yet Mohammed Ali knew nothing of the affair. And when the Bride of the Sea struck the ship of Mohammed Ali with her staff, crying: Let everything in this boat be in the sea and under the sea even as it was on the land and over the land, and let nothing be harmed by the sea, and let nothing be drowned by the sea, the buck rat and the he-flea heard her words and came beneath her spell, and they did not drown in the sea, nor were they harmed by it and they lived beneath the water even as they had lived on land, the buck rat eating of the fruit and the he-flea eating of the buck rat. But neither of them were happy, for the buck rat could find no doe and the he-flea could find no she-flea beneath the waters of the sea.

Yet when the buck rat saw the sacks of diamonds, he thought: These are for the shore! So he hid in one of the sacks, and, in a like manner, the he-flea with him. And Mohammed Ali el Berki departed for the shore, and the sacks of diamonds were carried by Pages of the Sea, and Mohammed Ali and the sea-youths swam after the manner of fish until they reached the beach and came out onto the sands. Then Mohammed Ali went and bought donkeys, and he loaded the sacks upon the donkeys and carried them to his house. And his wife and his sons cried out in astonishment when they saw Mohammed Ali, for they said: We thought you drowned, and your body lost in the sea!

Mohammed Ali el Berki said to his wife: My ship was carried by a storm to a far country and I was washed up upon a desolate beach. And there I lived in misfortune and distress until, one day, I saw a bird. And I caught the bird, meaning to kill it and eat it for my supper. But when I took my knife to slay the bird I was verily astonished, for in its beak was a large and perfect diamond of great price. Then I released the bird and followed where it led, and it flew for two days through a savage and desolate land, and thus we went, over hills and through deserts and across rivers and through forests, and under trees, the bird flying and I running, until we came to a great cavern leading into the very heart of the earth, and the bird entered the cavern and I followed. And in that cavern was an ogre, the height of ten men. And the ogre seized me in the grip of death and was about to slay me and eat me. But I said: Do you then eat your guests instead of giving them roast sheep and hot rice? And the ogre was amazed, and he said: What is roast sheep? I said: It is delicious and it crackles in the mouth! Then the ogre said: Bring me roast sheep and hot rice! But before he would release me he made me swear upon the Holy Quran that I would return to him with a roast sheep and a dish of rice, so bring me these things that I may return to him to fulfil my oath, and let them be well and delicately cooked, else he will surely slay me. And these diamonds I have brought you as the price of the meat and from my love of you.

And the wife of Mohammed Ali el Berki took the sacks from her husband, and she put them in a place of safety, and she wept, thinking: My beloved husband has to return to a terrible ogre in a far and desolate land! And as she put the sacks away she noticed that they were wet with the water of the sea, and she thought: Perhaps they were dropped in the sea when they were taken from the boat to the shore. For she did not know that her husband had come from beneath the sea.

Then the wife of Mohammed Ali el Berki commenced to prepare roast sheep and hot rice, and the smell of the roasting meat came to the nostrils of the rat which was in one of the sacks of diamonds. And the rat gnawed through the sack and came out from it and with him came the he-flea. And the he-flea was also hungry and he was tired of rat's blood, so he hopped from the rat and he hopped across the floor to the wife of Mohammed Ali el Berki, and he hopped onto her leg and drank of her blood until he was satisfied. And when he was satisfied with the blood he hopped up her leg and he climbed into her bag-trousers, thinking to search for a she-flea that he might love her. But the wife of Mohammed Ali el Berki became aware of the he-flea and she caught him with her fingers and she dropped him into a bowl of water that he might drown, but the he-flea was used to water and accustomed to it, so he dived and swam in the bowl of water after the manner of an insect of the sea, and the wife of Mohammed Ali el Berki gazed at the he-flea in astonishment, for she had never seen a flea swimming before.

And the he-rat could not resist the odours of the roasting sheep, for it was long since he had tasted mutton. So he ran across the floor when the woman had turned her back on him, and he started to eat scraps of meat from the floor. But the wife of Mohammed Ali el Berki saw the rat, and she called to her cat that she might chase the rat. And the cat came running in great jumps upon the rat, so that the rat did not know how to escape from her or

where to find refuge. But the rat saw the great jar of water
which stood in that house, and, since he was accustomed
to water and he lived in it, he dived into the jar and he
swam around beneath the water as a fish. And the wife of
Mohammed Ali el Berki gazed at the rat in astonishment,
for she thought: Rats can swim on top of the water, they do
not dive and swim as fish! Then how has my husband
brought with him a rat and a flea which swim as fish?
Perhaps he has not told me the truth, and he has not informed me fully of where he has been and from whence he
has come?

So the wife of Mohammed Ali el Berki left her house and
she went to a magician who was skilled above all the magicians, and she showed him the diamonds and she informed
him concerning the rat and the flea, and she said: Where
has Mohammed Ali el Berki been and what has he done?
And after meditation and consultation with the Jinn and
with ogres and Inns, the magician said: Your husband has
been to the palace of the King of the Sea, and he is
married to the Daughter of the Sea, and she is even now
swelling with his child.

And anger came to the heart of the woman, the wife of
Mohammed Ali el Berki, and she said: He would give of
my cooking to this woman of the sea! But I shall prepare
for him another dish! And the woman, in her anger, called
her nine sons and acquainted them with the perfidy of
their father, and she said: Bring rats and bring fleas, for
the dish of mutton which your father shall carry to his
concubine of the sea shall consist of living rats and biting
fleas. And the boys, the sons of Mohammed Ali el Berki,
set themselves to hunting rats, for what sport do boys love
better? And they returned and filled the great copper
cooking vessel with five hundred rats and a she-rat, and
with thousands upon thousands of the fleas. And the
woman, the wife, put the lid on and sealed the great vessel,
wrapping it around with sheets and with towels, but a little
of the meat which was cooked she put on a plate, and
she went in to her husband and she said: Eat of this meat,
then take the vessel to the ogre, that he may eat, for I have
prepared a dish such as was never cooked before, and it
never was eaten before!

And Mohammed Ali el Berki ate of the meat and he
relished its taste, for what dish is better than a tender
sheep? And he became glad with his wife and he thanked
her exceedingly, and he loaded the copper vessel on a
donkey and he set out for the beach. And when he came to

the sea he found pages and youths of the sea waiting for him, and they took the pot from him and carried it on top of the sea. And before they plunged the pot beneath the water the Bride of the Sea came and she struck the pot with her staff, that the meat might not spoil in the water. And she said: Let nothing be drowned by the sea and let nothing be spoiled by the sea!

And it came about that the King of the Sea and the Queen of the Sea, and the Bride of the Sea, and all of the Court assembled to eat of the mutton and the rice, and Mohammed Ali el Berki lifted the lid from the pot. Then there came out five hundred rats and a she-rat and thousand upon thousand of the fleas. And the fleas did not drown in the sea, and they bit the King of the Sea and they bit his Queen. And the rats did not drown and they started to eat all that there was of food in that palace. And the King of the Sea was angered with exceeding anger, so that the very oceans rose up to the skies, and Mohammed Ali el Berki was thrown out from the sea onto the beach, even, as you might say, on the beach of Benghazi. And the fish-girl Marjan, whose stomach was swollen, wept.

And Mohammed Ali el Berki found himself cast up on the beach, nor could he return to the sea, for the waves roared and hurled themselves at him in the most terrible of cries. So he was forced to return to his home, and to his wife, and to his nine sons, and even to his daughter he was forced to return. And the fish-girl Marjan gave birth in her season to a fine boy, and he had legs and even toes after the fashion of human legs, but he could only live and breathe beneath the water. And the fish-girl Marjan greatly desired that her husband should return to see his son, yet she could not prevail on the wrath of the King of the Sea, and his anger was terrible, since all his palace and his court was overrun with rats and with fleas. But it came about that after the passage of many, many years Mohammed Ali el Berki was walking on the beach near the sea in the season of summer, and he saw his sea bride, and with her a handsome youth, whom he knew to be his son. But when he approached the sea to plunge in to kiss and embrace them, the waters were shaken by a great storm, even as they had been shaken before. Then Mohammed Ali el Berki grieved with exceeding grief, and yet he was glad in his heart that he had a fine son in the sea. And he made his nine sons of the land into sea captains and he sent them on voyages, saying: If you are in trouble on the sea, then call on your brother who lives in the

sea. And they went on journeys and they returned with
exceeding wealth. And as to the rats of the sea, from that
day to this very day, should any ship start on any journey,
though it is clean and new-built, and though there is not
in it a single rat, rats will come into it out of the sea.
And as for the fleas of the sea, if you go to any beach and
drive your fingers into the sands you will find them, and
these things persist, since they are signs of a woman's
jealousy.

TRANSLATED BY C. G. CAMPBELL

NAGIB MAHFOUZ: ZAABALAWI

[from *Zābalawī*]

Nagib Mahfouz was born in Cairo in 1911 and took a degree in philosophy from Cairo University. He began to write historical novels in the thirties; then, in 1945, he wrote the first of a series of novels in which he has recorded contemporary Egyptian life with great skill, detail and wry humor. In 1956 and 1957 he published his trilogy, in twelve hundred pages, about an Egyptian middle-class family during the period between the two wars. His more recent novels are shorter, often allegorical in tone, and show an increasing preoccupation with technique. He is certainly the most successful novelist in the Arab world today.

Finally I became convinced that I had to find Sheikh Zaabalawi.

The first time I had heard of his name had been in a song:

"What's wrong with the world, O Zaabalawi?
They've turned it upside down and made it insipid."

It had been a popular song in my childhood and one day it had occurred to me—in the way children have of asking endless questions—to ask my father about him.

"Who is Zaabalawi, Father?"

He had looked at me hesitantly as though doubting my ability to understand the answer. However, he had replied:

"May his blessing descend upon you, he's a true saint of God, a remover of worries and troubles. Were it not for him I would have died miserably—"

In the years that followed I heard him many a time sing the praises of this good saint and speak of the miracles

243

he performed. The days passed and brought with them many illnesses, from each one of which I was able, without too much trouble and at a cost I could afford, to find a cure, until I became afflicted with that illness for which no one possesses a remedy. When I had tried everything in vain and was overcome by despair, I remembered by chance what I had heard in my childhood: Why, I asked myself, should I not seek out Sheikh Zaabalawi? I recollected that my father had said that he had made his acquaintance in Khan Gaafar at the house of Sheikh Kamar, one of those sheikhs who practised law in the religious courts, and I therefore took myself off to his house. Wishing to make sure that he was still living there, I made enquiries of a vendor of beans whom I found in the lower part of the house.

"Sheikh Kamar!" he said, looking at me in amazement. "He left the quarter ages ago. They say he's now living in Garden City and has his office in al-Azhar Square."

I looked up the office address in the telephone book and immediately set off to the Chamber of Commerce Building where it was located. On asking to see him I was ushered into a room just as a beautiful woman with a most intoxicating perfume was leaving it. The man received me with a smile and motioned me towards a fine leather-upholstered chair. My feet were conscious of the costly lushness of the carpet despite the thick soles of my shoes. The man wore a lounge suit and was smoking a cigar; his manner of sitting was that of someone well satisfied both with himself and his worldly possessions. The look of warm welcome he gave me left no doubt in my mind that he thought me a prospective client, and I felt acutely embarrassed at encroaching upon his valuable time.

"Welcome!" he said, prompting me to speak.

"I am the son of your old friend Sheikh Ali al-Tatawi," I answered so as to put an end to my equivocal position.

A certain languor was apparent in the glance he cast at me; the languor was not total in that he had not as yet lost all hope in me.

"God rest his soul," he said. "He was a fine man."

The very pain that had driven me to go there now prevailed upon me to stay.

"He told me," I continued, "of a devout saint named Zaabalawi whom he met at Your Honour's. I am in need of him, sir, if he be still in the land of the living."

The languor became firmly entrenched in his eyes and it

would have come as no surprise to me if he had shown the door to both me and my father's memory.

"That," he said in the tone of one who has made up his mind to terminate the conversation, "was a very long time ago and I scarcely recall him now."

Rising to my feet so as to put his mind at rest regarding my intention of going, I asked:

"Was he really a saint?"

"We used to regard him as a man of miracles."

"And where could I find him today?" I asked, making another move towards the door.

"To the best of my knowledge he was living in the Birgawi Residence in al-Azhar," and he applied himself to some papers on his desk with a resolute movement that indicated that he wouldn't open his mouth again. I bowed my head in thanks, apologized several times for disturbing him and left the office, my head so buzzing with embarrassment that I was oblivious to all sounds around me.

I went to the Birgawi Residence, which was situated in a thickly populated quarter. I found that time had so eaten into the building that nothing was left of it save an antiquated façade and a courtyard which, despite its being supposedly in the charge of a caretaker, was being used as a rubbish dump. A small insignificant fellow, a mere prologue to a man, was using the covered entrance as a place for the sale of old books on theology and mysticism.

On asking him about Zaabalawi he peered at me through narrow, inflamed eyes and said in amazement: "Zaabalawi! Good heavens, what a time ago that was! Certainly he used to live in this house when it was livable in, and many was the time he would sit with me talking of bygone days and I would be blessed by his holy presence. Where, though, is Zaabalawi today?"

He shrugged his shoulders sorrowfully and soon left me to attend to an approaching customer. I proceeded to make enquiries of many shopkeepers in the district. While I found that a large number of them had never even heard of him, some, though recalling nostalgically the pleasant times they had spent with him, were ignorant of his present whereabouts, while others openly made fun of him, labelled him a charlatan, and advised me to put myself in the hands of a doctor—as though I had not already done so. I therefore had no alternative but to return disconsolately home.

With the passing of the days like motes in the air my

pains grew so severe that I was sure I would not be able to hold out much longer. Once again I fell to wondering about Zaabalawi and clutching at the hopes his venerable name stirred within me. Then it occurred to me to seek the help of the local Sheikh of the district; in fact, I was surprised I hadn't thought of this to begin with. His office was in the nature of a small shop except that it contained a desk and a telephone, and I found him sitting at his desk wearing a jacket over his striped *galabia*. As he did not interrupt his conversation with a man sitting beside him, I stood waiting till the man had gone. He then looked up at me coldly. I told myself that I should win him over by the usual methods, and it wasn't long before I had him cheerfully inviting me to sit down.

"I am in need of Sheikh Zaabalawi," I answered his enquiry as to the purpose of my visit.

He gazed at me with the same astonishment as that shown by those I had previously encountered.

"At least," he said, giving me a smile that revealed his gold teeth, "he is still alive. The devil of it is, though, he has no fixed abode. You might well bump into him as you go out of here; on the other hand you might spend days and months in fruitless search of him."

"Even you can't find him!"

"Even I! He's a baffling man, but I thank the Lord that he's still alive!"

He gazed at me intently, and murmured:

"It seems your condition is serious."

"Very!"

"May God come to your aid! But why don't you go about it rationally?"

He spread out a sheet of paper on the desk and drew on it with unexpected speed and skill until he had made a full plan of the district showing all the various quarters, lanes, alleyways, and squares. He looked at it admiringly and said, "These are dwelling houses, here is the Quarter of the Perfumers, here the Quarter of the Coppersmiths, the Mouski, the Police and Fire Stations. The drawing is your best guide. Look carefully in the cafés, the places where the dervishes perform their rites, the mosques and prayer rooms, and the Green Gate, for he may well be concealed among the beggars and be indistinguishable from them. Actually, I myself haven't seen him for years, having been somewhat preoccupied with the cares of the world and was only brought back to those most exquisite times of my youth by your enquiry."

I gazed at the map in bewilderment. The telephone rang and he took up the receiver.

"Take it," he told me, generously. "We're at your service."

Folding up the map, I left and wandered off through the quarter, from square to street to alleyway, making enquiries of everyone I felt was familiar with the place. At last the owner of a small establishment for ironing clothes told me: "Go to the calligrapher Hassanein in Umm al-Ghulam —they were friends."

I went to Umm al-Ghulam, where I found old Hassanein working in a deep, narrow shop full of signboards and jars of colour. A strange smell, a mixture of glue and perfume, permeated its every corner. Old Hassanein was squatting on a sheepskin rug in front of a board propped against the wall; in the middle of it he had inscribed the word "Allah" in silver lettering. He was engrossed in embellishing the letters with prodigious care. I stood behind him, fearful to disturb him or break the inspiration that flowed to his masterly hand. When my concern at not interrupting him had lasted some time, he suddenly enquired with unaffected gentleness: "Yes?"

Realizing that he was aware of my presence, I introduced myself.

"I've been told that Sheikh Zaabalawi is your friend and I'm looking for him," I said.

His hand came to a stop. He scrutinized me in astonishment.

"Zaabalawi! God be praised!" he said with a sigh.

"He is a friend of yours, isn't he?" I asked eagerly.

"He was, once upon a time. A real man of mystery; he'd visit you so often that people would imagine he was your nearest and dearest, then would disappear as though he'd never existed. Yet saints are not to be blamed."

The spark of hope went out with the suddenness of a lamp by a power cut.

"He was so constantly with me," said the man, "that I felt him to be a part of everything I drew. But where is he today?"

"Perhaps he is still alive?"

"He's alive, without a doubt. He had impeccable taste and it was due to him that I made my most beautiful drawings."

"God knows," I said, in a voice almost stifled by the dead ashes of hope, "that I am in the direst need of him and no one knows better than you of the ailments in respect of which he is sought."

"Yes—yes. May God restore you to health. He is, in truth, as is said of him, a man, and more—"

Smiling broadly, he added: "And his face is possessed of an unforgettable beauty. But where is he?"

Reluctantly I rose to my feet, shook hands and left. I continued on my way eastwards and westwards through the quarter, enquiring about him from everyone who, by reason of age or experience, I felt was likely to help me. Eventually I was informed by a vendor of lupine that he had met him a short while ago at the house of Sheikh Gad, the well-known composer. I went to the musician's house in Tabakshiyya, where I found him in a room tastefully furnished in the old style, its walls redolent with history. He was seated on a divan, his famous lute lying beside him, concealing within itself the most beautiful melodies of our age, while from within the house came the sound of pestle and mortar and the clamour of children. I immediately greeted him and introduced myself, and was put at my ease by the unaffected way in which he received me. He did not ask, either in words or gesture, what had brought me, and I did not feel that he even harboured any such curiosity. Amazed at his understanding and kindness, which boded well, I said: "O Sheikh Gad, I am an admirer of yours and have long been enchanted by the renderings of your songs."

"Thank you," he said with a smile.

"Please excuse my disturbing you," I continued timidly, "but I was told that Zaabalawi was your friend and I am in urgent need of him."

"Zaabalawi!" he said, frowning in concentration. "You need him? God be with you, for who knows, O Zaabalawi, where you are?"

"Doesn't he visit you?" I asked eagerly.

"He visited me sometime ago. He might well come now; on the other hand I mightn't see him till death!"

I gave an audible sigh and asked: "What made him like that?"

He took up his lute. "Such are saints or they would not be saints," he said laughing.

"Do those who need him suffer as I do?"

"Such suffering is part of the cure!"

He took up the plectrum and began plucking soft strains from the strings. Lost in thought, I followed his movements. Then, as though addressing myself, I said: "So my visit has been in vain!"

He smiled, laying his cheek against the side of the lute.

"God forgive you," he said, "for saying such a thing of a visit that has caused me to know you and you me!"

I was much embarrassed and said apologetically: "Please forgive me; my feelings of defeat made me forget my manners!"

"Do not give in to defeat. This extraordinary man brings fatigue to all who seek him. It was easy enough with him in the old days when his place of abode was known. Today, though, the world has changed and after having enjoyed a position attained only by potentates, he is now pursued by the police on a charge of false pretences. It is therefore no longer an easy matter to reach him, but have patience and be sure that you will do so."

He raised his head from the lute and skilfully led into the opening bars of a melody. Then he sang:

"I make lavish mention, even though I blame myself,
    of those I have loved,
For the words of lovers are my wine."

With a heart that was weary and listless I followed the beauty of the melody and the singing.

"I composed the music to this poem in a single night," he told me when he had finished. "I remember that it was the night of the Lesser Bairam. He was my guest for the whole of that night and the poem was of his choosing. He would sit for a while just where you are, then would get up and play with my children as though he were one of them. Whenever I was overcome by weariness or my inspiration failed me he would punch me playfully in the chest and joke with me, and I would bubble over with melodies and thus I continued working till I finished the most beautiful piece I have ever composed."

"Does he know anything about music?"

"He was the epitome of things musical. He had an extremely beautiful speaking voice and you had only to hear him to want to burst into song. His loftiness of spirit stirred within you—"

"How was it that he cured those diseases before which men are powerless?"

"That is his secret. Maybe you will learn it when you meet him."

But when would that meeting occur? We relapsed into

silence and the hubbub of children once more filled the room.

Again the Sheikh began to sing. He went on repeating the words "and I have a memory of her" in different and beautiful variations until the very walls danced in ecstasy. I expressed my wholehearted admiration and he gave me a smile of thanks. I then got up and asked permission to leave and he accompanied me to the outer door. As I shook him by the hand he said, "I hear that nowadays he frequents the house of Hagg Wanas al-Damanhouri. Do you know him?"

I shook my head, a modicum of renewed hope creeping into my heart.

"He is a man of private means," he told me, "who from time to time visits Cairo, putting up at some hotel or other. Every evening, though, he spends at the Negma Bar in Alfi Street."

I waited for nightfall, and went to the Negma Bar. I asked a waiter about Hagg Wanas and he pointed to a corner which was semisecluded because of its position behind a large pillar with mirrors on its four sides. There I saw a man seated alone at a table with a bottle three-quarters empty and another empty one in front of him; there were no snacks or food to be seen and I was sure that I was in the presence of a hardened drinker. He was wearing a loosely flowing silk *galabia* and a carefully wound turban; his legs were stretched out towards the base of the pillar, and as he gazed into the mirror in rapt contentment the sides of his face, rounded and handsome despite the fact that he was approaching old age, were flushed with wine. I approached quietly till I stood but a few feet away from him. He did not turn towards me or give any indication that he was aware of my presence.

"Good evening, Mr. Wanas," I said with amiable friendliness.

He turned towards me abruptly as though my voice had roused him from slumber and glared at me in disapproval. I was about to explain what had brought me to him when he interrupted me in an almost imperative tone of voice which was nonetheless not devoid of an extraordinary gentleness: "First, please sit down, and, second, please get drunk!"

I opened my mouth to make my excuses but, stopping up his ears with his fingers, he said: "Not a word till you do what I say."

I realized that I was in the presence of a capricious

drunkard and told myself that I should go along with
him at least halfway.

"Would you permit me to ask one question?" I said
with a smile, sitting down.

Without removing his hands from his ears he indicated
the bottle.

"When engaged in a drinking bout like this I do not
allow any conversation between myself and another unless,
like me, he is drunk, otherwise the session loses all
propriety, and mutual comprehension is rendered impossible."

I made a sign indicating that I didn't drink.

"That's your lookout," he said offhandedly. "And
that's my condition!"

He filled me a glass which I meekly took and drank.
No sooner had it settled in my stomach than it seemed
to ignite. I waited patiently till I had grown used to its
ferocity, and said: "It's very strong, and I think the time
has come for me to ask you about—"

Once again, however, he put his fingers in his ears.

"I shan't listen to you until you're drunk!"

He filled up my glass for the second time. I glanced at it
in trepidation; then, overcoming my innate objection, I
drank it down at a gulp. No sooner had it come to rest
inside me than I lost all will power. With the third glass I
lost my memory and with the fourth the future vanished.
The world turned round about me and I forgot why I had
gone there. The man leaned towards me attentively but I
saw him—saw everything—as a mere meaningless series
of coloured planes. I don't know how long it was before
my head sank down onto the arm of the chair and I
plunged into deep sleep. During it I had a beautiful dream
the like of which I had never experienced. I dreamed that
I was in an immense garden surrounded on all sides by
luxuriant trees, and the sky was nothing but stars seen
between the entwined branches, all enfolded in an
atmosphere like that of sunset or a sky overcast with cloud.
I was lying on a small hummock of jasmine petals which
fell upon me like rain, while the lucent spray of a fountain
unceasingly sprinkled my head and temples. I was in a
state of deep contentedness, of ecstatic serenity. An
orchestra of warbling and cooing played in my ear. There
was an extraordinary sense of harmony between me and
my inner self, and between the two of us and the world,
everything being in its rightful place without discord or
distortion. In the whole world there was no single reason

for speech or movement, for the universe moved in a rapture of ecstasy. This lasted but a short while. When I opened my eyes consciousness struck at me like a policeman's fist and I saw Wanas al-Damanhouri regarding me with concern. In the bar only a few drowsy people were left.

"You have slept deeply," said my companion; "you were obviously hungry for sleep."

I rested my heavy head in the palms of my hands. When I took them away in astonishment and looked down at them I found that they glistened with drops of water.

"My head's wet," I protested.

"Yes, my friend tried to rouse you," he answered quietly.

"Somebody saw me in this state?"

"Don't worry, he is a good man. Have you not heard of Sheikh Zaabalawi?"

"Zaabalawi!" I exclaimed, jumping to my feet.

"Yes," he answered in surprise. "What's wrong?"

"Where is he?"

"I don't know where he is now. He was here and then he left."

I was about to run off in pursuit but found I was more exhausted than I had imagined. Collapsed over the table, I cried out in despair: "My sole reason for coming to you was to meet him. Help me to catch up with him or send someone after him."

The man called a vendor of prawns and asked him to seek out the Sheikh and bring him back. Then he turned to me.

"I didn't realize you were afflicted. I'm very sorry—"

"You wouldn't let me speak," I said irritably.

"What a pity! He was sitting on this chair beside you the whole time. He was playing with a string of jasmine petals he had round his neck, a gift from one of his admirers, then, taking pity on you, he began to sprinkle some water on your head to bring you round."

"Does he meet you here every night?" I asked, my eyes not leaving the doorway through which the vendor of prawns had left.

"He was with me tonight, last night and the night before that, but before that I hadn't seen him for a month."

"Perhaps he will come tomorrow," I answered with a sigh.

"Perhaps."

"I am willing to give him any money he wants."

Wanas answered sympathetically: "The strange thing is

that he is not open to such temptations, yet he will cure you if you meet him."

"Without charge?"

"Merely on sensing that you love him."

The vendor of prawns returned, having failed in his mission.

I recovered some of my energy and left the bar, albeit unsteadily. At every street corner I called out "Zaabalawi!" in the vague hope that I would be rewarded with an answering shout. The street boys turned contemptuous eyes on me till I sought refuge in the first available taxi.

The following evening I stayed up with Wanas al-Damanhouri till dawn, but the Sheikh did not put in an appearance. Wanas informed me that he would be going away to the country and wouldn't be returning to Cairo until he'd sold the cotton crop.

I must wait, I told myself; I must train myself to be patient. Let me content myself with having made certain of the existence of Zaabalawi, and even of his affection for me, which encourages me to think that he will be prepared to cure me if a meeting between us takes place.

Sometimes, however, the long delay wearied me. I would become beset by despair and would try to persuade myself to dismiss him from my mind completely. How many weary people in this life know him not or regard him as a mere myth! Why, then, should I torture myself about him in this way?

No sooner, however, did my pains force themselves upon me than I would again begin to think about him, asking myself as to when I would be fortunate enough to meet him. The fact that I ceased to have any news of Wanas and was told he had gone to live abroad did not deflect me from my purpose; the truth of the matter was that I had become fully convinced that I had to find Zaabalawi.

Yes, I have to find Zaabalawi.

TRANSLATED BY DENYS JOHNSON-DAVIES

AHMED ALI: TWILIGHT IN DELHI

[from *Twilight in Delhi*]

*This novel, a favorite of E. M. Forster's, was expert-
ly written in English and later required great talent to
translate into Urdu. "My purpose," the author wrote,
"was to depict a phase of our national life and the
decay of a whole culture, a particular mode of thought
and living, now dead and gone already before our
eyes." In its happy marriage of pattern and episode,
it marks a high command of the form of the novel.*

> *Is it a storm, or is it life?*
> *We die of living and the strife.*
> Khwaja Mir Dard

It was the terrible summer of nineteen hundred and
eleven. No one had experienced such heat for many years.
Begam Jamal complained that she had never known such
heat in all her life. Begam Nihal said she had never experienced such a summer ever since 1857, the year of the
"Mutiny." The temperature rose higher and higher until
it reached one hundred and fifteen in the shade. From
seven in the morning the loo began to moan, blowing
drearily through the hopeless streets. The leaves of the
henna tree became sered and wan, and the branches of
the date palm became coated with sand. The dust blew
through the unending noon; and men went out with their
heads well covered and protected. The pigeons flew for a
while and opened their beaks for heat. The crows cawed
and the kites cried and their voices sounded so dull.
    The sky lost its colour and became dirty and bronzed.
The loo did not stop even at night. The stars flickered in
the sky behind the covering layer of dust. The sand rained
down all night, came between the teeth, covered the beds,
and sleep did not come near parched humanity.

Tempers rose and from all around came the loud voices of women quarrelling, husbands beating their wives, mothers their children, and there seemed no rest for man.

Fires broke out every now and then. At such times the sky was made red with the flames that shot up from the burning earth. Men died of sunstroke; and even birds were not immune from the destructive influence of the sun, and many pigeons died.

Outside the city, beyond the Fort and beyond the Mori Gate, workmen were digging away in the scorching heat of May levelling or raising the earth, beautifying the ground in preparation for the Coronation of a new and foreign king. But that was still far off and no one seemed to be concerned.

Inside the city the wind blew free through the length and breadth of Chandni Chowk, raised dust in the streets and by-lanes, lashed the stalwart trees that stood in rows in the middle of the bazar from Fatehpuri to the Fountain and beyond. Men shut themselves up inside the houses or in shops. At noon the city seemed deserted and dead but for the grating noise of tram cars that plied throughout the day, though very few people used them. In the evenings men came out when the sun had gone down and the water had been sprinkled, and the city hummed with noise.

Mir Nihal, wearing a muslin coat so made that one of his breasts showed naked through it, and red shoes with flowers embroidered in white on the toes, walked out of his shop of Haji Noor Elahi & Sons, Lace Dealers. As he set foot in the street a hot gust of wind blew, and Mir Nihal put a bandana on his neck to protect it from the sun. From a housetop nearby a pigeon-flier shouted excitedly: "Ao, ao." Automatically Mir Nihal looked up. Although it was still very hot the sky was full of pigeons. Suddenly Mir Nihal remembered that he had forgotten to leave water inside the loft for his pigeons, and he quickened his pace.

He would have liked to go home via Babban Jan's, for she had been ill, but his pigeons worried him. So he came straight down Chandni Chowk towards the Clock Tower to go through Balli Maran, the nearest way home. As he passed the Clock Tower he saw a number of camel carts wind their way, creaking, groaning, moving slowly like snails, from the Company Gardens to Khari Baoli, the grain market. He felt thirsty, and at the turn of Balli

Maran he stopped to drink water from the sabeel.[1] Men had started going about and the shopkeepers were sprinkling water in front of their shops.

As he passed through Balli Maran his nostrils were filled with the smell of drugs and medicines. This was the street of druggists and Hakims. With the smell the thought of death came into his mind. There was an aroma of camphor in the air, and for some unknown reason he began to think of Babban Jan. Her thought was sad and sweet, like the memory of some dear one dead, coming from somewhere far away, ripping open the veils of the unconscious, saddening the heart.

A wave of self-pity surged in his breast. He felt he was getting old—he was sixty-two. He tried to suppress the feeling. But a peculiar heaviness appeared in his head, a pressure of blood that wants to burst out of its restricting channels of veins and arteries. For a moment everything went black in front of his eyes. He thought it was the result of his constipation. Or was it heatstroke? This seemed more plausible to Mir Nihal.

So, when he reached the Kucha Pandit, he bought a pice worth of unripe mangoes to have them roasted in the oven and have fresh sherbet made. The fruit and vegetable seller, a fat young woman with expansive thighs and breasts that could feed the whole of Hindustan, with a face disfigured with deep pock marks, a sharp tongue and a loud throat, started telling him that her melons were extra fine. She had just received a parcel from Lucknow, she said. Or would he care to have some mulberries? Mir Nihal said "no." "Then take some pomegranates. My man has just brought them from Qandahar."

Mir Nihal was in no mood to buy anything, and he went along, receiving greetings from the people of the mohallah and replying to them. As he was going through Jangli Kuan he saw Nisar Ahmad hurrying to the mosque. He was a tall, well-built man, somewhere on the other side of fifty. He wore a shirt and paijama of homespun, a cane cap brownish in colour and dirty at the edges, and a bandana over his shoulder. His head was close-cropped and made his forehead look broad. His expansive fan-shaped beard was dyed red with henna, and his moustaches were shaved on the upper lip in accordance with Islamic laws. His nose was big, jutting out on his face like a rock, and a

[1]Place where water is kept for drinking.

callosity had formed on his forehead on account of constantly rubbing it on the ground at prayer, and shone ashy grey from a distance on his dark face. He was called Balal Habshi (the Negro companion of Mohammad who was renowned for his azaan); and they had many things in common—their dark complexions and their golden voices. Nisar Ahmad sold ghee for a living, but it was said that he was a shady businessman and his ghee was not pure.

But his azaan compensated for his faults, and everyone blessed him and said he would go straight to heaven for calling the faithful to prayer. There is no doubt that when he called the evening azaan he filled the hearts with reverence and awe. Just as the sun had set, his golden voice would rise gradually in the air, and, rippling with the glory of Islam, would unfold its message to the Mussalmans, bringing with it a sense of the impermanence of life and the transience of the world. His voice could be heard far and wide in several mohallahs, rising above the din and noise of the town, leaping to the stars. Then slowly it would come to an end, bringing with it peace and silence, acting as a lullaby to the tired hearts of men.

Mir Nihal wished to overtake him to ask him to send some ghee for the pigeons. He did not take the ghee from home for fear of Begam Nihal, who would have shouted at him and complained. But Nisar Ahmad was ahead of him, and at the turn of Mohallah Niyaryan he was lost to sight.

Just then Sheikh Mohammad Sadiq peeped out of his shop and, seeing Mir Nihal, came to greet him. He made gold thread, and on his right leg he wore a short leather legging over his paijama on which he used to roll his cone-shaped bobbin. The thread would be hanging from the ceiling and Sheikhji would catch the long point of the bobbin and roll it on his leg, and the bobbin would go dancing and spinning for a while until the thread was spun. Then he would wind it up, draw more thread from the reel, and the whole process would be repeated once again.

Slowly Sheikh Mohammad Sadiq walked towards Mir Nihal. His beard was conical and small, and his bobbed hair was dyed red with henna and presented a funny contrast to his half-black and half-grey beard. As he came forward his red paijama-string dangled in front of him, trailing right down to the ground, and as he walked it moved to and fro.

"Assalaam-alaikum,[2] Mir Saheb," he said from a distance. "How are you?"

"Waalaikum-assalaam,"[3] Mir Nihal replied. "I am alive. How have *you* been keeping?"

"I am all right," said Sheikh Mohammad Sadiq, and he started walking with Mir Nihal towards Mohallah Niyaryan. "I have been thinking of coming to you, but I was so entangled in worries that I could not come."

"Is everything all right?" Mir Nihal enquired.

"It's your kindness. Everything is all right otherwise, but there is a little matter about which I wanted to talk to you."

They had come to the turn of the lane, and Mir Nihal stopped to listen to Sheikhji's story. From the other side came Fazal Khan, karkhandar, and as he came near he flung a greeting at Mir Nihal and enquired: "Is everyone all right at home?"

"Allah be thanked," Mir Nihal replied. "*You* are doing well?"

"Your graciousness—thanks."

Fortunately he did not stop, and went away.

Sheikh Mohammad Sadiq caught hold of his small beard in his right hand, shy and nervous at broaching the subject. A kite came dragging along, striking against the roofs and walls and was entangled in some wooden planks and tin sheets which were lying on a roof nearby. Sheikhji mustered courage and spoke out: "I have a niece. Her parents have both died, and I am anxious about her marriage. You'll forgive my presumptuousness, but—"

Sheikhji hesitated for a moment. The kite got disentangled and the owner pulled it home.

"If you will give your consent," Sheikhji continued, "I shall marry her to your servant Ghafoor."

Mir Nihal cleared his throat and asked: "How old is the girl?"

"She is about thirteen or fourteen, but she is so healthy that she looks much older."

Mir Nihal muttered "Umph" and pondered.

"Don't you think she is too young for Ghafoor?" he said at last.

"What you are saying is but too true," Sheikhji replied with humility and submission. "But what I say is that it is

[2] Peace be with you.
[3] Peace be with you also.

so difficult to get a good match for her. And my wife is worrying my life out of me with reminders about the girl's marriage. If you have no objection. . . ."

Mir Nihal did not seem to approve of the idea, but he was in a hurry to get home. The pigeon-fliers were shouting more loudly and in greater numbers, and were constant reminders of his own birds to Mir Nihal. That is why he summarily dismissed the affair by saying: "You speak to Ghafoor about it. The matter concerns him, you know."

"What you are saying is all right, but what I say is that he is your servant—and what is your idea?"

To which Mir Nihal replied by repeating the well-known saying: "When husband and wife are willing, what can the Qazi do?"

Sheikhji took this to be the consent and, smiling broadly, he caught hold of Mir Nihal's hand in both of his and began to shake it warmly. From behind came Mast Qalandar, a mad faqir, almost naked but for a strip of cloth tied to a string round his waist hiding his private parts. His matted beard, full of dust and soup and dirt, was tousled, looking like a bulbul's nest. His nails were long and black with filth, and his bare feet were dirty. But his body, hairy like a bear's, looked plump and healthy; and from his bushy face his small eyes sparkled. There was a look of madness on his face, yet people considered him a divine, a faqir very high up in the mystical order, as the name given to him, Qalandar, signified. He was a favourite with the gamblers, who always consulted him for lucky numbers. Most of the time he sat near the tombs of Haray Bharay (the evergreen one) and Sarmad at the foot of Jama Masjid, and seldom came into the city. He constantly cried the same mysterious saying: "When there is such pleasure in throwing it out how great would be the bliss in keeping it."

His cries came from a distance, and as he came near, Mir Nihal said good-bye to Sheikh Mohammad Sadiq and went home.

From a small, dilapidated house came the voice of a woman sharply reprimanding a girl: "O thou, Fatto, may God's wrath fall upon thee. Where hast thou died?"

And a dog ran after a cat, chasing her away.

Mir Nihal was worried, feeling heavy in the head, anxious about the birds. The thought of Babban Jan came back to his mind again and with it a Rubai of Sarmad, the mystic faqir and Persian poet who was beheaded by Aurangzeb:

I've lost religion in quite a novel way,
Throwing faith for drunken eyes away:
And all my life in piety spent I've flung
At the altar for that idol-worshipper's joy. . . .

CHAIRIL ANWAR: SEVEN POEMS

[from various sources]

Although Anwar wrote only some seventy poems and died at the age of twenty-six in 1949, he is recognized as Indonesia's only unqualifiedly great poet to date.[1] He began to compose his mature poetry during the Japanese occupation, in 1942. He was one of the organizers of the journal Gelanggang *(The Arena), serving as one of its editors, and his poems came to embody the spirit of the remarkable literary "Generation of '45." His verse was greatly influenced by Western poetic forms and Western sensibilities, yet it is profoundly rooted in Indonesian cultural traditions and modern spiritual problems.*

Tuti's Ice Cream

Between present and future happiness
The abyss gapes.
My girl is licking at her ice cream:
This afternoon you're my love,
I adorn you with cake and Coca-Cola
Oh wife-in-training.
We have stopped the clock's ticking.

You kissed skillfully, indelibly.
—When we cycled I took you home
—Your blood was hot, soon you were a woman,
And the stiff old man dreamed dreams
That leaped over the moon.

Every day's beau invited you on,
Every day's beau was different.

[1]See Burton Raffel, *The Development of Modern Indonesian Poetry*, State University of New York Press, 1967, pages 80–110.

Tomorrow we'll meet and not know each other:
Heaven is this minute's game.

I am like you, everything ran by,
Me and Tuti and Greet and Amoi . . .
Dilapidated hearts.
Love's a danger that quickly fades.

In Vain

The last time you came
You brought bright flowers,
Red roses, white jasmine,
Blood and holiness,
And spread them in front of me
With a decisive look: for you.

We were stunned
And asked each other: what's this?
Love? Neither of us understood.

That day we were together.
We did not touch.

But my heart will not give itself to you,
And does not care
That you are ripped by desolation.

Twilight at a Little Harbor
For Sri Ajati

This time no one's looking for love
Between the sheds, the old houses, in the make-believe
Of poles and rope. A boat, a *prau* without water,
Puffs and blows, thinking there's something it can catch.

The drizzle comes harder and darkens. There's an eagle
      flapping,
Pushing sulkily off, and the day swimming silkily
To meet temptations yet to come. Nothing moves.
And now the sand and the sea are asleep, the waves are
      gone.

There's no one else. I'm alone. Walking,
Combing the cape, still drowning the hope

Of just once getting to the end of it and saying goodbye
   to everything
From the fourth beach, where the last sob could be
   hugged tightly to me.

My Love's on a Faraway Island

My love's on a faraway island,
A sweet girl, doing nothing for lack of anything better.

The *prau* slides quickly along, the moon gleams,
Around my neck I wear a charm for my girl;
The wind helps, the sea's clear, but I know
I'm not going to reach her.

In the calm water, in the gentle wind,
In the final sensation, everything goes swiftly.

Fate takes command, saying:
"Better steer your *prau* straight into my lap."

Hey! I've come this way for years!
The *prau* I'm in is going to crash!
Why is Fate calling
Before I have a chance to hug my girl?

My sweet on a faraway island,
If I die, she'll die for lack of anything better.

At the Mosque

I shouted at Him
Until He came.

We met face to face.

Afterwards He burned in my breast.
All my strength struggles to extinguish Him.
My body, which won't be driven, is soaked with sweat.

This room
Is the arena where we fight,

Destroying each other,
One hurling insults, the other gone mad.

To a Friend

Before emptiness draws closer
And the final treachery leaps at us from behind,
While blood runs and feeling beats,

And despair has not bloomed and there is no fear
Remember the evening fades, without warning,
A red sail dipping into darkness,
And, friend, let's part now, here:
The emptiness that pulls at us also strangles itself!

So
Empty the glass,
Pierce, traverse, invert the world,
Love women, but leave the flatterers,
Rope the wildest horse, spur him swiftly,
Tie him to neither noon nor night
And
Undo what you've done,
End without inheritance, without family,
Without requesting forgiveness,
Without granting it!

So
Again
Let us part:
The final agony will draw us into an empty sky.
Once more, friend, one line more:
Shove your sword to the hilt
Into those who've diluted the pureness of honey! ! !

Heaven

Like my mother, and my grandmother too,
Plus seven generations before them,
I also seek admission to heaven,
Which the Moslem Party and the Mohammedan Party
    say has rivers of milk
And thousands of houris all over.

But there's a contemplative voice inside me,
Stubbornly mocking: Can you ever
Get dry after a soaking in the blue sea,

After the sly temptations waiting in every port?
Anyway, who can say for sure
That there really are houris there
With voices as rich and husky as Nina's, with eyes that
    flirt like Jati's?

TRANSLATED BY BURTON RAFFEL AND NURDIN SALAM

MUHAMMAD AGA KHAN: LOOKING FORWARD

[from *World Enough and Time*]

The late Aga Khan (1877–1957) was one of the most remarkable Islamic leaders of modern times. As Imam of the Khoja Ismailis, he directed his large, advanced, and far-flung community with enlightenment and foresight. As an international statesman, friend and adviser of the great, he was truly a celebrity among celebrities.

His autobiography contains a great deal of wisdom based on experience; it is also steeped with Islamic spirituality and, despite its disclaimers of prophecy, prophetic.

All my life I have looked forward. Large-scale prophecy, however, is as dangerous as it is easy, and true prophetic vision is rare indeed. It is a rarity more than ever marked in an epoch such as ours, in which science has placed in our reach material and natural powers undreamed of fifty short years ago. But since the human mind and the human imagination are as yet by no means fully equipped to master the immense forces which human ingenuity has discovered and unleashed, it is not too difficult to foresee at least some of the political and social reactions of nations as well as individuals to this enormous scientific and technical revolution and all its accompanying phenomena.

India, the country of my birth and upbringing, has been for centuries a land of extreme poverty, misery and want, where millions are born, live and work and die at a level far below the margin of subsistence. A tropical climate, aeons of soil erosion, and primitive and unskilled methods of agriculture have all taken their toll of suffering, patient, gentle but ignorant mankind. The Indian peasant has survived and multiplied but in face of the most ferocious and formidable handicaps. Many years ago, in my first book, *India in Transition,* I gave this account of the day-to-day life of the ordinary Indian peasant under British rule:

A typical rural scene on an average day in an average year is essentially the same now as it was half a century ago. A breeze, alternately warm and chilly, sweeps over the monotonous landscape as it is lightened by a rapid dawn, to be followed quickly by a heavy molten sun appearing on the horizon. The ill-clad villagers, men, women, and children, thin and weak, and made old beyond their years by a life of underfeeding and over-work, have been astir before daybreak, and have partaken of a scanty meal, consisting of some kind or other of cold porridge, of course without sugar or milk. With bare and hardened feet they reach the fields and immediately begin to furrow the soil with their lean cattle, of a poor and hybrid breed, usually sterile and milkless. A short rest at midday, and a handful of dried corn or beans for food, is followed by a continuance till dusk of the same laborious scratching of the soil. Then the weary way homeward in the chilly evening, every member of the family shaking with malaria or fatigue. A drink of water, probably contaminated, the munching of a piece of hard black or green *chaupati,* a little gossip round the peepul tree, and then the day ends with heavy, unrefreshing sleep in dwellings so insanitary that no decent European farmer would house his cattle in them.

The Raj has gone, but in essentials the life and lot of the humble villager of rural India have scarcely changed since I wrote these words. Education, hygiene, welfare schemes, plans for village "uplift" have but scratched the surface of the problem, hardly more deeply or more efficiently than the peasant's own wooden plough scratches the sunbaked soil of India. Nor is the lot of his urban kinsman, working in one of the great and ever growing industrial cities like Bombay or Calcutta, much better. At his factory, in his home, the Indian industrial worker endures, and takes for granted, utterly appalling conditions. From steamy, overcrowded mill or factory he trudges to the shanty or tenement, equally overcrowded, equally unhealthy, which serves him as his home. His diet, though more varied than that of his cousin in the country, is pitifully meager by any Western standard. Around him are the increasing distractions of a great city, but they have little meaning for him. His amenities are few, his luxuries nonexistent.

During the years of British rule it was relatively easy to shrug off responsibility for the economic *malaise* of India, to put all the blame on imperialist exploitation, and to say, "When we get our independence, then we shall put economic conditions right." The imperialists have gone; the period of alien exploitation is over. But can economic injustice be so easily righted? India's population is steadily and rapidly increasing, yet at the present rate—and in spite of all manner of schemes for soil conservation, irrigation, better use of land, intensive and planned industrialization—it is unlikely that more than half the natural increase in population can be economically absorbed. India's problem, like China's, is one of economic absorptive capacity. Pakistan's problem, since she has the empty but potentially rich acres of Baluchistan to fill with her surplus population, is less pressing. Doubtless in India, as in China, the extension of education and growing familiarity with the use of the vote and the processes of democracy will give rise to eager and energetic efforts to find political solutions to the gravest economic problems. Hundreds upon hundreds of millions of human beings in India and in China live out their lives in conditions of extreme misery. How long will these vast masses of humanity accept such conditions? May they not—as realization dawns of their own political power—insist on an extreme form of socialism, indeed on communism, though not on Soviet Russian lines and not under Soviet leadership? And may not that insistence be revolutionary in its expression and in its manifestations?

Yet in India, as well as in China, if every "have" in the population were stripped of wealth and reduced to the level of the lowest "have not," of the poorest sweeper or coolie, the effect on the general standard of living—the general ill-being—would be negligible. There are far too few "haves," far too many "have nots," in both countries for even the most wholesale redistribution of wealth as it now stands. Reform, to be real and effective, must strike much deeper. These are thoughts grim enough to depress anyone who possesses more than the most superficial knowledge of Asia's problems and difficulties.

There is one major political step forward that should be taken by the Governments of India and Pakistan, which would have a significant and beneficial effect on the life and welfare of their peoples. This is the establishment of a genuine and lasting *entente cordiale* between the two countries, such as subsisted between Britain and France from 1905 to 1914. Even more pertinent analogies are offered by Belgium and Holland, and Sweden and Norway. Here are two pairs of neighboring sovereign states, once joined and now separated. The separation of the Low Countries offers the nearest parallel, since this was effected on the specific grounds of religious difference. I have earlier likened the Hindu and Muslim communities of the old Indian Empire to Siamese twins; as such they were, before they were parted, hardly able to move; now separate, surely they ought to be able to go along together as companions and friends, to their mutual benefit and support.

Here, however, it is for India, with its far greater population, resources, and developed industries, to show the same political judgment as Sweden showed toward Norway after their separation—that is to say, a final and sincere acceptance of the partition as desirable and in itself as at last opening the door to a real understanding between the two culturally different peoples of the subcontinent.

Even a small minority can make great mischief if it keeps up and repeats the political slogans of unity which may have had a sense at one time but which today can only prevent that good neighborly relation on which future co-operation in international politics depends.

In problems such as water, both east and west between the two republics of India and Pakistan, refugee property and other financial claims and counterclaims should be settled now in a way that the weaker country of the two shall not feel that it has been browbeaten and unjustly treated by its vast and powerful neighbor.

The problem of Kashmir should also be faced as an honest attempt to bring about by plebiscite, under international auspices, a final settlement on the basis of the triumph of the popular will. Were India to adopt consistently toward Pakistan the policy adopted by Sweden toward Norway, by Holland toward Belgium, not only for years but for decades, not only peace in Southern Asia but the full weight for international peace and good will necessarily will increase to an extent of which we at present can have little idea. The great role to be played as bridge between West and East beyond the frontiers of Pakistan and India can be accomplished only if and when these two neighbors are themselves capable of co-

operation and such fair dealing toward each other as will
convince the rest of the world that they have a claim to be
listened to and seriously considered.

The alternative to an Indian policy of understanding
and the encouragement of water and other economic needs
of Pakistan, not only justly, but with free comprehension,
can be that the neighbor will turn in other directions for
alliances and friendships—the result of which must lead
to these two neighborly powers, instead of looking outward
and working for world peace, watching each other, ever
on the lookout for danger and discord rather than for
peaceful and economic independence and development.

I do not think that the countries of the Near East,
with the possible exception of Egypt, face any population
problems which, granted courage, resolution and ingenuity,
should prove insuperable.

All that the people of countries such as Iran, Iraq, Syria,
the Lebanon, Yemen and even Saudi Arabia need is
knowledge—knowledge of new techniques, knowledge of
engineering, knowledge of agriculture. They have room
and resources enough. Science properly applied can re-
populate their empty lands and make their barren spaces
flourish; can plant cities, fertilize crops; can set up industries and develop their immensely rich mineral and
raw material potentialities. Here there was once the Garden
of Eden; historians and archaeologists have shown that this
region was at one time fertile, rich and populous. So it
can be again, if the powers and the resources available to
mankind now are properly employed. The Arab lands
have been devastated by centuries of folly, by waste and
extravagance due to ignorance; the pitiful condition of
their peoples today is a condemnation of their past. There
is no need to look further than Israel to realize what
courage and determination, allied to skill and urgent need,
can achieve. The Arabs are no whit inferior to any race
in the world in intelligence and potential capacity. A single
generation's concentrated and devoted attention to the real
needs of education for all, of scientific and technical as
well as academic teaching, training and discipline, could
revolutionize the Arab world. Self-help is better by far
than grants in aid, and better than perpetual outpouring by
the United States of its surplus production. The Arabs' only
danger lies in continued apathy and ignorance in a swiftly changing world, and in a social and economic outlook
and practices unadapted to the challenging realities of our
time.

I have little fear about the impact of the future of the British Crown Colonies in Africa. We have seen the noble work of Great Britain in West Africa. In East and Central Africa the problem is at present complicated by the presence of a European settler population. I believe that there can be a healthy and satisfactory adjustment, provided all sections in these multiracial communities—indigenous Africans and immigrant Europeans and Asians—face the simple, fundamental fact that they are all dependent upon each other. No one section can dismiss any other from its calculations, either about contributions to past development or about plans for the future. The immigrant, be he European or Asian, has no hope of prosperity without the Africans; the African cannot do without the European farmer or the Asian trader, unless he wants to see his standard of living fall steeply, and with it all hope of exploiting and enhancing the natural wealth of the land in which all three have their homes and must earn their bread.

To a Muslim there is one quietly but forcibly encouraging element in this situation. Wherever the indigenous population is Muslim, there is remarkably little racial antagonism or sense of bitterness against the European, in spite of the European's obvious economic superiority. Islam, after all, is a soil in which sentiments of this sort do not take root or flourish easily. This is not a shallow and fatalistic resignation; it is something much more profound in the essence of the teaching of Islam—a basic conviction that in the eyes of God all men, regardless of color or class or economic condition, are equal. From this belief there springs an unshakable self-respect whose deepest effects are in the subconscious, preventing the growth of bitterness or any sense of inferiority or jealousy by one man of another's economic advantage.

Islam in all these countries has within it, I earnestly believe, the capacity to be a moral and spiritual force of enormous significance, both stabilizing and energizing the communities among whom it is preached and practiced. To ignore Islam's potential influence for good, Islam's healing and creative power for societies as for individuals, is to ignore one of the most genuinely hopeful factors that exists in the world today.

But what of the recurrent, intractable issue of peace or war? Few epochs in recent history have been more devastating and disastrous than (to quote a phrase of Sir

Winston Churchill's) "this tormented half-century." Is the long torment at last over?

I can only hope fervently, with all my being, that this is so; that the nations and their leaders are sincerely and actively convinced not only of the negative proposition that a Third World War would effect the destruction of civilization, perhaps indeed of humanity, but of its positive corollary that it now lies within men's power enormously and rapidly to enhance and increase civilization and to promote the material well-being of millions who now rank as "have nots." The only chance of nations and individuals alike among the "have nots" lies in the preservation of peace. Europe needs a century or more of recuperation after the agony and havoc that its peoples have endured, and recuperation means peace. The industrial and productive capacity of North America—the United States and Canada—already vaster than anything the world has ever seen, is increasing fast; North America needs markets, and markets mean peace. The underdeveloped countries, in Africa, Asia and South America, need over the years a vast and steady inflow of capital investment—to build and develop their communications, to exploit their resources, to raise their standard of living—and investment on this scale and to this end calls for peace. War, in face of such circumstances and so numerous and so imperative a series of needs, would be madness. But I must admit that if we look back at the history of the past fifty years, this has not been a consideration that has deflected the nations and their leaders from catastrophic courses. All the hardly won prosperity and security, all the splendid and beckoning hopes of the last quarter of the nineteenth century counted for nothing when the crucial test came. Pride and folly swayed men's hearts. The world's state today is the result of pride and folly.

As Germany did for so long, Russia now supplies the civilized world's great enigma, the riddle to which there seems no sensible or satisfactory answer. One factor in Russia's perplexing equation is obvious and known—the factor whose results can only be happy, peaceful and prosperous. The other—the perpetual "x"—is grim and incalculable. Long ago Lord Palmerston said that Russian history taught this lesson: the Russians must expand, and they will go on expanding until they encounter some force —a nation or a combination of nations—powerful enough to stop them. From its beginnings in the Grand Duchy of Moscow, Russia has expanded steadily and remorselessly.

Is expansion still the dominant motive in Russian policy? There are some somber indications that this is one of the many characteristics which Communist Russia possesses in common with Czarist Russia and that her appetite for expansion is still not glutted.

Yet why should this be so? Are there not other more peaceful factors at work? Russia's empty lands, within her own borders, are greater by far than those that opened up, decade after decade, in front of the pioneers who extended the United States from small, precarious beginnings along the Atlantic seaboard. Russia has no need of overseas colonies, no need, now that aerial communications have developed so swiftly and so powerfully, for those "windows on warm seas" which once mattered so much. Inside her own frontiers, if her leaders can genuinely be convinced that no one menaces the Soviet Union, that no one harbors aggressive, imperialist designs against her, her people may live at peace for centuries. Will these realistic and wholesome considerations carry the day, or will suspicion, blind hatred, pride and folly wreak new and more terrible havoc? As in the German people before the Second World War there was the dreadful, Wagnerian death wish, driving a great and superbly talented nation to self-immolation, so is there in the heart of all men some dark, satanic evil still lusting for destruction? These are the stern riddles of our time, and each of us seeks his own answers to them.

But these issues and questions concern men in the aggregate, great bodies of men in national and racial groups. The biggest group, however, is composed only of the number of individuals in it. If it is possible to bring happiness to one individual, in him at least the dark and evil impulses may be conquered. And in the end may not the power of good in the individual prevail against the power of evil in the many?

I can only say to everyone who reads this book that it is my profound conviction that man must never ignore and leave untended and undeveloped that spark of the Divine which is in him. The way to personal fulfillment, to individual reconciliation with the Universe that is about us, is comparatively easy for anyone who firmly and sincerely believes, as I do, that Divine Grace has given man in his own heart the possibilities of illumination and of union with Reality. It is, however, far more important to attempt to offer some hope of spiritual sustenance to those many who, in this age in which the capacity of faith is nonexistent in the majority, long for something beyond themselves, even if it seems second best. For them there is the possibility of finding strength of the spirit, comfort and happiness in contemplation of the infinite variety and beauty of the Universe.

Life in the ultimate analysis has taught me one enduring lesson. The subject should always disappear in the object. In our ordinary affections one for another, in our daily work with hand or brain, most of us discover soon enough that any lasting satisfaction, any contentment that we can achieve, is the result of forgetting self, of merging subject with object in a harmony that is of body, mind and spirit. And in the highest realms of consciousness all who believe in a Higher Being are liberated from all the clogging and hampering bonds of the subjective self in prayer, in rapt meditation upon and in the face of the glorious radiance of eternity, in which all temporal and earthly consciousness is swallowed up and itself becomes the eternal.

MOCHTAR LUBIS: THE MERDEKA MAN

[from *Twilight in Djakarta*]

The author of this remarkable novel was born in Sumatra and was a thoughtful observer of the last decades of the Dutch government of his country and an individualistic commentator on the conflicting ideologies which arose to take its place. A fearless newspaper publisher and editor, he won many awards and was often imprisoned.

Twilight in Djakarta is the story of a young Indonesian diplomat who returns to his homeland and is caught up in its political and moral tensions. The plot generally moves more swiftly than it does in this passage, but this one seems particularly appropriate to the emphasis of the present anthology.

They had been debating in the room for over two hours already; the problem they were discussing was turned over time and again, returning to its starting point, but it still looked as if the end was nowhere in sight. Suryono looked around him and was amazed: were all these friends really convinced of what they were saying, and were they serious in believing that what they were doing here was of benefit to the nation? He felt somewhat trapped, because Ies Iskaq had once challenged him by saying that if he was so completely dissatisfied, why didn't he join them, to think about the nation's problems, and she brought him several times to these meetings.

There were only six of them in the room. Ies, himself, Pranoto, the well-known essayist, who often wrote on Indonesia's cultural problems and was considered to be the driving force behind this small club. His face was that of a thinker and he always spoke with sincerity. Achmad, a labour leader, and Yasrin, a poet, who as time went on felt that there was no chance for him to grow and develop

in his own country, and Murhalim, a young provincial
comptroller who was constantly enraged by the conditions
in his office.

"Is there a crisis, or isn't there?" said Pranoto. "Actually,
the fact that this question is being raised at all shows that a
feeling of responsibility already exists in society. And . . ."

Suryono stopped listening to Pranoto's exposition and
thought of how time and again he had heard such dis-
cussions—about the function of culture in building up the
country, of the individual's loneliness in Indonesian society
and where was Indonesian music going, and he recalled a
particularly heated debate about Europeans having reached
a dead end, and how the debate finished with a question
from one of the people in the gathering—who was it? . . .
he forgot—why were we worrying whether the peoples of
Western Europe were stalemated or not; were we West
Europeans?

He was aware of Ies sitting at his side, her fine face, the
full curves of her breasts, and in his imagination he saw
her without a badju on, lying beside him in bed, and was
comparing her with Fatma. The young woman, feeling
his stare, turned her head to glance at Suryono. What she
saw in his face caused her to blush and she quickly
turned away. Suryono woke with a start and heard Yasrin
saying, "I received an invitation to visit Peking at the
expense of the Ministry of Education. In my conversation
with the minister I explained my desire to go to R.R.T.[1] to
study how they develop art among the masses over there.
In my opinion, the problem of social integration in our
nation is very closely connected with the development of
a national culture. I even think that the problem of our
society is a cultural problem."

"Just what do you mean by national culture?" asked
Murhalim. "I know—people are already sick and tired of
hearing this problem discussed, but why get excited about
the problem of a national culture? Why do people want to
synthesize regional cultures in order to produce one national culture? Why do people want to synthesize Western
dancing with the Srimpi[2] dance, or nationalize the
Srimpi? Why must gamelan[3] music be 'national-orches-

[1]*Republik Rakjat Tionghwa* = Chinese People's Republic.
[2]Originally a court dance, Srimpi is the classical dance for women
in Central Java.
[3]Javanese orchestra composed mainly of percussion instruments.

trated' with the addition of a viola, piano and cello? Why don't we view the problem from an angle in which the gamelan is national music, as the Sudanese angklung and ketjapi[4] are equally national music, and the S›rimpi dance of Central Java, the dances of Bali, the plate and hand-kerchief dances of Sumatra, the tjakalele[5] of the Moluccas, the pakarene[6] of Sulawesi, etc., all are national dances, because aren't they all the property of the Indonesian peo-ple, but only of different regional origin? I believe the problem does not involve national culture but the In-donesians, who are not as yet mature enough to feel them-selves as one nation and who still differentiate between the regions."

"I protest, I protest," said Achmad. "What Murhalim just said is surely nice to hear. But this means being blind to history, and to reality as it actually is. The problem of national culture *does* arise, because the Indonesian people indeed do not have a national consciousness. This is why a national culture must be created: to achieve our national integration."

"Is it possible to organize a national culture when the people don't have a national consciousness, as you've just said? Which comes first, a national culture or a national consciousness?" retorted Murhalim.

"Ah, your thinking is rather naïve, brother," said Achmad. "It's decadent bourgeois thinking. It is necessary to establish a concept of national culture at the top and then to spread it downwards. This is why I agree with brother Yasrin's plan to study the development of the peo-ple's culture in R.R.T. He will probably learn a lot and be inspired by their example."

"But maybe what is possible in R.R.T. cannot be applied in Indonesia," interposed Ies.

"What do you mean?" asked Achmad.

"In R.R.T., power is in the hands of the Communists and everything is run by a dictatorship. We in Indonesia have high respect for democracy."

"What does democracy mean today to the Indonesian people?" asked Achmad. "It is the voice of the bourgeois class wanting to retain its power over the ignorant and

---

[4]*Angklung:* percussion instrument made of bamboo tubes; *ketjapi*: a type of lute.

[5]*Tjakalele:* a war dance in the islands of East Indonesia.

[6]*Pakarene:* ritual dances in South Celebes (Sulawesi), especially in the regions of Makasar.

confused masses. How do we stand with our democracy? Is the provisional parliament democratic? Are our people already capable of realizing a democracy? Can you answer that honestly?"

"Eh . . . certainly not ripe yet, nevertheless . . ." said Murhalim.

"Nah, there you have that lack of certainty, the lack of courage of Indonesians to face the true reality. That's why our country is confused. That's why a moral crisis, a cultural crisis and all sorts of crises arise. Permit me to speak, and I hope Murhalim and Ies will refrain from interrupting me before I have really finished."

Achmad drew breath, looked around with the air of a man confident of his coming victory.

"According to Marx and Engels, it is the system of production which determines the process of social, political and intellectual life of man. This is the very root of our crisis. Because the system of production in our country is not only imperialistic but the height of capitalism, all sorts of crises are certain to occur, so long as their roots are not eradicated. And is any effort made to eradicate them, or to attempt to eradicate them? No! You, brothers, are worrying about a cultural crisis, but the discussion is all up in the clouds, because you don't want to face reality. The bourgeois spirit causes all this, brothers."

"I protest," shouted Ies.

Pranoto pounded on the table.

"Let Achmad finish speaking first," he said.

Achmad looked around again, and this time his expression conveyed that it's done, he must win. The little wheels in his mind strained, and all the arguments that had to be advanced became clear and precise.

"It is not man's consciousness that determines the condition of the self, or the personal condition, but it's the social self or the social situation which determines the consciousness of the individual. And because the system of production determines also the social life of man, it is clear therefore that a certain type of production system, such as capitalism, is a chain that constricts the social self of man, which further means pushing self-consciousness towards a conception of individuality. So it's clear that capitalism directly enslaves the human soul, and that from such a system of production inevitably arise all sorts of crises, especially because of the conflicts among peoples who wish to free themselves from enslavement to this capitalism. So, if we discuss cultural crisis, we really should be discussing the basis of our economy."

"But you seem to propose that Indonesia should become a Communist state?" said Ies. "Our state is based on Pantjasila."[7]

"Ha, Pantjasila," said Achmad. "I can muster arguments which will convince people with equal success that the Pantjasila aims in fact at an Islamic state, or a Christian state, or a socialist-welfare state, or at a Communist state. I'm not going to discuss the Pantjaslia, because its philosophy is not fully thought out; but how can we debate here? Ah, brothers, I beg you not to interrupt me. Permit me to speak until I have finished. As I said before, you, brothers, are not realistic in viewing the problem. We cannot discuss the cultural crisis which confronts us without touching on the economic system which still prevails in our country. The political development, law, philosophy, religion, literature, art and so forth are all based on economic development, so said Engels."

"Brother Achmad, have you finished?" asked Murhalim.

"Yes."

"May I ask a question?"

"Please," replied Achmad.

"I want to ask only one thing," said Murhalim. "Are you, brother Achmad, a Communist, or a member of the Communist party?"

"What connection is there between my being a Communist or a member of the Communist party and the problem we're discussing?" asked Achmad resentfully.

"If brother Achmad is a member of the Communist party, then it would be futile to continue this debate," said Murhalim, "because, to the end of days there would be no meeting of minds between us. I believe in democracy. Marxism, as practised by Communists, not only doesn't bring freedom and happiness to man, but ends up by bringing enslavement and loss of humanity. What brother Achmad wishes is that a dictatorship of the proletariat be established in Indonesia. But brother Achmad has forgotten that human beings are not machines who can be ordered to become parts of a production system. Next to materialism, there are also spiritual values of no less importance for ensuring the good way of life. If a man's stomach may not be

---

[7]The Five Principles: Belief in God, Nationalism, Humanism, Sovereignty of the People and Social Justice, proclaimed in 1945 by President Sukarno as the basis of the Indonesian State.

empty, neither may his soul be starved, and it must be able to live and flourish in freedom. Brother Achmad wants an economic system wholly controlled by the state, one hundred per cent. Such a totalitarian system must, of necessity, control the lives and thoughts of people, because without such absolute control and authority it would be impossible to attain what brother Achmad wishes for. I can agree that some parts of an economic system can influence the cultural development of a people. But one cannot completely disregard the human factors. The peoples of Persia, India, Egypt, Rome, Greece attained the peaks of their cultural glory under a system of absolute monarchy, which, according to Communist theory, could not possibly produce highly prized values. The painter Picasso, who glorifies the Communists, is himself the product of a bourgeois society and of capitalistic Western Europe. And I want to ask further, where are those cultural products that are supposedly coming out of Russia today? But—to return to my question —are you a Communist?"

"Your question implies a confession that you're unable to carry on the debate. I am not a Communist, but if conditions in our country should continue as they are today, with a leadership which continues to deceive the people, with corruption on the rampage, with disintegration and confusion, then I shall become a Communist."

Murhalim shrugged his shoulders.

"It's a bit difficult to continue a debate when one is accused of inability to continue it."

"I am not an expert on Islam," intervened Ies, "but I want to introduce a thought for all of us to consider: could not Islam be made the mainstay of our people's spiritual uplift? A modernized Islam, with a new dynamism?"

"Ha, Islam, what naïveté. Very naïve," interposed Achmad quickly. "I once talked to a man who came from a Middle East country and had visited its Islamic university, one of the highest, most widely acclaimed centres for the study of modern Islam in the world today. Do you know, sister, what he said? He was very disappointed. Disappointed no end. What he found was incredible dirt, people sleeping on dirty floors and nothing organized. And what did this Islam bring to these Arab countries? All we see is that one class of society exploits the masses who for hundreds of years have lived on the brink of starvation and in darkest ignorance."

"But this is not yet reason enough to reject the idea of seeking a new dynamism in Islam," Ies replied. "Probably,

with sufficient conscious stimulation, some Islamic thinkers
capable of finding it could emerge in Indonesia, too! The
conditions we see today in Islamic countries are not the
fault of Islam, but of some Moslems who disregard the
teachings of their religion. They make the study of Islam
a completely dead thing—no different than if one made a
mynah bird recite the verses of the Holy Quran, or from
putting the verses of the Quran on gramophone records
and then letting them play day and night. Since the majority
of our people adhere to the religious teachings of Islam,
and if some Islamic leaders would come forth bringing a
new dynamism into Islam, couldn't Islam then become a
tremendous force in the development of our people?"

"Theory! Vain hope! Impossible!" exclaimed Achmad
heatedly. "There isn't a single proof in history that religion
can bring about a good human society. Christianity at the
time of its greatest glory, Islam at the time of its greatest
glory, Buddhism at the time of its greatest glory, which of
these really succeeded in eliminating the contrasts between
the classes and bringing justice to humanity? The time of
Islam's glory was, as we saw, an era of royal power;
enslavement is still the order of the day, so where is your
just society? As Christianity flourished with its crusades,
so also the Spanish Catholic Church going to South
America has spread death and hatred."

"Brother Achmad appears to be completely antireligion,"
interposed Murhalim. "And, to criticize religion, he uses
Communist clichés. What Ies meant was to seek out and
develop the valuable principles contained in Islamic religion, just as there are valuable principles in any religion.
Values which now are buried and dead should be revived,
given a new life. That was the problem suggested by Ies's
question. Could Islam with a new dynamism be used to
become the mainstay for the development of our people?
This question was posed, I believe, because with the exception of you, brother Achmad, all of us here reject Communism with its totalitarian system as a means to build up
our nation."

"I don't reject Communism," said Suryono, speaking up
for the first time. "Why should Communism be rejected?
Look at Russia where it succeeded in freeing the people
from feudal oppression and provided them with livelihood.
Look also at R.R.T., how tremendous the progress which
has been initiated by Mao Tse-tung in all fields—the liberation of the people from the oppression and corruption of

Chiang Kai-shek's clique. If it can be done there, why not here?"

"Suryono, don't play!" Ies exclaimed. "I know you. You don't believe your own words!"

"You're right, Ies," replied Suryono. "Of course I don't believe what I've just said. Has it ever occurred to anyone that we do not live today in an atomic age, but in an age of unbelief? An age of unbelief caused by the deep frustration felt by mankind since the end of the last world war, when they saw that this war would not end all wars either? Isn't it evident that the Americans are afraid of their own atom and hydrogen bombs, do not believe in themselves, and the Russians, too, don't dare trust each other, that the Asians do not trust the West, that the West fears and doesn't trust Asia? Malan's racialism in South Africa, the white-skin policy in Australia, suspicion against foreigners in Indonesia and in other Asian countries, discrimination against Negroes in America—all this underlies this absence of faith. Because people don't trust each other they do not believe that human beings are equal and that they can and must be able to live together. The Communist is like this, the imperialist is like this, the democrat is like this, the merdeka[8] man is like this. They're all the same. There's little use spending oneself on exchanges of ideas, as we do here. Isn't it best to take care of oneself, seek one's own happiness in any way one chooses and to the devil with the world?"

"You're joking!" said Ies accusingly.

"No, he's not joking," spoke Achmad with a light smile. "It's quite true what he said about that nonbelief. But he forgot to clarify the cause of the lack of faith in the world today. It is the evil outcome of capitalism and imperialism which still——"

"And therefore we should all become Communists," broke in Murhalim.

Achmad glanced at Murhalim with great resentment.

"It's hard to exchange ideas in an intelligent manner with people who are as prejudiced as brother Murhalim here." He pretended to be plaintive.

"I want to intervene before the discussion strays off elsewhere," said Suryono, a smile playing on his lips. "If this discussion should be continued without a change of di-

---

[8]*Merdeka*, lit. freedom, is a much-used Indonesian slogan and greeting, hence "merdeka man" implies an Indonesian.

rection we are sure to get absolutely nowhere, because, friends, you're all taking the wrong view of the problem. Achmad, who adheres to historic materialism, is wrong; our friend who wanted to put forward Islam is also wrong. The root of the matter is man himself. That which is called crisis of leadership, cultural crisis, economic crisis, moral crisis, crisis in literature, is nothing but man's crisis. That's why an Indonesian must first of all realize that he exists and that his fate is in his own hands. That his life is not determined by society, is not determined by his family, not by the economic system, but that he has enough inner strength to determine himself."

"Ah, existentialist! Pessimistic bourgeois ideas!" sneered Achmad promptly.

Suryono laughed and looked at him.

"I admit frankly that what I've just said is lifted straight out of Sartre," he said. "But, of course, only people who are half-informed on existentialism always assert that it is a pessimistic philosophy. Yet, it is quite the contrary. Existentialism is the most optimistic of philosophies because it says that man, and not outside influences, can determine his own self. Sartre said it in *L'existentialisme est un humanisme*—have you read it, brother Achmad?" he asked, taunting, which made Achmad look at him furiously, and Suryono, smiling, continued, "In fact, Sartre himself opposed Marxism, because Marxism conceals the truth that man is fully responsible for his attitudes and choices. Sartre's argument is that the individual is fully responsible for what he is and what he does. That's why there is no other philosophy that is more optimistic than this existentialism, optimistic in the recognition of the individual's capacity to determine himself and to act as an individual, which is the only hope for humanity, as only by acting can man survive."

Pranoto coughed lightly, looked around, saw that Achmad was tearing to jump into the debate again and quickly said, "Ah, before we knew it, it's almost seven o'clock already. I'm really sorry to have to adjourn our meeting at a time when the discussion was becoming so very interesting, especially since Suryono, who kept quiet at the beginning, has now jumped into the arena with both feet. Although we have not arrived at any conclusion, I believe that many valuable ideas have been expressed, whether one agreed with every one of them or not. That such ideas are present, as well as the readiness of us all to discuss them and to listen, shows that we have high enough expectations from this exchange of ideas that it will enable each of us to clarify for himself the essence of the ideas touched upon here. I think that the most fortunate man among us is brother Achmad because to him everything is already clear. For him the road to our people's development and human happiness is Communism—while the others are still questioning and still searching for the way which seems best according to their views and convictions."

"I cannot discern the good fortune in Achmad's situation. His thoughts are no longer free," interjected Murhalim.

They laughed, and Achmad joined in laughing with them. Pranoto stood up and said, "Before we adjourn— remember that the meeting next week is on Wednesday."

Outside, Suryono said to Ies, "I will see you home, Ies."

"It's not necessary," said Ies. "I have a bicycle."

"Leave it here, I have Father's Dodge. Father just bought himself a new Cadillac! Tomorrow's time enough to pick up the bicycle, or get your younger brother to fetch it."

Ies looked very hesitant.

"You're angry with me," Suryono said. "You suspect that I was being sarcastic and was making fun of them with this existentialism?"

Ies regarded him for a moment and then said, "All right, you see me home."

They rode in Suryono's father's car, a new Dodge. "Aduh, it's embarrassing to be seen in such a luxurious car," sighed Ies. "They will suspect me of riding with a black marketeer or a corrupter."

"Ah, why these allusions?" Suryono asked. "If Father is wallowing in money made in business, why throw it into my face?"

"Forgive me, I'm wrong," said Ies, and, sincerely regretful, she lightly patted Suryono's neck and playfully wiggled the edge of his ear, gently.

No little startled, Suryono glanced at Ies, a thrill passing through him, but he quickly suppressed it. He was afraid to disturb the mood in the car. Never yet had he felt so close to Ies.

"I swear I wasn't mocking with this existentialism, Ies," he said. "I really, really believe that man has the strength to determine what and who he is."

"Ah, I'm already tired of pondering these involved problems," said Ies. "I just want to rest." And she leaned her head on his shoulder. "Let's not go home directly," said Ies. "Let's first take a little ride."

Suryono, happily, smiled and pressed Ies's hand with warmth.

GAMAL ABDEL NASSER: A ROLE IN SEARCH OF A HERO

[from *Falsafat al-thawrah*, The Philosophy of the Revolution]

Important books need not be badly written; and President Nasser's reflections on the Egyptian revolution of 1952, while inviting and receiving no acclaim as great literature, nonetheless revealed another remarkable talent on the part of their author. Its language is not so blunt and military as some expected it to be, and, in fact, its introspective probings and straightforward diction make up a timely and representative expression. Whatever else might be said, the book itself and its elaborations have certainly been seminal, for better or worse.

The age of isolation is gone.

And gone are the days in which barbed wire served as demarcation lines, separating and isolating countries from one another. No country can escape looking beyond its boundaries to find the source of the currents which influence how it can live with others, and so forth.

And no state can escape trying to determine its status within its living space and trying to see what it can do in that space, and what is its field of activities and its positive role in this troubled world.

Sometimes I sit in my study reflecting on the subject, asking myself: What is our positive role in this troubled world, and where is the place in which we should fulfill that role?

I review our circumstances and discover a number of circles within which our activities inescapably must be confined and in which we must try to move.

Fate does not jest and events are not a matter of chance —there is no existence out of nothing. We cannot look at the map of the world without seeing our own place upon it, and that our role is dictated by that place.

Can we fail to see that there is an Arab circle surrounding us—that this circle is a part of us, and we are a part of it, our history being inextricably part of its history?

These are facts and no mere idle talk. Can we possibly ignore the fact that there is an African continent which Fate decreed us to be a part of, and that it is also decreed that a terrible struggle exists for its future—a struggle whose results will be either for us or against us, with or without our will? Can we further ignore the existence of an Islamic world, with which we are united by bonds created not only by religious belief, but also reinforced by historic realities? As I have said once, Fate is no jester.

It is not without significance that our country is situated west of Asia, in contiguity with the Arab states with whose existence our own is interwoven. It is not without significance, too, that our country lies in northeast Africa, overlooking the Dark Continent, wherein rages a most tumultuous struggle between white colonizers and black inhabitants for control of its unlimited resources. Nor is it without significance that, when the Mongols swept away the ancient capitals of Islam, Islamic civilization and the Islamic heritage fell back on Egypt and took shelter there. Egypt protected them and saved them, while checking the onslaught of the Mongols at ʿAin Jalut. All these are fundamental realities with deep roots in our lives which we cannot—even if we try—escape or forget.

I do not know why I recall, whenever I reach this point in my recollections as I meditate alone in my room, a famous tale by a great Italian poet, Luigi Pirandello— *Six Characters in Search of an Author*. The pages of history are full of heroes who created for themselves roles of glorious valor which they played at decisive moments. Likewise the pages of history are also full of heroic and glorious roles which never found heroes to perform them. For some reason it seems to me that within the Arab circle there is a role, wandering aimlessly in search of a hero. And I do not know why it seems to me that this role, exhausted by its wanderings, has at last settled down, tired and weary, near the borders of our country and is beckoning to us to move, to take up its lines, to put on its costume, since no one else is qualified to play it.

Here, let me hasten to say that this role is not one of leadership. It is rather a role of interaction with, and responsibility to, all the above-mentioned factors. It is a role such as to spark this tremendous power latent in the area surrounding us—a role tantamount to an experiment, with the aim of creating a great strength which will then undertake a positive part in the building of the future of mankind.

There can be no doubt that the Arab circle is the most important, and the one with which we are most closely linked. For its peoples are intertwined with us by history. We have suffered together, we have gone through the same crises, and when we fell beneath the hooves of the invaders' steeds, they were with us under the same hooves.

We are also bound in this circle by a common religion.

The center of Islamic learning has always moved within the orbit of its several capital cities—first Mecca, then shifting to Kufa, then to Damascus, next to Baghdad, and finally to Cairo.

Lastly, the fact that the Arab states are contiguous has joined them together in a geographical framework made solid by all these historical, material and spiritual factors.

So far as I can recall, the first glimmers of Arab awareness began to steal into my consciousness when I was a student in secondary school. I used to go out on a general strike with my comrades every year on the second of December to protest the Balfour Declaration which Britain had made on behalf of the Jews, giving them a national home in Palestine, thus tyrannously wresting it from its rightful owners. And at that time, when I asked myself why I went out on strike with such zeal, and why I was angry about this act by a country I had never seen, I could find no answer except in the echoes of sympathetic emotion.

Then a kind of understanding began to develop when I became a student in the Military Academy, where I studied in particular the history of all past military campaigns in Palestine and in general the history of the area and its conditions which have made of it during the past hundred years an easy prey for the fangs of hungry beasts. Things grew still clearer and the underlying realities became apparent when, in the General Staff College, I began to study the late Palestine campaign and the problems of the Mediterranean in detail.

The result was that when the Palestine crisis began, I was utterly convinced that the fighting there was not taking place on foreign soil, nor was our part in it a matter of sentiment. It was a duty necessitated by self-defense. . . .

If we consider next the second circle—the continent of

Africa—I may say without exaggeration that we cannot, under any circumstances, however much we might desire it, remain aloof from the terrible and sanguinary conflict going on there today between five million whites and 200 million Africans. We cannot do so for an important and obvious reason: we are *in* Africa. The peoples of Africa will continue to look to us, who guard their northern gate, and who constitute their link with the outside world. We will never in any circumstances be able to relinquish our responsibility to support, with all our might, the spread of enlightenment and civilization to the remotest depths of the jungle.

There remains another important reason. It is that the Nile is the life artery of our country, bringing water from the heart of the continent.

As a final reason, the boundaries of our beloved brother, the Sudan, extend far into the depths of Africa, bringing into contiguity the politically sensitive regions in that area.

The Dark Continent is now the scene of a strange and excited turbulence: the white man, representing various European nations, is again trying to redivide the map of Africa. We shall not, in any circumstance, be able to stand idly by in the face of what is going on, in the false belief that it will not affect or concern us.

I will continue to dream of the day when I will find in Cairo a great African institute dedicated to unveiling to our view the dark reaches of the continent, to creating in our minds an enlightened African consciousness, and to sharing with others from all over the world the work of advancing the welfare of the peoples of this continent.

There remains the third circle, which circumscribes continents and oceans, and which is the domain of our brothers in faith, who, wherever under the sun they may be, turn, as we do, in the direction of Mecca, and whose devout lips speak the same prayers.

When I went with the Egyptian delegation to the Kingdom of Saudi Arabia to offer condolences on the death of its great sovereign, my belief in the possibility of extending the effectiveness of the Pilgrimage, building upon the strength of the Islamic tie that binds all Muslims, grew very strong. I stood before the Kaʿba, and in my mind's eye I saw all the regions of the world which Islam has reached. Then I found myself saying that our view of the Pilgrimage must change. It should not be regarded only as a ticket of admission into Paradise after a long life, or

as a means of buying forgiveness after a merry one. It
should become an institution of great political power and
significance. Journalists of the world should hasten to cover
the Pilgrimage, not because it is a traditional ritual afford-
ing interesting reports for the reading public, but because
of its function as a periodic political conference in which
the envoys of the Islamic states, their leaders of thought,
their men learned in every branch of knowledge, their
writers, their captains of industry, their merchants and their
youth can meet, in order to lay down in this Islamic-
world-parliament the broad lines of their national policies
and their pledges of mutual cooperation from one year to
another.

Pious and humble, but strong, they should assemble,
stripped of greed, but active; weak before God, but mighty
against their problems and their enemies; longing for an
afterlife, but convinced of their place in the sun, a place
they must fill in this existence.

I remember that I mentioned some of these thoughts to
His Majesty, King Saʿud, and he said to me, "It is indeed
the real *raison d'être* of the Pilgrimage." To tell the truth,
I myself am unable to imagine any other *raison d'être*.

When I consider the 80 million Muslims in Indonesia,
and the 50 million in China, and the millions in Malaya,
Siam and Burma, and the nearly 100 million in Pakistan,
and the more than 100 million in the Middle East, and the
40 million in the Soviet Union, together with the other
millions in far-flung parts of the world—when I consider
these hundreds of millions united by a single creed, I emerge
with a sense of the tremendous possibilities which we might
realize through the cooperation of all these Muslims, a
cooperation going not beyond the bounds of their natural
loyalty to their own countries, but nonetheless enabling
them and their brothers in faith to wield power wisely and
without limit.

And now I go back to that wandering mission in search
of a hero to play it. Here is the role. Here are the lines,
and here is the stage. We alone, by virtue of our place, can
perform the role.

MUHAMMAD KAMEL HUSSEIN: THE APOSTLES' SELF-REPROACH

[from *Qaryah Ẓālimah*, The Unjust City]

> The Unjust City *is a novel, or, perhaps more accurately, a series of character studies and reflections taking fictional form, about the Passion of Christ. Somewhat startlingly, it is the work of a prominent Moslem surgeon and educator. Almost never have Moslem authors chosen to stop at that theme, and Hussein's treatment of it won him the State Prize for Literature in Cairo in 1957 and prompted some alert Christian writers to pronounce it the most profound encounter with Christian problems on the part of a Moslem in recent years.*
>
> *Partly fetched from Freud, as the author explains, the central theme of the book is the tortured inability of Christ's followers to prevent the crucifixion, a bad dream which the author finds to shed unique illumination on Christian history. "The best Christian in his most sublime moments," he says, "is a sad man."*[1]
>
> *In the passage included here, one of the Magi is given the floor to summarize the indecision of the Apostles.*

The wise man who was their guest sat silently listening to their discussion without making his views known. But at this point he intervened to say, while they gave him close attention: "Much of what I have heard has surprised me. I have been apprehensive to see how far short you come in fulfilling the Sermon on the Mount. We listened to it and understood its import and I thought that it had penetrated your innermost souls and purified your conscience. I was convinced none of you would take a course of action inconsistent with its principles. Now I realise that you still regard it only as a noble exhortation

---

[1] See the "Author's Note," in Hussein, *City of Wrong* (Amsterdam, 1959), pages 223–225.

whose directives are to be followed only when feasible, and neglected when they conflict with the weakness and evil in man's nature.

I have also noted in much of what you have said that the emotions actuating you are not such as the master commended to you. In other people who have not listened to the master or known his guiding word, they might well be the most lofty sentiments. But in your case, your motives must be absolutely irreproachable. Motives are worthy or detestable, according to whether they coincide with or contravene conscience. I have heard you argue that it is your love for the master Christ that compels you to take reprisals against those who wrong him. But the real truth is that what drives you to them is hatred of his foes, not love for him. These two are sharply contrasted, though it is often supposed that they are mutually necessary. In their confusion of this score, people imagine that love on their part for a friend can only be by dint of their hating his enemy. To love one's country, for example, means, on this view, hating its enemies. But in fact there is a vast difference between the two attitudes. Love never invites to evil. If I find love calling for evil-doing I know that in the heart of the person in question it has turned into hatred of his enemy. This is an error into which most people fall. You must be wary of it. So easy is the confusion that only a very fine sensitivity of conscience is aware of it, and is zealously vigilant for the good in all its purity.

You have invoked also the principle of the triumph of the right through force. But what else is this on your part but a confusing of right with power? It is a delusion into which most people fall. Right recognises itself as bound by obligations; indeed it could be said in its very nature to be these limits. Force, however, in the nature of the case overreaches these limits as far as it can go. As and when proceeding together it is only temporarily so. Those who defend the right by force do so only until they gain their end. Then force alone becomes their master passion. Claims about force as the means to right are usually short-lived claims. They last only awhile. Then force, in full career, needs no sanction from right. All who have recourse to force as a means to the right soon discover that they have merely invoked the right as a means to force. So the idea that what is manifestly right should be defended by force should have no place in your motivation. Otherwise your fate will be that when you have righted the right you will be resting upon force alone. That is precisely what your religion forbids.

You should realise that as long as the right is put in an inferior position it is all the same whether it be force or falsehood to which it is made subservient.

Furthermore, I heard some of you remark that fear of what people say of you was a motive for action to be taken. It is true enough that there are those who believe that fear of this kind is a powerful factor in inducing people to do what is right. The error is very prevalent. Fear of being thought ill of is a very different thing from the desire after virtue. Such fear, as is the case with hatred, may sometimes lead to admirable actions and then quite soon after lead irretrievably to evil. It is in no way fitting that what you do should be motivated by fear.

Then, too, I heard one of you taking pride in his bravery and readiness for sacrifice, out of his anxiety for a good reputation and prestige. One of you remarked that you would find a place in history and that posterity would hold you forever in glorious remembrance. This is indeed a strange motive for action, though by many it is highly valued as an incentive to well-doing. But it is a pagan way of talking; it is the very sort of hollow vaunting and self-magnification the master forbade you. It is a stupid impulse by which only fools are guided. It has no validity as a motive for goodness, but is, in fact, very close to evil.

I have no wish to summon you to any particular line of action or to urge any course upon you. You know better than I the issues before you and are more competent to decide them. But I warn you: watch yourselves, scrutinise the motives behind what you do. If they are evil you will ultimately land in evil, even though you have been motivated by immediate good. I warn you against force and where it may lead you. If you kill or harm anyone in going through with what force prescribes, you will thereby transgress the bounds of conscience. That is the supreme disloyalty to your religion, whatever justification you may think you have for it.

On the point raised by some of you as to the role of that reason with which God has endowed us and the place of our free will, if it is our job to ignore our reason in plain issues like this one, my view is that you should be guided by reason so long as it keeps within the limits of conscience. You must understand that there are laws which the soul must not transgress unless it is to suffer disease. For in that respect the soul resembles the body, though, of course, the principles of soul health are more subtle and less easily understood. The harm, too, that results from flouting them in less evident than the diseases of the body and more far-reaching. The true unison of our powers of choice, the obligations under which we are laid by these laws of the soul and the behests of reason, is the problem of problems in the life of man. It may bring the problem home to our minds if we borrow the parable of a man in a boat. He has full freedom of movement and action, as his mind and his reason may determine, but always on condition that he stay within the boat and the limits of the laws of nature that relate to it. Otherwise he will drown."

At this point the disciple returned whom they had sent to the master to find out his mind and bring back to them his directions. They clamoured around him for news, each hoping that his opinion would be the one to be vindicated. The messenger said: "He commands you to go aside for worship and prayer and to leave him until God fulfills His purpose for him. He bids you go abroad into the world, calling men to his truth. He says he will meet you after three days in one of the villages of Galilee and that whatever be the suffering that befalls him on the morrow, it is by the will of God and it is not for us to resist it. He warns you against violence and reproaches you for your attitudes at the time of his arrest."

When they knew that these were his definite instructions and that they were final, their minds were put to rest in that they had a directive they could not possibly transgress. But the decision threw them into profound sorrow, whether their policy had been action or inaction, violence or non-resistance. Equally hard on all was this call for surrender and acquiescence in the worst. Many of them wept.

They had no compensating satisfactions, such as come with decisive action—the thrill of sacrifice in the cause of truth and the lust of revenge on the enemies of religion. Faith and obedience—these only were left to them. They submitted to his command with sorrowing and despairing hearts. They made up their minds to leave Jerusalem, the city of wrong. But there was in their hearts an utter sadness, a regretful reproach, at being obliged to abandon their prophet to the clutches of evil men, who would wreak their will on him. They were well-nigh broken at the thought of this inescapable choice between tragic inaction and the violation of their prophet's will.

The messenger said to them: "I paid the closest attention to what he said. My view is that we should occupy our-

selves wholly in worship and prayer, however distraught by
anxiety we may be. We must be led by that mountain
sermon. It proved so grievous to us that we forgot it, or
so exacting that we pretended to. Maybe it is well for us to
heed the words of this wise man. He drank in that sermon
and believed what it said with a far firmer faith than ours.
It is our duty to follow his advice and wisdom."

When they heard that, they clung all the more wistfully
to this man of wisdom, so untroubled by doubt and distress
or indecision. They clung as a drowning man might to his
rescuer. They sensed that somehow his absolute faith would
be their refuge, that they would find in him the inspiration
to lighten, perhaps, the burden of grief during three long
days. Through these they had to await their master's return,
God having meanwhile raised him to Himself. They gave
themselves to prayer and devotion, seeking respite thus
from the bitter weight of grief they bore.

There can be no doubt that the decision of the disciples
was the right one, by the criteria of revelation and religion,
and by reference to the things that transcend the capacity
of the human mind fully to understand. Nor is there any
doubt that they were mistaken in fearing the collapse of
the Christian religion when their master was no more with
them. In fact, by this action of theirs in holding back from
forcibly inducing his victory, they rendered a great service
to the Christian message. In that day's events, the Christian
religion defined its principles and formulated its philosophy.
Its dominant characteristics were there and then fashioned.
It was those events which gave rise to the most impressive
of its tenets about forgiveness and redemption. From them
came also that sadness which is a ruling element in the
character of the greatest adherents of Christianity, their
fear of sin, their love of self-reproach and abasement,
their sense of the importance of the sin of Adam and their
belief that it had to do with the anguish Christ underwent
that mankind might be saved from its consequences. Perhaps all these hallmarks of Christianity are simply an echo
of the great sin of the apostles' self-reproach, as if Christians are expiating this sin until the end of time.

But of all that the disciples knew nothing. And apart
from revelation they could not know it.

From the purely human point of view, however, there is
no doubt that what they did was wrong. They left the right
in all its unmistakability to suffer outrage. They exposed
their religion to extinction, their prophet to foul wrong, and

themselves to destruction. Nobody knows what would have
happened to Christianity had they succeeded in rescuing
him by force. But the fact remains that without doubt
the line of action their reason had approved and the
guidance deriving from their reflection and their intuitions
were alike invalid.

If then the disciples, though the finest of men, were not
saved from error after consultation and debate and having
at hand all that makes for right guidance, the people of
Israel have some excuse also if they proved to be mis-
guided. They took the Christian religion for a piece of sedi-
tion, which would quickly have destroyed the pillars of
their religion, their law and their nation. They supposed
that the man was a sorcerer and his followers criminals.
They proceeded upon purely human and self-made criteria
and from human emotions in no way stamped with that
ardent faith that characterised the disciples. If both groups,
disciples and Jews, erred and went astray, what can man
do in his desire to avoid error, as long as he proceeds in
what he does upon human reason alone?

To the present day, Christianity has not freed itself, and
perhaps never will, from the entail of that sorrow and
regret which haunted the souls of the disciples because
of all that they were lacking in relationship to Christ at
the time they held back from saving him. They have been
destined to bear the reproach of the great sin—the sin of
abandoning Christ to his foes, to his oppressors and per-
secutors. It seemed to them that they were commanded
to withhold themselves from rescuing their prophet only
because they did not deserve to be his witnesses.

And thus a dread of falling into sin, an apprehensiveness
about evil-doing, has become a dominant feature of the
Christian spirit. And so it will always remain. For Christians have no way of atoning for what happened on that
day.

TRANSLATED BY KENNETH CRAGG

MOHAMMED REZA SHAH PAHLAVI: MY FATHER

[from *Mission For My Country*]

Probably no Islamic monarch in modern times was more forceful than Reza Khan, who ruled as Shah of Iran between 1925 and 1941. A dynamo of a man, he blazed wide and unpopular trails through tradition in order to bring his country to the type of modernity he thought right for it. In his efforts to modernize, paradoxically, he became the most absolute monarch Iran had known for centuries. In a conscious attempt to avoid much of what was going on in Ataturk's Turkey, he nevertheless ran into formidable opposition both at home and abroad.

His son and successor on the Peacock Throne, studded with the gems which Nadir Shah brought from India, has written a remarkable analysis and appreciation of his father's character and achievement.

Everybody, even among his enemies, agreed that my father possessed a most amazing personality. He could be one of the pleasantest men in the world, yet he could be one of the most frightening. As I have already said, strong men often trembled just to look at him. He had an almost devastating ability to assess human nature. As though he possessed some secret electronic ray, he could almost instantly size up a man's strengths or weaknesses, his integrity or his slipperiness. No wonder many men feared to look him in the eye.

Yet contrary to what many believed, my father was kind and tenderhearted, especially towards his family. His forbidding sternness seemed to melt into love, kindness, and easy familiarity when he was with us. Especially with me, his acknowledged successor to the throne, he would play lightheartedly. When we were alone together, he would sing me little songs; I don't remember his ever doing this in front of others, but when only the two of us were there, he would often sing to me.

Especially remarkable was his simplicity of taste and of personal conduct. Many a self-made man tries to impress others with an ostentatious display of material wealth. Moreover, Oriental monarchs have not generally been known for the simplicity of their habits. But my father proudly shunned the Qajar tradition of lavish luxury.

Even after he became Emperor, he usually wore a simple army uniform tailored in the Russian Cossack style. His homemade stockings were not of very good quality, and he preferred well-worn short boots, which I remember were often in very poor condition. Besides a handkerchief, he carried in his pocket a silver cigarette case containing Persian cigarettes. He was meticulous about personal cleanliness.

In part because of a digestive complaint, his food was of the simplest. For breakfast he had only tea; usually he took none of the fruit or cheese or bread or eggs that most Persians then enjoy. For the other two meals he normally ate rice and boiled chicken, the same thing day after day. In his office he used to drink more tea at regular intervals from a common glass tumbler with a saucer.

Apart from relaxation with his family, my father almost never devoted any time to recreation. Perhaps once or twice a year he would go hunting for two or three hours. Mainly he got his exercise through walking. In my memory it seems as if he was *always* walking, either pacing up and down in his office or inspecting troops or projects on foot, or in the late afternoon, taking long walks in his garden. Often he would hold audiences while walking; those whom he received were on such occasions expected to pace up and down with him. And whenever Reza Shah was walking he was also thinking.

My father's simplicity carried over into his religion. Because he was always hounding certain sections of the clergy, many people thought that he was not religious; but I know that is untrue. He pushed the clergy into the background because at that time many of them were hindering the country's progress and interfering too much in affairs of state. If he had not treated them somewhat toughly, it might have taken three or four times as long as it did to carry out his programme of modernizing the country.

But that does not mean that he had no use for priests or for religion. He always respected the more progressive and enlightened clergy, and he named all of his sons after the Imam Reza, whom he esteemed highly as one of the descendants of our sainted Ali. Naturally his sons received additional names to distinguish them from each other, but as one of his given names each had that of Reza. My father often visited the shrine at Meshed where the Imam Reza is buried. Also, when he desired success in some project, he would swear, earnestly and never profanely, in the name of God or of one of our saints. This is our way of requesting divine assistance.

Surely no man ever believed more in his country than did my father. He was patriotic almost to excess, for sometimes he took a provincial view of accomplishments outside Iran. So complete was his dedication to his country that he believed the Persian culture surpassed all others in every respect.

No man was ever more zealous in seeking to modernize his country. This might seem contrary to his unqualified love for our existing culture, but he didn't regard it so. My father admired Persia's great past, and he wanted to keep those of our ancient ways of living which were not incompatible with modern progress. But he was convinced that Persia's national integrity, as well as the welfare of her people, demanded rapid modernization. Although his travels abroad were so limited, my father was always filled with visions of modern factories, power plants, dams, irrigation systems, railways, highways, cities, and armies. Just how he did it I don't know, but he always seemed to know of the latest industrial, economic, and military advances abroad. It must have been a combination of his hard-won reading habit, plus his penchant for asking searching questions.

My father was not only sober and hard-working, but more than intelligent. He spoke very little, but his terse sentences contained all the pertinent facts and were always to the point. Although he was not, by our modern standards, by any means an educated man, it was amazing how easily he could grasp the essentials of any problem, whether an engineering impasse on the trans-Iranian railway construction project or a matter of foreign policy.

He was notable for the earnestness of his utterances. He had confidence in himself and in what he said, and his words expressed a conviction and belief which came from his heart and which almost invariably moved his listeners deeply. He possessed amazing self-control. Contrary to common opinion, I think that during his entire reign he never really lost his temper. He was often angry when he thought it necessary, but he never lost control.

Equally significant was his marvellous sense of political timing. He possessed the great statesman's knowledge of when to do, or when to avoid doing, any particular thing. In less than one minute he could decide upon a major action, or he could if necessary wait ten years before acting. Many of his thoughts and ideas were turned over in his mind for a long time before he gave them practical expression; in an uncanny way he always seemed to know just when the time was ripe.

In his energy and endurance my father surpassed the ordinary man. He hurled himself unstintingly into the work of modernization, and he expected others to do the same. He totally reorganized the Government's administrative departments, and his spirit of discipline and selfless service began to pervade the whole structure. Often he would appear unheralded at some Government office just at the opening hour. Woe betide any functionaries who arrived late!

For example, on one occasion Reza Shah arrived at our Ministry of Finance just after opening time and ordered all the doors closed. A number of sleepy officials, including the minister, found themselves locked out; they were all promptly sacked. That was just one of many blows my father struck at slothfulness and procrastination. It was Reza Shah who not only pioneered our railway system but had the trains running on time; it always delights me to see the photograph of him aboard a Persian passenger train, looking at his watch and wearing the pleased expression which indicated that the train was arriving exactly on schedule. For the first time in modern Persian history he awakened the people to the importance of punctuality.

Proverbially, to get things done in Persia, one must both reward and punish. My father relied more on punishment than he did on reward or even encouragement. In his view there was no reason to wax sentimental about a man who was doing something well, because that was his duty. On the other hand if my father learned of a man who was doing something poorly or dishonestly, he would live to regret it. Oriental psychology in these matters differs from that of the West, and my father's methods for getting things done showed no little realism in the light of our authoritarian tradition. But in recent years, as our society has become more democratized, other techniques for motivating people have begun to yield better returns than the means my father used.

To inspire his people to ever greater efforts, my father relied essentially upon his own force of character. This appeal was by no means wholly negative. Persians dedicated themselves to his projects because they believed in him, respected him, and feared him. In the early part of his reign he had the love of his people, but later, after he had been obliged to apply much coercion as the price of progress, love gave way to respect and deference. Throughout his reign he had a tremendous hold upon his people.

My father did much to revive interest in Persia's great past, and he appealed to the people to modernize their country in a manner worthy of its ancient glory. On the other hand, although he carried out so many ambitious and progressive projects, he never promulgated any comprehensive development programme such as our present Second Seven-Year Plan or the third plan, to run for five years, which we are now drawing up. Without benefit of any overall plan or system of priorities, he would plunge enthusiastically into one new project after another. The marvel is that his headlong modernization drive added up to such a rational pattern of national progress.

Granted that some of his projects were more wisely conceived than others, and that his methods for marshalling his people behind his schemes were a bit too rough-and-ready, still he achieved phenomenal results. And results he was determined to have. When one surveys his work and his impact upon the country, it is hard to believe that he reigned only some sixteen years; indeed, it seems incredible that the tremendous advances I have described in the last chapter could have been achieved in a period so brief.

To know the character of a man, it is well to examine his sense of humour, if he has one. I am sure that many Persians, recalling my father's reign, would tell you that he possessed no sense of humour whatever. But that is not true. He would joke with me in the most informal and affectionate manner. And even outside his family circle he would often laugh uproariously. I think the thing that amused him most was the ridiculous attitudes of pomposity and of hypocritical fawning respect often assumed by his subjects.

I have mentioned that he was one of the greatest mind

readers. He knew by the looks and attitudes and gestures of people exactly what they were thinking. He couldn't easily be fooled, and when he perceived hypocrisy or sham deference in his officials or courtiers he would laugh in their faces. He derived great, even if sardonic, amusement from that sort of thing. I think his scorn of pretence gave my country a tonic it badly needed, for court etiquette and even the exaggerated courtesies practised here by ordinary people had too often become hollow phrases and meaningless gestures. Form rather than substance was stressed. In Persia we had badly overworked our poet Saadi's proverb which says, "Well-meaning falsehoods are better than a truth which leads to a quarrel." My father was too blunt and honest to put up with that sort of thing, and it tickled him immensely to see others found out when they tried it.

You might think that my father's military career would have given him a taste for off-colour stories. But I never heard him tell such tales. In fact, except with me, I don't think he ever indulged in any informal, easygoing humour. Those who came in contact with him either were trembling before him or looked up to him in a way that ruled out that kind of rapport. Except with me, his mental dominance and force of personality made lighthearted humour impossible.

The same applied to friendship. Of course he had many acquaintances, and I recall his being quite friendly with one of my uncles. But such an imposing personality as his virtually shut the door on close friendships, for people wouldn't dare think of approaching him on an equal footing. I think that was his problem.

I have often wondered if he felt lonely. I don't think so. I think his nature was such that he did not need any close friends. His ideas and his work were his constant companions, and they were all he required. Yet it is possible that later, when his circle of advisers became ever narrower, a few intimates might have helped him to keep in touch with the world.

DRISS BEN HAMED CHARHADI: AT MUSTAPHA'S CAFÉ

[from *A Life Full of Holes*]

This autobiographical narration of a young Moroccan was tape-recorded in Maghrebi (northwest African) Arabic and translated by Paul Bowles, the American writer. It is said to be the first "novel" in Maghrebi.

The narrator's themes are poverty, survival and— a rarely made point in modern Islamic literature— the impossibility of loneliness without leisure. He expresses the monotony of living, but also its infinite turns, beauties, and opportunities for humor. The book has all the spontaneity of youth and something of the captivating, and at best matchless, techniques of storytelling in classical Islamic folk literature.

To place this episode in its proper setting, the protagonist's mother had remarried when he was eight; a stepbrother was preferred, and, in spite of sporadic sojourns under his mother's roof, he was always on his own. "He is as unlike his contemporaries," one critic said of him, "as a sacramental wafer is unlike the slices in a loaf of packaged white bread. . . . He worries and worries that Morocco is abandoning its traditions and will end up as one more godless and immoral blue-jean civilization."

My mother's husband would not let me live at home, and so I went to stay at Mustapha's café again. And one day we heard that the Sultan was coming back to us. Have you heard the news? they were saying. No, I haven't heard anything. The Sultan's coming back, and the French are going to give us our freedom. And the day after he comes to Tanja will be the Festival of the Throne! Ah, what a day that's going to be! The biggest day of the year!

Who knows? I said.

I was not working then. My clothes were ripped and ragged and very dirty. One afternoon I went home to

Souani to see my mother. When I got there I was hungry, and she gave me some food. If her husband had been there she could not have given me anything. But he was not at home. When I finished eating, I said to her: Look. If my brother has an extra pair of pants and a shirt, I'd like to have them for a few days. Until the festival is over. Then I can give them back.

She brought them to me. Here are the trousers and the shirt. But when the feast is finished give them back to me.

I'm afraid your husband's going to make trouble, I told her. They're his son's clothes.

No. Just take them. Don't worry about that. It'll be all right. If he says anything, I'll tell him I took them.

Ouakha, I said. I put on the shirt and the trousers, and she gave me half a loaf of bread. Go now.

I went out. Everybody in the city was happy, everywhere in the streets. They were going to get their freedom. One man was saying: The Nazarenes[1] are leaving! I'm going to have a big house on the Boulevard, and it will be all mine. Mine! Another was saying: I'm going to be a commissaire! And they were all telling each other they were going to be rich, and no one would ever have to ask for alms in the street again. They were all talking. But not one of them knew how to read or write.

The men of all the quarters in town were out collecting money to pay for the festival. In each quarter they would look for a big house where they could have the music and dancing. They filled the houses with mattresses and rugs and decorated them with palm branches and flowers. Flowers everywhere. In Souani a man was building a big new house, but it was still not finished, and no one was living in it. The people in that part of the town asked him if they could use his house for the festival. Yes, good! he said. They could have it. Each family in the quarter gave something for the feast. One gave a rug, another a mattress, another cushions or haitis to hang along the wall, or just money to buy food and tea.

The festival lasted three days. The first day the men were all sitting on one side of the big room and the boys were on the other side. The women were in the street outside the doorway, because they were not allowed in. But there were five or six chairs in the street by the door, and when the women came by, they would say to the men:

[1] Or "Christians." There is nothing particularly invidious about the term in Arabic, and indeed its usage with this literal translation might be regarded as one of the translator's idiosyncrasies. [Ed.]

What is this? Here we are in the Festival of the Throne, and you're all inside eating. Aren't you going to give us anything? The men would say: Of course. Here you are. Sit down. The chairs were always full. When one woman got up, another sat down. Spanish women came by, too, and sat and had a glass of tea.

I was inside with the other boys, eating and laughing and drinking tea. We kept eating. It was all free. In the afternoon my mother's husband came by, looking for me. Have you seen Ahmed, my wife's son? Someone said: He's sitting inside, I think.

Go and get him, said my mother's husband. If he's in there, tell him I'm looking for him.

The boy came in and said: Ahmed. Your mother's husband wants to see you.

I went outside.

As soon as I saw him, I said to myself: Ah! He's going to say something about these clothes. I went over to him, and he said: Why did you put on your brother's pants and shirt?

Because today and tomorrow and the next day we have the festival. When it's over I'll take them back to the house. I'm not going to hurt them.

You'll do it now. Go and put on your own dirty pants.

Ouakha, I said. I could not say that my mother had given me the clothes. She had to tell him that. And I went home and took off the shirt and the trousers, and put on my own clothes that were torn and stiff with mud. My mother never had time to wash and mend them. When I had dressed I went back to the big house where the festival was going on. I sat down again. The boys around me began to whisper: Look at Laraïchi's son. Look at the clothes he has on. A little while ago he was wearing good pants and a new shirt. What's happened to him? And one boy said to me: Why did you change your clothes? Did you think the festival was over?

No, I said. I changed because I'm going to stay here all night. Until tomorrow morning. And I didn't want to get the other pants dirty.

Another boy said: Look at these clothes I'm wearing. They're all new. Everything. Look.

Yes, I said. Wear them in good health.

The three days of festival went by, and I went on wearing my old clothes. And the people began to empty the big house, taking away all the things they had brought for the feast. The wall coverings, the rugs, the teapots, the

stoves, everything. After it was all gone, I said to myself:
Now the holiday is over. I've eaten and slept for three days
here in the big house. I'm going down to Mustapha's café
and see if there's any news. Maybe some work for me.
Perhaps in the Calle de Italia I can find somebody who
needs a porter to pull a cart.

I was living again in the café. Some days I found a man
who needed a cart, and I worked. And some days I found
nothing. But Mustapha always gave me two or three rials
each afternoon. To help him I would get up early in the
morning and build the fire for the qahouaji. I would take
the chairs outside and put them in the alley while I swept
the floor. Then I sprinkled water around on the floor inside and outside the door.

I stayed there six or seven months, working like that,
and I got to know all the men who came to the café.
There were thieves, pickpockets, all kinds of men. I used
to listen to them when they talked. One day I said to one of
them: Why don't you let me go with you sometime?

No. You wouldn't know anything. You don't know anything about stealing.

Why don't you let me try? I said. But they would not
listen.

One day I was hungry. I went home and knocked on
the door. My brother opened it. When I went in I found
only him and my mother in the house. I said hello to my
mother.

Are you hungry? she asked me.

Yes.

She gave me a little food and some bread. Here you are.
Eat. When I had finished she said: Look, son. There's a
Nazarene who keeps pigs, and he needs somebody to work
for him. You're there living in the town. Sometimes you
eat, and sometimes you don't. Wouldn't you be better off
working for him and always eating there at his house?
You'd sleep there too, and it would be better than where
you are now.

Yes, I said. Where is he, this Nazarene?

He lives in Oued Bahrein.

Do you know him?

Yes. Your stepfather met him and told him you were
working in the city. And he said you could work there
with his pigs.

Ouakha. Who's going to take me to see him?

Wait until your stepfather comes home. He'll take you.

We sat there talking, the three of us, and after a while my mother's husband came back.

Labess, he said. How have you been?

My mother told him: He's come so you can take him to see the Spaniard.

I had gone home because I was hungry, but she did not tell him that.

That one's going to work? said my mother's husband. He never works.

I told him: You're not the one who's going to do the work. I am. Just take me there. Don't worry about whether I ever work or don't ever work.

All right. Tomorrow morning. I'll take you to see him.

So I slept there at home that night. And in the morning I got up and had breakfast. Then he and I started out, walking to the Nazarene's farm. When we got to the orchard, my mother's husband began to call out: Pépe! Pépe! Then a man answered: Na'am? The Nazarene knew how to speak Maghrebi.

Here's the boy I told you about, said my mother's husband.

The Nazarene was young and short and fat. Have you ever worked with garbage? he asked me.

Yes. Once I worked with it at the Monopolio on the beach.

Good. I'll give you two rials a day and your food, and you can sleep here.

Ouakha, I said.

You have to go into the city every morning with the donkey and fill the panniers with garbage and bring it back.

My mother's husband said: All right. I'm going now. Good-bye. You stay here.

Ouakha. And so he went away. And I stayed there with the Spaniard. He lived in the house with his father, his mother, his brother and his sister. Five of them lived there together.

I slept in the stall where they kept the straw. The next morning the Nazarene knocked on my door. Ya, Ahmed! he said. Buenos días.

Buenos días, I said.

Go to the kitchen. The coffee's ready for you. I'll get the donkey harnessed while you have your breakfast.

Ouakha. I went and washed my face. Then I went to the kitchen. Buenos días, Maria, I said.

Buenos días, hijo.

I sat down in a chair. She gave me a cup of coffee with milk, and some bread and butter. Then I went out. I cut a branch from a tree and shook it at the donkey. Let's go! I shouted. I was going to walk beside the donkey.

Pépe said: No, hombre! Ride him now. But when he's carrying the garbage, walk beside him.

So I started out to the town riding the donkey. Riding, riding, until I got to the Boulevard. Then I tied him to a tree on a back street, took the basket down, and started to look for garbage.

I was looking, too, for policemen because I knew it was forbidden to pick up garbage in the street. The police said the garbage belonged to the city. If they caught someone stealing it to carry away with him, they fined him and sent his donkey to the slaughterhouse. But I knew about this before I went to take it. I made friends with the garbage collectors, and sometimes I would help them carry the garbage to their carts. I had no trouble.

When I would find a pile of garbage in front of a door, I would empty it into the basket. Then I would look all through it and pull out the papers and cans and things that the pigs could not eat, and put them back on the sidewalk. What stayed in the basket was all food: potato peelings, banana skins, old bread, lettuce and things like that. When the basket was full of food I took it back to the donkey and emptied it into one of the panniers. Then I went and picked up more garbage, and I kept doing this until both the panniers were full. I filled the basket too, and put it on top of the saddle. Then I unhitched the donkey and started out for the farm. When I got back, I set the panniers on the floor. I took the harness off the donkey and hung it up. Then I led him out into the orchard and left him under a tree where he could eat flowers. It was the largest and finest orchard anywhere around. There were many big trees, and there were flowers everywhere on the ground underneath the trees.

The first day, when I had tied the donkey to a tree in the orchard, I went into the pigpen. I was going to give the pigs the garbage then, but the Nazarene called to me. No! First you must sweep out the pen. I swept all the dung into a corner, and poured the garbage onto the clean side. While the pigs were eating I carried the dung out to the manure heap in a wheelbarrow.

Each morning Pépe's mother went out to sell milk, and his sister went into the city to work. Some days I started out with them. They would put the milk cans into the

panniers on each side of the donkey. The two brothers
and the father stayed at home, feeding the cattle and cleaning out the stalls. In the morning they fed the pigs wheat
chaff, and in the afternoon they fed them the garbage I
brought back with me.

I stayed on there for a month and a half or two months,
and then I went down to the town and bought some new
clothes. I began to enjoy my work on the farm. I thought:
This is better than living in the city the way I've been
doing. In the café, I slept on the floor one night, in a
chair the next night, and I never slept well. Now I sleep
and eat well, too, and I feel better.

Today and tomorrow, today and tomorrow.

TRANSLATED BY PAUL BOWLES

SOMALI LOVE SONGS AND A REACTION

Little formal Islamic literature from the sub- or near-Saharan regions of Africa differed much in modern times from the encomiastic memorials to sheikhs which we sampled from Abdullah dan Fodio early in this book. They seemed mostly to be recitative, alliterative, and excessively reliant upon ancient conventions of Arabic prosody.

Yet recently a form of love song called balwo, as free as an uncommitted lovebird, was invented by a Somali lorry driver and was promptly attacked, in staunchly traditional strophes, by a pious sheikh. Examples of the songs, and a portion of the sheikh's refutation, are given below.

Love Songs

I

The oryx does not bring her young into the open,
Why are you doing this with your thigh?

II

A flash of lightning does not satisfy thirst,
What then is it to me if you just pass by?

III

It is the custom of the Somali,
To mock a man who has fallen in love.

IV

One does not hurry past a dying man,
Before I enter the grave, spare a word for me.

V

When you die you will enter the earth,
Let not the preacher then turn you from your love-
    song.

VI

Is it lightning far distant from me,
That I have strained for vainly?

VII

The girl for whom I have withered like a stick,
Are you telling me to despair of ever attaining?

VIII

My heart is single and cannot be divided,
And it is fastened on a single hope; Oh you who might
  be the moon.

IX

Until I die I shall not give up the love-song,
Oh God, forgive me my shortcomings.

X

Oh bottles, pour out your medicines,
And when you have emptied, resound with a love-
  song.

XI

If a potion tastes bitter,
And yet brings relief, would you give it up?

XII

Oh doctor, I have a pain in my heart,
Give me treatment, but don't put me in the hospital!

The Evils of the Balwo

Sheikh Mahammad Hasan

Oh my God, my God, have mercy on us and save us
  from the *balwo*.
The evil *balwo* songs came, bringing corruption and
  spreading sin,
And God was displeased with those who wrought
  such wrongfulness.

They wasted their substance in frivolity and dissipa-
tion,
They gathered together in debauchery and hungered
after what is prohibited.

Women who became like devils lured them astray,
As holy tradition says: "They are the snares of the
devil."

Turn away from them, pay no heed to them, and
abandon their places of song.

Flee from these vain things, forsake them; their possession brings no happiness;
Abandon them, and those who seek them. Unhappy
is the place of song!

TRANSLATED BY B. W. ANDRZEJEWSKI AND I. M. LEWIS.

TAIEB SALEH: THE DOUM TREE OF WAD HAMID

*This young Sudanese writer attended Khartoum and
Exeter Universities, and has worked in broadcasting
in the Sudan and in Britain. The technique of his
fiction, on which he has concentrated, is modern and
highly polished. It is dramatic, meaningfully episodic,
reverential, just a bit cynical, relaxedly social-minded,
and withal the type which marks modern Islamic
literature as perfectly in control of itself.*

Were you to come to our village as a tourist, it is likely,
my son, that you would not stay long. If it was in wintertime, when the palm trees are pollinated, you would find
that a dark cloud had descended over the village. This,
my son, would not be dust, nor yet that mist which rises
up after rainfall. It would be a swarm of those sandflies
which obstruct all paths to those who wish to enter our
village. Maybe you have seen this pest before, but I swear
that you have never seen this particular species. Take this
gauze netting, my son, and put it over your head. While
it won't protect you against these devils, it will at least
help you to bear them. I remember a friend of my son's,
a fellow student at school, whom my son invited to stay
with us a year ago at this time of the year. His people
come from the town. He stayed one night with us and
got up next day, feverish, with a running nose and swollen
face; he swore that he wouldn't spend another night with
us.

If you were to come to us in summer you would find
the horseflies with us—enormous flies the size of young
sheep, as we say. In comparison to these the sandflies are
a thousand times more bearable. They are savage flies, my
son: they bite, sting, buzz, and whirr. They have a special
love for man and no sooner smell him out than they
attach themselves to him. Wave them off you, my son—
God curse all sandflies.

And were you to come at a time which was neither
summer nor winter you would find nothing at all. No

doubt, my son, you read the papers daily, listen to the radio, and go to the cinema once or twice a week. Should you become ill you have the right to be treated in a hospital, and if you have a son he is entitled to receive education at a school. I know, my son, that you hate dark streets and like to see electric light shining out into the night. I know, too, that you are not enamoured of walking and that riding donkeys gives you a bruise on your backside. Oh, I wish, my son, I wish—the asphalted roads of the towns—the modern means of transport—the fine comfortable buses. We have none of all this—we are people who live on what God sees fit to give us.

Tomorrow you will depart from our village, of this I am sure, and you will be right to do so. What have you to do with such hardship? We are thick-skinned people and in this we differ from others. We have become used to this hard life, in fact we like it, but we ask no one to subject himself to the difficulties of our life. Tomorrow you will depart, my son—I know that. Before you leave, though, let me show you one thing—something which, in a manner of speaking, we are proud of. In the towns you have museums, places in which the local history and the great deeds of the past are preserved. This thing that I want to show you can be said to be a museum. It is one thing we insist our visitors should see.

Once a preacher, sent by the government, came to us to stay for a month. He arrived at a time when the horseflies had never been fatter. On the very first day the man's face swelled up. He bore this manfully and joined us in evening prayers on the second night, and after prayers he talked to us of the delights of the primitive life. On the third day he was down with malaria, he contracted dysentery, and his eyes were completely gummed up. I visited him at noon and found him prostrate in bed, with a boy standing at his head waving away the flies.

"O Sheikh," I said to him, "there is nothing in our village to show you, though I would like you to see the doum tree of Wad Hamid." He didn't ask me what Wad Hamid's doum tree was, but I presumed that he had heard of it, for who has not? He raised his face, which was like the lung of a slaughtered cow; his eyes (as I said) were firmly closed, though I knew that behind the lashes there lurked a certain bitterness.

"By God," he said to me, "if this were the doum tree of Jandal, and you the Moslems who fought with Ali and Muʾawiya, and I the arbitrator between you, holding your

fate in these two hands of mine, I would not stir an inch!"
And he spat upon the ground as though to curse me and
turned his face away. After that we heard that the Sheikh
had cabled to those who had sent him, saying: "The
horseflies have eaten into my neck, malaria has burnt up
my skin, and dysentery has lodged itself in my bowels.
Come to my rescue, may God bless you—these are people
who are in no need of me or of any other preacher." And
so the man departed and the government sent us no
preacher after him.

But, my son, our village actually witnessed many great
men of power and influence, people with names that rang
through the country like drums, whom we never even
dreamed would ever come here—they came, by God, in
droves.

We have arrived. Have patience, my son; in a little while
there will be the noonday breeze to lighten the agony of
this pest upon your face.

Here it is: the doum tree of Wad Hamid. Look how it
holds its head aloft to the skies; look how its roots strike
down into the earth; look at its full, sturdy trunk, like the
form of a comely woman, at the branches on high resembling the mane of a frolicsome steed! In the afternoon,
when the sun is low, the doum tree casts its shadow from
this high mound right across the river so that someone
sitting on the far bank can rest in its shade. At dawn,
when the sun rises, the shadow of the tree stretches across
the cultivated land and houses right up to the cemetery.
Don't you think it is like some mythical eagle spreading
its wings over the village and everyone in it? Once the
government, wanting to put through an agricultural scheme,
decided to cut it down; they said that the best place for
setting up the pump was where the doum tree stood. As
you can see, the people of our village are concerned solely
with their everyday needs and I cannot remember their ever
having rebelled against anything. However, when they
heard about cutting down the doum tree they all rose up
as one man and barred the district commissioner's way.
That was in the time of foreign rule. The flies assisted
them too—the horseflies. The man was surrounded by
the clamouring people shouting that if the doum tree were
cut down they would fight the government to the last man
while the flies played havoc with the man's face. As his
papers were scattered in the water we heard him cry out:
"All right—doum tree stay—scheme no stay!" And so

neither the pump nor the scheme came about and we kept our doum tree.

Let us go home, my son, for this is no time for talking in the open. This hour just before sunset is a time when the army of sandflies becomes particularly active before going to sleep. At such a time no one who isn't well-accustomed to them and has become as thick-skinned as we are can bear their stings. Look at it, my son, look at the doum tree: lofty, proud, and haughty as though—as though it were some ancient idol. Wherever you happen to be in the village you can see it; in fact, you can even see it from four villages away.

Tomorrow you will depart from our village, of that there is no doubt, the mementoes of the short walk we have taken visible upon your face, neck and hands. But before you leave I shall finish the story of the tree, the doum tree of Wad Hamid. Come in, my son, treat this house as your own.

You ask who planted the doum tree?

No one planted it, my son. Is the ground in which it grows arable land? Do you not see that it is stony and appreciably higher than the riverbank, like the pedestal of a statue, while the river twists and turns below it like a sacred snake, one of the ancient gods of the Egyptians? My son, no one planted it. Drink your tea, for you must be in need of it after the trying experience you have undergone. Most probably it grew up by itself, though no one remembers having known it other than as you now find it. Our sons opened their eyes to find it commanding the village. And we, when we take ourselves back to child-hood memories, to that dividing line beyond which you remember nothing, see in our minds a giant doum tree standing on a riverbank; everything beyond it is as cryptic as talismans, like the boundary between day and night, like that fading light which is not the dawn but the light directly preceding the break of day. My son, do you find that you can follow what I say? Are you aware of this feeling I have within me but which I am powerless to express? Every new generation finds the doum tree as though it had been born at the time of their birth and would grow up with them. Go and sit with the people of this village and listen to them recounting their dreams. A man awakens from sleep and tells his neighbour how he found himself in a vast sandy tract of land, the sand as white as pure silver; how his feet sank in as he walked so that he could only draw them out again with difficulty;

how he walked and walked until he was overcome with
thirst and stricken with hunger, while the sands stretched
endlessly around him; how he climbed a hill and on reaching the top espied a dense forest of doum trees with a
single tall tree in the centre which in comparison with
the others looked like a camel amid a herd of goats; how
the man went down the hill to find that the earth seemed
to be rolled up before him so that it was but a few steps
before he found himself under the doum tree of Wad
Hamid; how he then discovered a vessel containing milk,
its surface still fresh with froth, and how the milk did
not go down though he drank until he had quenched his
thirst. At which his neighbour says to him, "Rejoice at
release from your troubles."

You can also hear one of the women telling her friend:
"It was as though I were in a boat sailing through a
channel in the sea, so narrow that I could stretch out my
hands and touch the shore on either side. I found myself
on the crest of a mountainous wave which carried me upwards till I was almost touching the clouds, then bore me
down into a dark, fathomless pit. I began shouting in my
fear, but my voice seemed to be trapped in my throat.
Suddenly I found the channel opening out a little. I saw
that on the two shores were black, leafless trees with thorns,
the tips of which were like the heads of hawks. I saw the
two shores closing in upon me and the trees seemed to be
walking towards me. I was filled with terror and called
out at the top of my voice, "O Wad Hamid!" As I looked
I saw a man with a radiant face and a heavy white beard
flowing down over his chest, dressed in spotless white and
holding a string of amber prayer beads. Placing his hand
on my brow he said: "Be not afraid," and I was calmed.
Then I found the shore opening up and the water flowing
gently. I looked to my left and saw fields of ripe corn,
water wheels turning, and cattle grazing, and on the shore
stood the doum tree of Wad Hamid. The boat came to
rest under the tree and the man got out, tied up the boat,
and stretched out his hand to me. He then struck me
gently on the shoulder with the string of beads, picked
up a doum fruit from the ground and put it in my hand.
When I turned round he was no longer there."

"That was Wad Hamid," her friend then says to her,
"you will have an illness that will bring you to the brink
of death, but you will recover. You must make an offering
to Wad Hamid under the doum tree."

So it is, my son, that there is not a man or woman,

young or old, who dreams at night without seeing the doum tree of Wad Hamid at some point in the dream.

You ask me why it was called the doum tree of Wad Hamid and who Wad Hamid was. Be patient, my son—have another cup of tea.

At the beginning of home rule a civil servant came to inform us that the government was intending to set up a stopping place for the steamer. He told us that the national government wished to help us and to see us progress, and his face was radiant with enthusiasm as he talked. But he could see that the faces around him expressed no reaction. My son, we are not people who travel very much, and when we wish to do so for some important matter such as registering land, or seeking advice about a matter of divorce, we take a morning's ride on our donkeys and then board the steamer from the neighbouring village. My son, we have grown accustomed to this, in fact it is precisely for this reason that we breed donkeys. It is little wonder, then, that the government official could see nothing in the people's faces to indicate that they were pleased with the news. His enthusiasm waned and, being at his wit's end, he began to fumble for words.

"Where will the stopping place be?" someone asked him after a period of silence. The official replied that there was only one suitable place—where the doum tree stood. Had you that instant brought along a woman and had her stand among those men as naked as the day her mother bore her, they could not have been more astonished.

"The steamer usually passes here on a Wednesday," one of the men quickly replied. "If you made a stopping place, then it would be here on Wednesday afternoon." The official replied that the time fixed for the steamer to stop by their village would be four o'clock on Wednesday afternoon.

"But that is the time when we visit the tomb of Wad Hamid at the doum tree," answered the man; "when we take our women and children and make offerings. We do this every week." The official laughed. "Then change the day!" he replied. Had the official told these men at that moment that every one of them was a bastard, that would not have angered them more than this remark of his. They rose up as one man, bore down upon him, and would certainly have killed him if I had not intervened and snatched him from their clutches. I then put him on a donkey and told him to make good his escape.

And so it was that the steamer still does not stop here

and that we still ride off on our donkeys for a whole morning and take the steamer from the neighbouring village when circumstances require us to travel. We content ourselves with the thought that we visit the tomb of Wad Hamid with our women and children and that we make offerings there every Wednesday as our fathers and fathers' fathers did before us.

Excuse me, my son, while I perform the sunset prayer—it is said that the sunset prayer is "strange": if you don't catch it in time it eludes you. *God's pious servants—I declare that there is no god but God and I declare that Mohamed is His Servant and His Prophet—Peace be upon you and the mercy of God!*

Ah, ah. For a week this back of mine has been giving me pain. What do you think it is, my son? I know, though, it's just old age. Oh, to be young! In my young days I would breakfast off half a sheep, drink the milk of five cows for supper, and be able to lift a sack of dates with one hand. He lies who says he ever beat me at wrestling. They used to call me "the crocodile." Once I swam the river, using my chest to push a boat loaded with wheat to the other shore—at night! On the shore were some men at work at their water wheels, who threw down their clothes in terror and fled when they saw me pushing the boat towards them.

"Oh people," I shouted at them, "what's wrong, shame upon you! Don't you know me? I'm 'the crocodile.' By God, the devils themselves would be scared off by your ugly faces."

My son, have you asked me what we do when we're ill?

I laugh because I know what's going on in your head. You townsfolk hurry to the hospital on the slightest pretext. If one of you hurts his finger you dash off to the doctor, who puts a bandage on and you carry it in a sling for days; and even then it doesn't get better. Once I was working in the fields and something bit my finger—this little finger of mine. I jumped to my feet and looked around in the grass where I found a snake lurking. I swear to you it was longer than my arm. I took hold of it by the head and crushed it between two fingers, then bit into my finger, sucked out the blood, and took up a handful of dust and rubbed it on the bite.

But that was only a little thing. What do we do when faced with real illness?

This neighbour of ours, now. One day her neck swelled up and she was confined to bed for two months. One night she had a heavy fever, so at first dawn she rose from her bed and dragged herself along till she came—yes, my son, till she came to the doum tree of Wad Hamid. The woman told us what happened.

"I was under the doum tree," she said, "with hardly sufficient strength to stand up, and called out at the top of my voice: "O Wad Hamid, I have come to you to seek refuge and protection—I shall sleep here at your tomb and under your doum tree. Either you let me die or you restore me to life; I shall not leave here until one of these two things happens."

"And so I curled myself up in fear," the woman continued with her story, "and was soon overcome by sleep. While midway between wakefulness and sleep I suddenly heard sounds of recitation from the Koran and a bright light, as sharp as a knife edge, radiated out, joining up the two riverbanks, and I saw the doum tree prostrating itself in worship. My heart throbbed so violently that I thought it would leap up through my mouth. I saw a venerable old man with a white beard and wearing a spotless white robe come up to me, a smile on his face. He struck me on the head with his string of prayer beads and called out: "Arise.""

"I swear that I got up I know not how and went home I know not how. I arrived back at dawn and woke up my husband, my son, and my daughters. I told my husband to light the fire and make tea. Then I ordered my daughters to give trilling cries of joy, and the whole village prostrated themselves before us. I swear that I have never again been afraid, nor yet ill."

Yes, my son, we are people who have no experience of hospitals. In small matters such as the bites of scorpions, fever, sprains, and fractures, we take to our beds until we are cured. When in serious trouble we go to the doum tree.

Shall I tell you the story of Wad Hamid, my son, or would you like to sleep? Townsfolk don't go to sleep till late at night—I know that of them. We, though, go to sleep directly the birds are silent, the flies stop harrying the cattle, the leaves of the trees settle down, the hens spread their wings over their chicks, and the goats turn on their sides to chew the cud. We and our animals are alike: we rise in the morning when they rise and go to sleep when they sleep, our breathing and theirs following one and the same pattern.

My father, reporting what my grandfather had told him, said: "Wad Hamid, in times gone by, used to be the slave of a wicked man. He was one of God's holy saints but kept his faith to himself, not daring to pray openly lest his wicked master should kill him. When he could no longer bear his life with this infidel he called upon God to deliver him and a voice told him to spread his prayer mat on the water and that when it stopped by the shore he should descend. The prayer mat put him down at the place where the doum tree is now and which used to be wasteland. And there he stayed alone, praying the whole day. At nightfall a man came to him with dishes of food, so he ate and continued his worship till dawn."

All this happened before the village was built up. It is as though this village, with its inhabitants, its water wheels and buildings, had become split off from the earth. Anyone who tells you he knows the history of its origin is a liar. Other places begin by being small and then grow larger, but this village of ours came into being at one bound. Its population neither increases nor decreases, while its appearance remains unchanged. And ever since our village has existed, so has the doum tree of Wad Hamid; and just as no one remembers how it originated and grew, so no one remembers how the doum tree came to grow in a patch of rocky ground by the river, standing above it like a sentinel.

When I took you to visit the tree, my son, do you remember the iron railing round it? Do you remember the marble plaque standing on a stone pedestal with "The doum tree of Wad Hamid" written on it? Do you remember the doum tree with the gilded crescents above the tomb? They are the only new things about the village since God first planted it here, and I shall now recount to you how they came into being.

When you leave us tomorrow—and you will certainly do so, swollen of face and inflamed of eye—it will be fitting if you do not curse us but rather think kindly of us and of the things that I have told you this night, for you may well find that your visit to us was not wholly bad.

You remember that some years ago we had Members of Parliament and political parties and a great deal of to-ing and fro-ing which we couldn't make head or tail of. The roads would sometimes cast down strangers at our very doors, just as the waves of the sea wash up strange weeds. Though not a single one of them prolonged his stay beyond one night, they would nevertheless bring us the news of the great fuss going on in the capital. One day they told us that the government which had driven out imperialism had been replaced by an even bigger and noisier government.

"And who has changed it?" we asked them, but received no answer. As for us, ever since we refused to allow the stopping place to be set up at the doum tree no one has disturbed our tranquil existence. Two years passed without our knowing what form the government had taken, black or white. Its emissaries passed through our village without staying in it, while we thanked God that He had saved us the trouble of putting them up. So things went on till, four years ago, a new government came into power. As though this new authority wished to make us conscious of its presence, we awoke one day to find an official with an enormous hat and small head, in the company of two soldiers, measuring up and doing calculations at the doum tree. We asked them what it was about, to which they replied that the government wished to build a stopping place for the steamer under the doum tree.

"But we have already given you our answer about that," we told them. "What makes you think we'll accept it now?"

"The government which gave in to you was a weak one," they said, "but the position has now changed."

To cut a long story short, we took them by the scruffs of their necks, hurled them into the water, and went off to our work. It wasn't more than a week later when a group of soldiers came along, commanded by the small-headed official with the large hat, shouting, "Arrest that man, and that one, and that one," until they'd taken off twenty of us, I among them. We spent a month in prison. Then one day the very soldiers who had put us there opened the prison gates. We asked them what it was all about, but no one said anything. Outside the prison we found a great gathering of people; no sooner had we been spotted than there were shouts and cheering and we were embraced by some cleanly dressed people, heavily scented and with gold watches gleaming on their wrists. They carried us off in a great procession, back to our own people. There we found an unbelievably immense gathering of people, carts, horses, and camels. We said to each other, "The din and flurry of the capital has caught up with us." They made us twenty men stand in a row and the people passed along it shaking us by the hand: the Prime Minister—the President of the Parliament—the President of the Senate—the member for such and such constituency—the member for such and such other constituency.

We looked at each other without understanding a thing

of what was going on around us except that our arms were aching with all the handshakes we had been receiving from those Presidents and Members of Parliament.

Then they took us off in a great mass to the place where the doum tree and the tomb stand. The Prime Minister laid the foundation stone for the monument you've seen, and for the dome you've seen, and for the railing you've seen. Like a tornado blowing up for a while and then passing over, so that mighty host disappeared as suddenly as it had come without spending a night in the village—no doubt because of the horseflies which, that particular year, were as large and fat and buzzed and whirred as much as during the year the preacher came to us.

One of those strangers who were occasionally cast upon us in the village later told us the story of all this fuss and bother.

"The people," he said, "hadn't been happy about this government since it had come to power, for they knew that it had got there by bribing a number of the Members of Parliament. They therefore bided their time and waited for the right opportunities to present themselves, while the opposition looked around for something to spark things off. When the doum tree incident occurred and they marched you all off and slung you into prison, the newspapers took this up and the leader of the government which had resigned made a fiery speech in Parliament in which he said: 'To such tyranny has this government come that it has begun to interfere in the beliefs of the people, in those holy things held most sacred by them.' Then taking a most imposing stance and in a voice choked with emotion, he said: 'Ask our worthy Prime Minister about the doum tree of Wad Hamid. Ask him how it was that he permitted himself to send his troops and henchmen to desecrate that pure and holy place!'

"The people took up the cry and throughout the country their hearts responded to the incident of the doum tree as to nothing before. Perhaps the reason is that in every village in this country there is some monument like the doum tree of Wad Hamid which people see in their dreams. After a month of fuss and shouting and inflamed feelings, fifty members of the government were forced to withdraw their support, their constituencies having warned them that unless they did so they would wash their hands of them. And so the government fell, the first government returned to power, and the leading paper in the country wrote: 'The doum tree of Wad Hamid has become the symbol of the nation's awakening.' "

Since that day we have been unaware of the existence of the new government, and not one of those great giants of men who visited us has put in an appearance; we thank God that He has spared us the trouble of having to shake them by the hand. Our life returned to what it had been: no water pump, no agricultural scheme, no stopping place for the steamer. But we kept our doum tree, which casts its shadow over the southern bank in the afternoon and, in the morning, spreads its shadow over the fields and houses right up to the cemetery, with the river flowing below it like some sacred legendary snake. And our village has acquired a marble monument, an iron railing, and a dome with gilded crescents.

When the man had finished what he had to say he looked at me with an enigmatic smile playing at the corners of his mouth like the faint flickerings of a lamp.

"And when," I asked, "will they set up the water pump, and put through the agricultural scheme and the stopping place for the steamer?"

He lowered his head and paused before answering me, "When people go to sleep and don't see the doum tree in their dreams."

"And when will that be?" I said.

"I mentioned to you that my son is in the town studying at school," he replied. "It wasn't I who put him there; he ran away and went there on his own, and it is my hope that he will stay where he is and not return. When my son's son passes out of school and the number of young men with souls foreign to our own increases, then perhaps the water pump will be set up and the agricultural scheme put into being—maybe then the steamer will stop at our village —under the doum tree of Wad Hamid."

"And do you think," I said to him, "that the doum tree will one day be cut down?" He looked at me for a long while as though wishing to project, through his tired, misty eyes, something which he was incapable of doing by word.

"There will not be the least necessity for cutting down the doum tree. There is not the slightest reason for the tomb to be removed. What all these people have overlooked is that there's plenty of room for all these things: the doum tree, the tomb, the water pump, and the steamer's stopping place."

When he had been silent for a time he gave me a look which I don't know how to describe, though it stirred within me a feeling of sadness, sadness for some obscure thing which I was unable to define. Then he said: "Tomorrow, without doubt, you will be leaving us. When you arrive at your destination, think well of us and judge us not too harshly."

TRANSLATED BY DENYS JOHNSON-DAVIES

MUHAMMAD HEJAZI: TWENTY-ONE SAYINGS

[from *Hazār Sokhan*, A Thousand Sayings]

Proverbs and aphorisms of all sorts have always been a natural and favored means of expression and recourse among all peoples. Everyone, from seer to after-dinner speaker, has quoted (or misquoted) the best or most apt sayings he has ever heard, usually careless of their sources. Bulky collections of such sayings have been studiously compiled for nearly every great literary tradition, and scholars have shown how many of them are really saying the same things, often borrowed from each other.

Over the long course of Islamic history, such sayings have not only formed a notable part of the daily speech of its peoples but have been a prominent feature and nourishment of higher forms of its literatures. The Islamic peoples, heirs as they are to so many ancient cultures, have correctly tended to consider their proverbs as enshrining one thing, at least, which is better for not being "modern": wisdom. Since we began our study with a selection of such sayings, it may be fitting that we end it that way.[1]

These sayings, destined though they may be to become proverbs, are the work of a distinguished modern writer. Senator Hejazi has contributed much to the development of his native literature, Persian, and to the intellectual as well as practical development of his native land, Iran. These sayings are not just bons mots; they reflect a great deal of wisdom echoing many appropriate and harmonious intellectual influences: ancient Iran, Greek philosophy, Sufism, French rationalism, and, above all, common sense bridled by art. As such they reflect, too, the spirit behind the best in modern Islamic literature, a literature which now stands proudly for itself and will be welcomed anywhere in the world where literature is appreciated.

---

[1] Cf. *Anthology of Islamic Literature*, pages 63–65.

Politics is the profession of those who have neither trade nor art.

Woman reaches love through friendship; man reaches friendship through love.

The flatterer takes us twice for a fool: first, we know he lies but we accept his lie; second, we try to believe that his lie is actually the truth.

Nature is the harmless and kind beloved of those who have been disillusioned by other beloveds.

Society punishes only the unsuccessful traitor.

The day the world turns our way, we are great philosophers and can close our eyes to possessions; but the day the world turns against us, we are bawling children, grasping for toys.

The problems of life are solved when we can solve them by ourselves.

Women are more afraid of old age than of death.

The most useful invention of human beings is the book.

Those who give advice are amazed that their wisdom does not always affect others; but the real amazement lies in the fact that most great advice does not even reach from the mouth of the advisor to his own ear.

The plan of life is designed by the heart and is executed by the mind.

Not to desire the advancement of a friend is partly due to jealousy, but is also partly due to the fact that we lose him as he advances.

Every individual has a special religion.

Death is a reality in which no living creature believes.

Cleverness is a wall between honesty and dishonesty; it is not apparent to which side the wall belongs.

He who can live with himself can also live with others.

If man was worthy of love the mystic would not have searched for God.

General opinion is the opinion of one or a few for which the public is held responsible.

Everyone tries to cover his madness, except one who is in love.

The secret of happiness is only a few words; yet we will not accept it from anyone, but must learn it from a lifetime of experience, when it is far too late.

Today I myself do not understand well what I wrote yesterday; why do I expect others to grasp the truth of the condition and purpose of my writings?

TRANSLATED BY BAHRAM JAMALPUR

Selected References

The best books on modern Islamic literatures have been written in modern Islamic languages. Some very good ones have been written in other European and Asian languages, too. But there is not a great deal to be read about them, good or bad, in English. The following list of suggested references, mainly historical, makes no pretension to completeness, proper coverage, or even good sense. It is included for the purpose of directing the interested general reader toward more information about the Islamic world in modern times. It does not list original texts or even works in foreign languages. For the serious, the bibliographies of periodical literature compiled by J. D. Pearson and J. F. Ashton, *Index Islamicus, 1906–1955* (Cambridge, 1958), *1955–1960* (Cambridge, 1962), *1961–1965* (Cambridge, 1967), will provide ample further references. The reader who wishes to trace the complete translations of works included in this anthology may do so by consulting the list of acknowledgements on pages v–vi.

ADAMS, C. C. *Islam and Modernism in Egypt.* London, 1933.

AHMAD, AZIZ. *Islamic Culture in the Indian Environment.* London, 1964.

———. *Islamic Modernism in India and Pakistan, 1857–1964.* London, 1967.

AHMED, J. M. *The Intellectual Origins of Egyptian Nationalism.* London, 1960.

ALI, SYED AMEER. *The Spirit of Islam.* London, 1939.

ANDERSON, J. N. D. *Islamic Lands in the Modern World.* New York, 1959.

ANDRZEJEWSKI, B. W., and LEWIS, I. M. *Somali Poetry.* London, 1964.

ANTONIUS, GEORGE. *The Arab Awakening.* London, 1938.

ARASTEH, R. *Education and Social Awakening in Iran, 1850–1960.* Leiden, 1962.

ARBERRY, A. J. *Modern Arabic Poetry.* Cambridge, 1949.

———. *The Legacy of Persia.* Oxford, 1953.

———. *Persian Poems.* London, 1954.

ARBERRY, A. J., and LANDAU, ROM, eds. *Islam To-Day*. London, 1943.

ARNOLD, T. W., and GUILLAUME, A., eds. *The Legacy of Islam*. London, 1931.

AVERY, PETER. *Modern Iran*. New York, 1965.

AZIZ, K. K. *Britain and Muslin India*. London, 1963.

BADEAU, JOHN S. *The Emergence of Modern Egypt*. New York, 1953.

————. *The American Approach to the Arab World*. New York, 1968.

BERGER, MORROE. *The Arab World Today*. Garden City, 1962.

BERQUE, JACQUES. *The Arabs: Their History and Future*. New York, 1964.

BINDER, LEONARD. *Religion and Politics in Pakistan*. Berkeley, 1961.

BLUNT, W. S. *The Future of Islam*. London, 1882.

BONNÉ, ALFRED. *State and Economics in the Middle East*. 2nd ed. London, 1955.

BROCKELMANN, CARL. *History of the Islamic Peoples*. New York, 1960.

BROWNE, E. G. *A Literary History of Persia*. 4 vols. London, 1924–1930.

————. *The Persian Revolution of 1905–1909*. Cambridge, 1910.

————. *The Press and Poetry of Modern Persia*. Cambridge, 1914.

————. *A Year Amongst the Persians (1887–88)*. London, 1893.

CRAGG, KENNETH. *Call of the Minaret*. New York, 1956.

————. *The Dome and the Rock*. London, 1964.

————. *Counsels in Contemporary Islam*. London, 1965.

CROMER, LORD. *Modern Egypt*. 2 vols. London, 1908.

DANIEL, NORMAN. *Islam, Europe and Empire*. Edinburgh, 1966.

DAVISON, R. H. *Reform in the Ottoman Empire*. Princeton, 1963.

ELWELL-SUTTON, L. P. *Modern Iran*. London, 1941.

Encyclopaedia of Islām. 1st ed. Leiden, 1913–38. 4 vols. and suppl. 2nd ed., 1954–.

FARIS, NABIH A., ed. *The Arab Heritage*. Princeton, 1963.

FRYE, RICHARD. *Islam and the West*. The Hague, 1957.

FYZEE, A. A. *A Modern Approach to Islam*. New York, 1964.

GARDET, LOUIS. *Mohammedanism*. Tr. by W. Burridge. New York, 1961.

GIBB, E. J. W. *A History of Ottoman Poetry*. 6 vols. London, 1900–1909.

GIBB, H. A. R. *Arabic Literature*. 2nd ed. Oxford, 1963.

————. *Modern Trends in Islam*. Chicago, 1947.

————. *Mohammedanism*. London, 1949.

————. *Studies on the Civilization of Islam*, ed. by S. Shaw and W. Polk. Boston, 1962.

————, ed. *Whither Islam?* London, 1932.

———, and BOWEN, H. *Islamic Society and the West.* 2 vols. London, 1950–1957.

———, and KRAMERS, J. H. *Shorter Encyclopaedia of Islam.* Leiden, 1953.

GLUBB, JOHN B. *Britain and the Arabs.* London, 1959.

GÖKALP, Z. *Turkish Nationalism and Western Civilization.* Tr. and ed. by N. Berkes. London, 1959.

GORDON, D. C. *North Africa's French Legacy, 1954–1962.* Cambridge, 1962.

GRANT, DOUGLAS, ed. *The Islamic Near East.* Toronto, 1960.

GROSECLOSE, ELGIN. *Introduction to Iran.* New York, 1947.

GRUNEBAUM, GUSTAVE E. VON. *Islam.* London, 1955.

———. *Islam: Essays in the Nature and Growth of a Cultural Tradition.* London, 1955.

———. *Modern Islam: The Search for Cultural Identity.* Berkeley, 1962.

———, ed. *Medieval Islam: A Study in Cultural Orientations.* 2nd ed. Chicago, 1953.

———, ed. *Unity and Variety in Muslim Civilization.* Chicago, 1955.

GUILLAUME, ALFRED. *Islam.* New York, 1956.

HAAS, WILLIAM S. *Iran.* New York, 1946.

HADDAD, GEORGE. *Fifty Years of Modern Syria and Lebanon.* Beirut, 1950.

HAIM, SYLVIA G. *Arab Nationalism, an Anthology.* Berkeley, 1964.

HALPERN, MANFRED. *The Politics of Social Change in the Middle East and North Africa.* Princeton, 1963.

HAZARD, HARRY W. *Atlas of Islamic History.* Princeton, 1954.

HEYD, U. *Foundations of Turkish Nationalism.* London, 1950.

HEYWORTH-DUNNE, J. *Introduction to the History of Education in Modern Egypt.* London, 1938.

HITTI, P. K. *The Arabs: A Short History.* Princeton, 1944.

———. *History of the Arabs.* 6th ed. London, 1956.

———. *Lebanon in History.* New York, 1957.

———. *The Near East in History.* Princeton, 1961.

———. *Syria: A Short History.* New York, 1959.

HOLLISTER, JOHN N. *The Shia of India.* London, 1953.

HOURANI, ALBERT H. *Syria and Lebanon.* London, 1946.

———. *Arabic Thought in the Liberal Age, 1798–1939.* London, 1962.

HOWARTH, HERBERT, and SHUKRALLAH, IBRAHIM. *Images from the Arab World.* London, 1944.

HUREWITZ, J. C. *Diplomacy in the Near and Middle East.* 2 vols. London, 1956.

IKRAM, S. M. *Muslim Civilization in India.* New York, 1964.

IRELAND, PHILIP W. *Iraq.* London, 1937.

———, ed. *The Near East, Problems and Prospects.* Chicago, 1942.

ISSAWI, CHARLES. *Egypt at Mid-Century*. London, 1947.

JOHNSON-DAVIES, DENYS. *Modern Arabic Short Stories*. London, 1967.

KARPAT, KEMAL. *Political and Social Thought in the Contemporary Middle East*. New York, 1968.

KAZEMZADEH, FIRUZ. *Russia and Britain in Persia, 1864–1914*. New Haven and London, 1968.

KEDOURIE, ELIE. *England and the Middle East, 1914–21*. London, 1956.

KERR, MALCOLM. *Islamic Reform: The Political and Legal Theories of Muḥammad ʿAbduh and Rashīd Riḍā*. Berkeley, 1966.

KIRK, GEORGE. *A Short History of the Middle East*. 5th ed. New York, 1959.

KNIGHT, E. F. *Turkey's Awakening: A History of the Turkish Revolution*. London, 1909.

KOHN, HANS. *Nationalism and Imperialism in the Hither East*. London, 1932.

KRITZECK, JAMES. *Approaches to Islam*. Notre Dame, 1970.

———. *Sons of Abraham*. Baltimore, 1965.

———, and LEWIS, WILLIAM H. *Islam in Africa*. New York, 1969.

———, and WINDER, R. B., ed. *The World of Islam*. 3rd ed. London, 1960.

LAMBTON, ANN K. *Landlord and Peasant in Persia*. London, 1953.

LANDAU, J. M. *Parliaments and Parties in Egypt*. Tel Aviv, 1953.

———. *Studies in the Arab Theater and Cinema*. Philadelphia, 1958.

LAQUEUR, W. Z., ed. *The Middle East in Transition*. London, 1958.

LENCZOWSKI, GEORGE. *Russia and the West in Iran, 1918–1948*. Ithaca, 1949.

———. *The Middle East in World Affairs*. 2nd ed. Ithaca, 1956.

LEVY, REUBEN. *Persian Literature*. London, 1928.

———. *The Social Structure of Islam*. Cambridge, 1957.

LEWIS, BERNARD. *The Arabs in History*. London, 1950.

———. *The Emergence of Modern Turkey*. London, 1961.

LEWIS, I. M., ed. *Islam in Tropical Africa*. London, 1966.

LIEBESNY, H. S. *The Government of French North Africa*. Philadelphia, 1943.

LLOYD OF DOLOBRAN, VISCOUNT. *Egypt Since Cromer*. 2 vols. London, 1933–34.

LONGRIGG, S. H. *Syria and Lebanon under French Mandate*. London, 1958.

MALIK, HAFEEZ. *Moslem Nationalism in India and Pakistan*. Washington, 1962.

MARDIN, ŞERIF. *The Genesis of Young Ottoman Thought*. Princeton, 1962.

MARTINOVITCH, N. N. *The Turkish Theatre*. New York, 1933.

MILLSPAUGH, ARTHUR C. *Americans in Persia*. Washington, 1942.

MILTON, D. L., and CLIFFORD, W. *A Treasury of Modern Asian Stories*. New York, 1961.

MORGAN, K. W., ed. *Islam: The Straight Path*. New York, 1958.

NICHOLSON, R. A. *Eastern Poetry and Prose*. Cambridge, 1922.

———. *A Literary History of the Arabs*. 3rd ed. Cambridge, 1953.

———. *Studies in Islamic Poetry*. Cambridge, 1921.

NUSEIBEH, H. Z. *The Ideas of Arab Nationalism*. Ithaca, 1956.

PATAI, RAPHAEL, ed. *The Republic of Syria*. 2 vols. New Haven, 1956.

———, ed. *Jordan*. New Haven, 1957.

PHILBY, H. ST. J. B. *Arabia*. New York, 1930.

PROCTOR, J. HARRIS, ed. *Islam and International Relations*. New York, 1965.

QUBAIN, FAHIM I. *The Renaissance of Iraq, 1950–1957*. New York, 1958.

RAFFEL, BURTON. *The Development of Modern Indonesian Poetry*. New York, 1967.

RAHMAN, FAZLUR. *Islam*. New York, 1967.

RAMSAUR, E. E. *The Young Turks*. Princeton, 1957.

ROOLVINK, ROELOF. *Historical Atlas of the Muslim Peoples*. Cambridge, 1957.

SAYEGH, F. A. *Arab Unity*. New York, 1958.

SHARABI, H. B. *Nationalism and Revolution in the Arab World*. Princeton, 1966.

SHUSTER, W. M. *The Strangling of Persia*. New York, 1920.

SMITH, WILFRED CANTWELL. *Islam in Modern History*. Princeton, 1957.

———. *Modern Islām in India*. London, 1946.

———. *Pakistan as an Islamic State*. Lahore, 1951.

STEVENS, GEORGIANA, ed. *The United States and the Middle East*. Englewood Cliffs, N.J., 1964.

STORRS, RONALD. *Orientations*. London, 1937.

SYKES, PERCY. *A History of Persia*. 3rd ed. New York, 1930.

TIBAWI, A. L. *American Interests in Syria, 1800–1901*. London, 1966.

TITUS, MURRAY. *Islam in India and Pakistan*. London, 1961.

TWITCHELL, K. S. *Saudi Arabia*. Princeton, 1947.

ULLAH, NAJIB. *Islamic Literature*. New York, 1963.

WILBER, D. N. *Iran: Past and Present*. 4th ed. Princeton, 1958.

WILLIAMS, JOHN A., ed. *Islam*. New York, 1961.

YOUNG, T. C., ed. *Near Eastern Culture and Society*. Princeton, 1951.

YOHANNAN, J. D. *A Treasury of Asian Literature*. New York, 1959.

ZEINE, Z. N. *Arab-Turkish Relations and the Emergence of Arab Nationalism*. Beirut, 1958.

————. *The Struggle for Arab Independence*. Beirut, 1960.

ZIADEH, NICOLA. *Syria and Lebanon*. London, 1957.

Other MENTOR Books of Special Interest

☐ **THE WHITE PONY: An Anthology of Chinese Poetry edited by Robert Payne.** A rich collection of Chinese poetry spanning three thousand years and covering every conceivable mood and subject.

(#MY1111—$1.25)

☐ **ISLAM IN MODERN HISTORY by Wilfred Cantwell Smith.** A noted scholar discusses the impact of Mohammedanism on Middle Eastern political life today.

(#MY1108—$1.25)

☐ **A TREASURY OF ASIAN LITERATURE, John D. Yohannan, editor.** A collection of Asian classics spanning 2500 years and encompassing China, India, Arabia, Iran, and Japan.

(#MW1063—$1.50)

☐ **BOOKS THAT CHANGED THE WORLD by Robert B. Downs.** Sixteen great books that changed the course of history are discussed here—books that caused people to revolt against oppression, start wars, and revolutionized man's ideas about himself and the world.

(#MQ1038—95¢)

More MENTOR Titles of Special Interest

☐ **THE ANCIENT MYTHS by Norma Loore Goodrich.** A vivid re-telling of the great myths of Greece, Egypt, India, Persia, Crete, Sumer, and Rome. (#MQ1012—95¢)

☐ **THE ANVIL OF CIVILIZATION by Leonard Cottrell.** This fascinating history of the ancient Mediterranean civilizations reveals the long-buried secrets of the early Egyptians, Hittites, Sumerians, Assyrians, Babylonians, Greeks and Hebrews, brought to light by archaeological discoveries. (#MY951—$1.25)

☐ **THE UPANISHADS: BREATH OF THE ETERNAL.** The wisdom of the Hindu mystics, translated by Swami Prabhavananda and Frederick Manchester. (#MQ921—95¢)

☐ **THE ANCIENT KINGDOMS OF THE NILE by Walter A. Fairservis, Jr.** The cultural and political history of Nubia, Egypt, and the Sudan from the earliest civilizations through the glories of the Pharaohs to British rule. Diagrams, maps and photographs. (#MW1182—$1.50)

☐ **THE ETERNAL MESSAGE OF MUHAMMAD by Abd-al-Rahmān Azzām.** A brilliant Arab patriot and Muslim scholar's remarkable interpretation of his religion. Already a classic in the world of Islam. Foreword by Vincent Sheean. (#MT634—75¢)
